Integrating Key Skills in Higher Education

Integrating Key Skills in Higher Education

Employability, Transferable Skills and Learning for Life

**Edited by
Stephen Fallows and Christine Steven**

**KOGAN
PAGE**

First published in 2000

Kogan Page Limited
120 Pentonville Road
London
N1 9JN
UK

Stylus Publishing Inc.
22883 Quicksilver Drive
Sterling
VA 20166-2012
USA

British Library Cataloguing in Publication Data

A CIP record for this book is available from the British Library.

ISBN 0 7494 3265 9

Typeset by Kogan Page
Printed and bound in Great Britain by Clays Ltd, St Ives plc

Contents

Part 3:   Conclusions

Part 4: Guidance on 'How to...'

Notes on contributors

Sue Bloy is employed as Personal and Professional Skills Coordinator at De Montfort University. She has been involved in key skills developments in higher education since 1990. As Enterprise Director under the Enterprise in Higher Education initiative, she was instrumental in introducing the university's model for personal transferable skills. More recently, under the development project 'Diagnosis, guidance and support and recording achievement of key skills in higher education', funded by the DfEE (Department for Education and Employment), she has coordinated a team of staff drawn from across the university. The project has resulted in the adoption of the national framework for key skills as benchmark outcomes within the university's modular scheme.

Maggie Boyle is the Student Development Officer at the University of Leeds and works in the Skills and Employability Unit, where she is developing accreditation routes for work-related learning. She has been working in the field of student development since the start of the Enterprise in Higher Education Project at Leeds in 1991. She is currently the manager of the Context Project, which promotes the use of case materials and simulations in the higher education curriculum.

Mary Chapple is a lecturer in the School of Nursing at the University of Nottingham. For the past two years she has been the Project Director of the DfEE Embedding Key Skills in a Traditional University Project. She has a background in nursing and nursing education both in the National Health Service and in higher education and she has published in the areas of teaching and learning and the evaluation of learning. She is currently the Acting Director of a new Pre-registration Diploma in Nursing Course that is one of 16 national demonstration sites.

Becka Currant is currently employed as the Student Development Coordinator at the University of Bradford. Her role encompasses designing, delivering and assessing student-led training programmes, along with encouraging students to maximize their own personal development whilst at university. Before joining the University of Bradford she was the sabbatical student union officer responsible for academic affairs at the University of East Anglia. She is the Student Advisor for the North Yorkshire branch of the Institute of Personnel and Development (IPD). She holds the IPD Certificate in Training Practice.

Dr Barbara de la Harpe is a lecturer in the Centre for Educational Advancement, Curtin University of Technology, where she is involved in professional development support for academic staff. She is currently the Educational Consultant for the Curtin Business School Professional Skills Project. She has an honours degree in Science and a graduate diploma and a PhD in Education. Her research interests are in student learning, writing and skill development. In 1999, the Faculty of Education at Curtin awarded her the Walter D Neal Medal for Excellence in Educational Research.

Sue Drew is a senior lecturer in the Learning and Teaching Institute at Sheffield Hallam University, where she has supported the integration of key skills into the curriculum since 1987. She is the joint author of two books and a CD ROM providing skills support materials, and also of a number of articles about key skills. From 1998 to 2000 she was the manager of the 'Key to Key Skills' Project funded by the Teaching and Learning Technology Programme (TLTP), for which Sheffield Hallam University was the lead institution.

Nancy Falchikov is a senior lecturer at Napier University, where she teaches psychology and researches aspects of student learning. She has also worked at the University of New South Wales, Sydney, and collaborates with colleagues in several Australian institutions of higher education. She has published widely on self- and peer assessment and group dynamics. Current research projects are in the fields of cooperative learning in tertiary education and student expectations of, and attitudes to, their own university education. She has recently completed a book on peer tutoring in higher education.

Dr Stephen Fallows is Reader in Educational Development at the University of Luton. This role is research-based and a key theme in his work is the evaluation of novel approaches to teaching and course delivery. Dr Fallows made the move to educational development from his original discipline of food policy via the use of computer-based teaching and these are both interests that he maintains. Dr Fallows's current responsibilities are concerned with the development of pedagogic and related research activity across all four faculties of the University.

Rigmor George is the Coordinator: Academic Development within the Flexible Learning Centre of the University of South Australia. This involves shaping the direction of both student support staff and academic professional development to achieve strategic objectives of the University such as graduate qualities. The approach has resulted in innovative ways of working with teaching staff to provide quality learning outcomes. Her research interests include higher education policy and practice, the theory and practice of distance education, approaches to inclusive curricula and sociolinguistics.

Dick Glover has a degree from the University of Cambridge and was once an engineer. He has worked in the metal industry, for CRAC and is now self-employed. In industry, he had a range of roles, all finally focusing on managing people, with technology skills a necessary background. Whilst in this role, he was a Young Manager on a CRAC Insight into Management course and steadily became more involved with CRAC. Eventually, he joined CRAC full-time, and managed the Insight Programme for eight years. He also pioneered work at CRAC that sought ways to take the technology of active learning into universities. Since leaving CRAC at the end of 1991, Dick has become a 'portfolio' worker, carrying out specific projects for a range of clients. These projects range from developing forms of active learning material to creating and running development programmes for staff in companies and universities.

Dr Judy Goldfinch is a senior lecturer in the School of Mathematical and Physical Sciences at Napier University in Edinburgh. She is currently holder of a five-year teaching fellowship in the university and is interested in the development and assessment of generic skills, with particular reference to team and IT skills, and to peer assessment. She is also working on the development and use of computer-based assessment.

Professor Milton Hakel has 34 years of experience as a university educator, author and researcher. This has included two years at the University of Minnesota, 17 years at Ohio State University, where he directed the Industrial and Organizational Psychology Programme, and six years as Chair of the Psychology Department at the University of Houston. Since 1991, Professor Hakel has served as the Ohio Board of Regents' Eminent Scholar in Industrial and Organizational Psychology at Bowling Green State University. He currently is a member of the Alverno National Council, having first become acquainted with the college and its innovative approach to higher education at a meeting of the Assessment Center Research Group in the mid-1970s. He recently completed two terms as a member of the Board of Governors of the Center for Creative Leadership, including a term as chair of the Board's Research Committee.

Dr Judith Harding is Associate Director of Learning Development in the Centre for Learning Development at Middlesex University. She works across the institution to develop contexts for discussion of learning and teaching issues, and is part of the team working with the Postgraduate Certificate in Higher Education course for new lecturers. She is also an art historian interested in problems of early medieval iconography and a practising artist who writes on contemporary textiles.

Len Holmes is currently Senior Lecturer in Organization and Employment Studies at the University of North London. He has a professional background in trainer training and development, and has worked in the private, public and voluntary sectors. From 1991 to 1996 he was Business School Faculty Coordinator for Enterprise in Higher Education. His first degree, from Nottingham University, was in Philosophy; he has an MPhil from Lancaster University and is currently completing a PhD with the Institute of Education, London University.

Professor Alan Jenkins is an educational developer at Oxford Brookes University. He is currently course leader for the ILT-accredited course for new teaching staff and is responsible for coordinating pedagogic research across the University. He was centrally involved in Oxford Brookes' Enterprise Programme, which sought to require all undergraduate courses to deliver five university-wide key skills. He was co-chair of the DfEE Ability Based Curriculum Network of UK institutions, which sought to spread good practice in delivering institution-wide policies for key skills. Previously he taught geography at Brookes and with his colleagues developed a department-wide integration of skills and disciplinary knowledge. He is currently adviser to the Geography Discipline Network's DfEE project on embedding key skills in geography curricula.

Phyllis Laybourn is a lecturer in the Department of Psychology and Sociology at Napier University, Edinburgh. Having studied for a degree and a PhD in psychology at the University of Dundee, she conducted post-doctoral research at the University of Oxford. She currently holds a teaching fellowship and balances her research interests in cognitive psychology (the areas of decision making and perception) with those in innovations in learning and teaching in higher education. She applies her knowledge of psychology to the understanding of the learning process and to help her find ways of facilitating student-centred learning.

Dr Donna Wood McCarty holds a BA in English and a PhD in Educational Psychology. She is an Associate Professor of Psychology at Clayton College & State University in a suburb of Atlanta, Georgia. Dr McCarty has extensive teaching experience at the undergraduate level and has had the opportunity to serve the university and the academic community in a variety of ways in addition to her teaching. She currently coordinates the academic assessment and faculty development programmes on her campus.

Holly McCausland is Senior Project Officer in the Flexible Learning Centre of the University of South Australia. In this role she provides executive support to the director and senior academic staff and contributes to initiatives for the improvement of teaching and learning. These have included a computer literacy strategy for commencing students, reward schemes for excellence in teaching and learning, and the development of frameworks to foster inclusivity and information literacy for lifelong learning. She has also coordinated services supporting the university's involvement in Open Learning Australia, and was manager of the print and editorial services section.

Dr Ellie McCreery earned her doctoral degree from Bowling Green State University in Interpersonal and Public Communication with a specialization in Industrial and Organizational Psychology. She is now Director of the university's Springboard initiative. Dr McCreery's teaching success over 22 years at the University of Toledo Department of Communication along with her breadth of consulting experience in public and private sector organizations form a substantial base of experience from which to lead the innovative, exciting, creative work awaiting her in Springboard's future.

Dr Catherine Milne is now working at the Graduate School of Education at the University of Pennsylvania. Until May 2000 she was the Tertiary Literacies Coordinator at the University of Wollongong. She has a PhD from Curtin University of Technology. At Wollongong, she was responsible for professional development in the areas of development and integration of generic skills/graduate attributes and the process of collecting evidence of that integration. She also had responsibility for developing and coordinating the compulsory introductory information, computer and statistical literacy programme. One of her interests is examining the construction of generic skills and comparing and contrasting the beliefs that are held about knowledge and skills.

Pete Mitton describes himself as 'an aged postgraduate research student'. He is based in the School of Informatics at the University of Bradford. He has been part of the Bradford student development team since his first undergraduate year when he became involved as a course representative. He has developed personally by progressing through the training stages outlined in his chapter. He has no formal training and development qualifications, but has learnt a great deal through observing and reflecting upon his own and others' experience.

Ted Nunan is an Associate Professor at the Flexible Learning Centre of the University of South Australia, where he coordinates research and scholarship activities. His most recent writing has been in the area of change in higher education, particularly in relation to the development, assessment, and recording of achievement of generic qualities of graduates. He has also written extensively on policy and implementation issues about open, distance and flexible learning.

Dr Kathleen O'Brien is the Vice President for Academic Affairs at Alverno College. She holds a MBA from Vanderbilt University and a PhD in management from the Graduate School of Business, University of Wisconsin–Madison. She has considerable experience in designing and implementing student performance assessments for specific courses and for different milestones in a student's academic progress. Recently, she has focused her work in this area on designing a Diagnostic Digital Portfolio system for the college. She has consulted on ability-based education and assessment throughout the United States and in other countries.

Dr Alex Radloff is Associate Professor in the Centre for Educational Advancement, Curtin University of Technology, where she coordinates professional development for academic staff. She has a Masters degree in Psychology and a PhD in Education. Her background is in educational psychology and her research interests are in self-regulation of learning and in the development of student communication skills, especially academic writing.

Christine Steven has experience teaching in secondary and further education as well as in higher education. Her subject specialism is computer science but she has maintained an interest in pedagogic issues and much of her research is in this area. She has considerable experience in designing and running courses in the area of computing and has always maintained that an important aspect is the enhancement of the students' other skills areas. Christine was for some years a teaching fellow at the University of Luton, where much of her work centred on issues of assessment, particular emphasis being on the use of computer-aided assessment packages and their effectiveness.

Dr Harry Tolley was formerly Senior Lecturer in Education at the University of Nottingham, where he was Director of Initial Teacher Training. For the past ten years he has worked as a consultant to a variety of organizations including the Commission for Racial Equality, the Council of Europe and the Civil Service. During that time he has continued to work in the university as a senior research fellow on a variety of projects. These were mainly concerned with the assessment and accreditation of work-based and prior learning, the validity and transferability of National Vocational Qualifications (NVQs) in the workplace and embedding key skills in higher education. He is currently Acting Director of the Centre for Developing and Evaluating Lifelong Learning (CDELL) in the School of Education at the University of Nottingham.

Gordon Weller is Head of the Work Based Learning Unit at the University of Luton. He joined the university in 1991 as part of the Enterprise in Higher Education initiative. Through EHE, he became interested in work-based learning, and has been involved in developing work-based learning modules and programmes. Latterly he has been involved in the Graduate Apprenticeship Scheme initiative, as a transferable model to other higher education institutions.

Jenny Westwood is currently working as an Academic Development Adviser at Napier University, having previously spent 13 years teaching in the further education sector. Her passion has always been, and continues to be, the empowerment of students. Her interests therefore lie in the promotion of a learner-focused educational environment. This includes the embedding of employability skills into the curriculum and extending the use of assessment as a learning tool, with particular emphasis on the use of self- and peer assessment and critical reflection for both staff and students.

Jean Williams is a lecturer in Interfaculty and Independent Studies at De Montfort University. Her current research interests include key skills in higher education, coaching education and sporting elites, and support systems for lifelong access to further and higher education. She extends interest across the range of the skills agenda from highly institutionalized formal modes of development to voluntary leisure activities. She is currently writing her PhD on women's football.

Preface

The impetus for the preparation of this book came from the editors' involvement at the University of Luton with the introduction of a curriculum that fully recognizes the need to develop, in every one of the university's students, the skills needed for smooth progression from higher education into employment.

The University of Luton's development of a skills-recognizing curriculum grew from the institution's involvement with the UK government-funded Enterprise in Higher Education initiative. The Enterprise scheme at Luton placed significant emphasis on building upon the institution's links with local and national employers. It was through the extended involvement with these employer partners in a variety of working groups and other settings that the university began to consider how best to equip its students for the world of work. In 1994, the formal decision was taken to implement a skills-recognizing curriculum. This was debated and then progressively introduced during the second half of the 1990s. In the summer of 1999 the first cohort of students graduated after following the skills-recognizing curriculum throughout their university studies. At graduation, University of Luton students are presented with a personalized detailed skills profile in addition to their normal degree certificates.

The University of Luton experience will be discussed in greater detail within the main text of the book. However, it should be recognized that this publication is much more than a record of the Luton work in the area of skills. It also highlights, through a series of focused case examples, the work that has taken place in other institutions around the world. The examples included can only provide snapshots of what is taking place. None of the institutions referred to is a static entity: each will be developing its provision further over the coming months and years. Similarly, there are numerous other institutions that might have provided alternative examples but space has necessarily been limited.

The book falls into four principal parts:

Part 1 is the scene-setter. Here the editors discuss many of the general issues that surround the development of the skills-recognizing curriculum.

Part 2 contains 17 case examples from 16 different institutions in three countries. This part is subdivided into three themes: institutional models, specific local approaches to skills development, and three personal reflections on issues relating to skills. The case examples have been chosen to reflect a range of institutional styles and circumstances. This section is preceded by a short introduction from the editors.

Part 3 summarizes some of the key observations that have emerged from the work presented by the contributors of the case examples. The case examples above are essentially focused on skills programmes rather than on the minutiae of specific modules or even courses. This leads to consideration of the issues to be addressed and questions that must be answered as an institution establishes a skills programme.

Part 4 provides the reader with specific advice on how a skills-recognizing curriculum might be implemented at the very personal and local level of the individual module or course. Whilst recognizing that there are clearly many alternative skills models, the editors utilize their experience with the University of Luton model as the framework for the discussions.

The book provides information for readers across the broad higher education spectrum. Higher education managers (deans, heads of department, course leaders) are provided with a series of practice-based examples and a clear consideration of the issues associated with the introduction of a skills development programmes in higher education. 'Front-line' teachers are provided with practical advice that may be applied in lectures, seminars, coursework and time-constrained assessments.

Contact details for all contributors are provided at the end of the book. For all contributors an e-mail address has been provided since this has been the principal mode of contact between the editors and authors; indeed, many of the contributors have only ever communicated with the editors in this manner.

Finally, there is an index.

We hope that you find this book useful. If readers know of alternative models of skills development in higher education please get in touch – there may be an opportunity for further volumes of this nature!

Part 1

Introduction to skills

1

The skills agenda

Stephen Fallows and Christine Steven
University of Luton
UK

INTRODUCTION

This book addresses issues that surround the skills debates that are current in higher education. Much of the content reflects the situation in the United Kingdom, since that is the location of the editors and the majority of contributors; however, contributions from the United States and from Australia serve to illustrate that the issues are global and the solutions transferable.

This chapter reviews the 'skills agenda' and begins by considering the reasons for the implementation of skills development programmes for students in higher education. It then considers the points of debate that have been common in institutions that have considered adopting or have adopted a skills development programme.

The chapter recognizes that for many of the points raised on the skills agenda there can be no definitive correct answer. The agenda sets the scene for debate within individual institutions; each has to consider the issues against such local matters as:

- nature of the student population (for instance school leavers or mature returners);
- management/organizational arrangements;
- diversity of courses offered;
- financial status of the institution;
- location of the institution;
- particular national priorities.

The intention is to give readers the necessary information from which to compile appropriate questions when the skills issue is addressed.

THE EXTERNAL CONTEXT

Internationally, the nature of higher education in modern universities is changing extremely rapidly as institutions are forced to take account of a number of major external factors. The developments described in this book derive from a number of such external factors.

- There is increasing international recognition that the transition from higher education to employment is not always straightforward. In the United Kingdom, the considerable increase in the number of students passing through the higher education system (Higher Education Statistics Agency (HESA), annual publication (a)) now means that the competition for established positions in traditional 'graduate employment' and the professions is fierce. As a consequence, the range and variety of jobs into which graduates are moving is becoming increasingly diverse.

    It is only a small minority of graduates who are able to gain employment that directly utilizes the academic content of their higher education curriculum (HESA, annual publication (b)). In some disciplines this fact is recognized from the outset by the students (for instance, very few students studying philosophy expect to gain full-time employment as a philosopher). However, for other disciplines there will be at least an initial expectation of directly related employment and students may take some time to recognize that their vocationally related degree may not lead to employment in the area. Unfortunately, academic staff, who by definition have gained employment within their discipline, may be the last to recognize this point.

    The above point applies regardless of the students' level of maximum attainment. School leavers do not expect to use directly the material studied at school when they get a job, but graduates often do and PhD graduates have often undertaken this qualification with the express purpose of gaining entry to often very limited job opportunities.

    Similarly, it is recognized in the UK that many new graduates may take as long as three years to reach employment at what they consider to be at graduate level (Connor *et al*, 1997, Elias *et al*, 1999). This situation applies to a wide variety of graduates and not only to those whose academic discipline does not have any obvious link to a particular job. Even those with vocationally related degrees can find that the possession of current technical expertise is insufficient to overcome the lack of practical on-the-job experience. Such statistics are repeated worldwide.

● It is increasingly recognized that, regardless of the subjects that are studied, the academic curriculum is essentially a vehicle through which other graduate attributes are delivered. Many of these attributes are largely constant regardless of the subject studied. For example, the essential information retrieval and analysis skills required to prepare a review of the background literature to a topic do not essentially differ from archaeology to zoology; similarly, these skills are directly transferable into a wide range of employment.

As above, this point can be applied regardless of the students' level of maximum attainment. The PhD can be considered to be the pinnacle of student academic achievement; it is also a demonstration of the application of a wide range of skills to a particularly high standard.

● The world of employment is also changing rapidly. Permanence is no longer a significant feature: established career paths have disappeared as businesses have adopted a flatter management structure; entire industries have relocated to other areas of the world; and new technologies have made established practice and experience irrelevant.

However, the story is not completely gloomy. New industries, often but not always technology-driven, have emerged as major employers: illustrative technology-based examples include the personal computer and mobile telephone industries. Similarly, many of those in employment today are engaged in jobs that simply did not exist 20 or even 10 years ago. As the pace of change continues to accelerate, new jobs, not yet thought of, will emerge with increasing rapidity whilst old jobs will inevitably disappear.

● Graduates are increasingly expected to 'hit the ground running'. The proportion of new graduates who will be given the chance to spend perhaps months 'learning the ropes' as graduate trainees is already much reduced and this proportion will decline still further. This fact will become increasingly apparent as the number of new graduates joining small to medium enterprises (SMEs) continues to rise. SMEs are already the main engines of growth in the UK economy and provide around 45 per cent of non-government jobs (Department of Trade and Industry (DTI), 1999). It has been suggested that SMEs will become the main employers of graduates and it has been estimated that in the very near future as many as 70 per cent of vacancies filled by graduates will be in these organizations (Bradford, 1999).

Each of the above points is a major consideration in the notion of a need for the population to be flexible and prepared for a lifetime of change and personal development. This fact is particularly true for graduates who will be expected to be the leaders of change rather than followers.

The concept of 'lifelong learning' is now central to official UK government thinking within the combined Department for Education and Employment (DfEE). The current (Labour) UK government has recognized that we now must live in a 'Learning Age' (DfEE, 1998) in which it will be the norm to engage in retraining and personal development throughout working life.

Similarly, the European Commission has for some time recognized the need to establish a 'Learning Society' which 1) takes account of the rapid changes that are taking place in Europe due to the internationalization of trade, the move to an information society and developments in science and technology, and 2) utilizes education and training to provide solutions through a mix of formal qualifications and personal skills (European Commission, 1995).

Higher education in particular must provide its graduates with the skills to be able to operate professionally within the environment required for the 'Learning Age' or 'Learning Society'. The UK National Committee of Inquiry into Higher Education (Dearing Commission, 1997) noted that:

> ... institutions of higher education [should] begin immediately to develop, for each programme they offer a 'programme specification' which... gives the intended outcomes of the programme in terms of:
>
> the knowledge and understanding that a student will be expected to have on completion;
>
> key skills: communication, numeracy, the use of information technology and learning how to learn;
>
> cognitive skills, such as an understanding of methodologies or ability in critical analysis;
>
> subject specific skills, such as laboratory skills.

The Dearing recommendation reflects the views of employer organizations. Research conducted in the United Kingdom for the Association of Graduate Recruiters (AGR) (1995) stressed the need for graduates to become self-reliant and able to take responsibility for their own careers. The AGR noted that many of the skills required of the self-reliant graduate were also those required of the self-reliant learner; the AGR thus concluded that there would be benefits within higher education from the promulgation of such capabilities.

The Higher Education and Employment Division of the DfEE noted in a Briefing Paper published in November 1997 that:

> ... studies of employer needs have repeatedly stressed the priority which they give to 'personal transferable skills'. When they recruit graduates they are typically seeking individuals not only with specific skills and

knowledge, but with the ability to be proactive, to see and respond to problems creatively and autonomously, and all the predicted trends in the world of employment suggest that these pressures will increase.

The DfEE agrees with the AGR that there is no conflict between the development of skills for employment and the development of skills for learning:

> The processes which make learning effective in a changing higher education also develop the qualities which are needed in the changing workplace.

The above text draws largely upon the authors' observations in the United Kingdom. However, it has to be recognized that the UK experience is not unique; the observations can be made in many if not all countries around the world. The observations can be distilled down to the following four key statements:

- A degree is not an immediate passport to a 'graduate-level' position.
- Most graduates do not directly utilize the content of their degree curriculum during employment.
- The degree curriculum is a means through which students can gain a range of skills that can be considered to be the key attributes of a graduate.
- All graduates must be ready for lifelong learning.

AN AGENDA FOR DEBATE

The above paragraphs indicate a clear demand for students to be provided with a range of skills that will equip them for their transfer from the world of education into the world of work. The next section addresses questions such as:

- What is meant by the general term 'skills'?
- What are the university's responsibilities?
- How should these responsibilities be met?

The answers to these questions are not straightforward and there can be no simple answers. The case examples that are presented in subsequent chapters provide verification that a range of different approaches are viable and fit for the purpose of addressing skills requirements.

What is meant by the general term 'skills'?

From the outset it must be recognized that there is no definitive definition that may be applied in all situations. Neither is there a single, universally accepted terminology:

- 'Skills necessary for employment and for life as a responsible citizen' – this seems to sum up what the numerous skills programmes are seeking. To the authors' knowledge, no institution utilizes this descriptive phrase.

- 'Transferable skills' – this is a term in common parlance within education. The implication in the term is that skills developed within one situation (education) are also useful when transferred into another situation (employment). (One trick to make this a correct assumption is to consider what is needed in a work situation and then apply this back into education – that is utilize a process that may be termed 'reverse transfer'. For example, it is recognized that the skill of writing reports, rather than essays, is valued by employers; so base certain of the assessments on report writing.)

- 'Key skills' – the word 'key' in this context is generally taken in the context of being important. However, the word has a useful second meaning as an instrument used to release a lock; this can be considered as a useful metaphor as these skills might help to 'unlock the doors' to employment.

- 'Common skills' – 'common' in this context refers to the universal nature of these skills: they are relevant to each and every student regardless of discipline and can be demonstrated within all programmes.

- 'Core skills' – here the implication is that the skills have to be central to the students' experience within higher education.

The above list is not exhaustive. Alverno College, in the United States, refers to the 'Abilities' that its students gain through their educational experience. Similarly, in Australia, the University of Wollongong refers to the 'Tertiary Literacies' that its graduates will have achieved. (Both of these institutions' programmes are described as case examples later in the book.)

Similarly, there is a good deal of debate about what the above terms should include. The case examples presented in later chapters provide an illustrative selection. There does seem to be a universal acceptance of a need for students to develop the following skills:

- Communication skills, using a range of approaches.
- Information management skills. Information management is central to higher education as students develop their ability to retrieve, evaluate, analyse and utilize information from a range of sources in an appropriate manner.

- Skills in using modern communications and information technologies such as e-mail, word-processing and data handling for a range of common tasks.

- People skills such as group working, ethics and recognition of diversity. These are described in a range of different ways but appear on all skills lists.

- Personal skills such as time management and recognition of personal responsibilities.

In addition to the above, it is common for skills expectations to include elements that can be referred to generically as 'citizenship skills'.

Most institutions have chosen to develop their own list of desired skills; however, De Montfort University has taken a different approach and has adopted the skills descriptors set out by the national Qualifications and Curriculum Authority (QCA). (See Chapter 14).The QCA approach to description of skills expectations is to utilize a system in which five levels are described. Levels 1–3 are intended for use within schools and further education. Level 3 achievement equates broadly with entry into higher education, whilst Levels 4 and 5 are deemed to be relevant to higher technical and professional circumstances and to study within higher education. The QCA model sets out defined standards for each skill at each Level; this allows for the formal assessment of skills at entry to higher education as well as subsequently (QCA, 2000).

Responsibilities for higher education

Universities and colleges have a responsibility to provide their students with a well-grounded education in the chosen discipline. But it is no longer to produce the 'boffin' who can work diligently and to independent good effect on an academic challenge. Today's circumstances demand the skills and abilities listed above and to ignore these would be a failure on the part of higher education.

It is possible to argue that the development and use of skills has always been a feature of education at all levels and particularly so within higher education. It is impossible for a student to prepare a competent item of academic work without utilizing certain skills. The following is a minimal listing:

- Researching the topic requires information retrieval skills.
- Relevant information must be selected from the totality of that which is available.
- There may be a need to analyse data using statistical or other methodologies.

- The materials must be presented in a manner that communicates the outcomes of the study in an appropriate manner.
- The task must be completed within the defined timescales.

The above applies universally throughout higher education no matter how traditional the institution. However, it is quite possible to envisage a higher education system in which other skills, such as group working, may not be utilized. Similarly, traditional higher education has placed great emphasis on assessment through the production of essays under time-constrained examination circumstances. This develops only a limited range of communication skills.

The skills requirements highlighted by employers apply across all disciplines, not least because few graduates take up employment that directly uses the discipline studied. Thus, it follows that skills provision should be universal with all students experiencing all elements.

However, there are those who would argue that (to cite a couple of stereotypical examples) those studying an arts discipline have no need to consider the skill of numerical analysis, whilst those studying mathematics have no need to develop expertise in certain communications skills. This position is rejected strongly by most skills advocates, who point to the fact that the future employment prospects for these graduates is unknown.

However, there is a strong argument in favour of additional skills being needed by those studying certain disciplines. For example, those studying a laboratory-based science subject will need to develop the skills needed to operate professionally in this specialist environment. Similarly, specific skills of oral communication will apply in certain disciplines – the 'bedside manner' of a good health professional depends to a substantial extent upon the development of oral communication and other interpersonal skills.

How should an institution's skills responsibilities be met?

As indicated above, and illustrated in the case examples that follow, there are several basic methodologies that can be adopted for the introduction of skills into the student experience. Several different examples are described in this book.

The University of Luton has chosen to embed its skills provision within the general curriculum with the intention that each and every module offered by the university can and should make a contribution to students' skills development. A single set of skills expectations applies regardless of the primary disciplines studied. This model suits an institution that has an extensive and well-established modular credit scheme, in which the students are afforded considerable choice in the construction of their degree programmes.

The University of Nottingham is building upon 'naturally occurring' skills to develop individual targeted skills programmes for a number of departments. This model is in accordance with the needs of a traditional university in which considerable autonomy is devolved to departments.

Middlesex University has introduced a skills module built around a template that can be 'tuned' to provide for the needs or desires of different discipline areas.

The three models used as examples and outlined above differ from each other in the following aspects:

- embedded system compared with specific and separate skills module;
- use or otherwise of a specific set of recognized descriptors;
- standard scheme versus programme tuned to discipline requirements;
- assessment of skills against recognized standards versus skills not formally assessed.

The skills model adopted at the University of Luton (see Chapter 2) recognizes that a student's skills develop during study in higher education and therefore it is considered reasonable to describe skills expectations for each of the three undergraduate levels of study. The key skills model set out by the QCA describes skills outcomes at five levels, of which only the two highest are appropriate for use within higher education.

Other institutional models define only a single level of skills development which equates to that expected to be achieved whilst participating in higher education and is often applied only at the earlier levels of study.

CONCLUDING COMMENT

It has been said previously and it will be said again later in this book: there is no universal skills development model that suits the entirety of higher education, or even the entirety of UK higher education. The sector is populated by independent institutions with individual identities and inspirations. There is generally strong resistance to imposed change and to that which was 'not invented here'. Hence the diversity of approaches that will be illustrated in this book.

REFERENCES

Association of Graduate Recruiters (AGR) (1995) *Skills for Graduates in the 21st century*, Association of Graduate Recruiters, Cambridge

Bradford, J (1999) An Employer's View, in *Developing Tomorrow's Workforce*, Report of 1999 Skills and Enterprise Network Annual Conference, Nottingham

Connor, B *et al* (1997) *What do graduates do next?* Grantham Book Services Ltd, The Institute for Employment Studies, University of Sussex

Department for Education and Employment (DfEE) (1998) *The Learning Age: a renaissance for a new Britain*, Command Paper Cm 3790, The Stationery Office, London

DfEE Higher Education and Employment Division (November 1997) *Getting the Most out of HE: Supporting learning autonomy*, DfEE Briefing Paper, Sheffield

Department of Trade and Industry (DTI) (1999) *SME Statistics for the UK 1997*, DTI SME Statistics Unit, Sheffield

Elias, P *et al* (1999) *Moving On – Graduate careers three years after graduation*, DfEE/Higher Education Careers Service Unit/Association of Graduate Careers Advisory Services/Institute for Employment Research, University of Warwick

European Commission (1995) *Teaching and Learning: Towards the learning society* available on the Internet at www.cec.lu/en/comm/dg22/dg22.html

Higher Education Statistics Agency (HESA) (annual publication) (a) *Higher Education Statistics for the UK*, HESA Services Ltd, Cheltenham

Higher Education Statistics Agency (HESA) (annual publication) (b) *First Destinations of Students Leaving Higher Education Institutions*, HESA Services Ltd, Cheltenham

National Committee of Inquiry into Higher Education (Dearing Committee) (1997) *Higher Education in the Learning Society*, Report of the National Committee of Inquiry into Higher Education, The Stationery Office, London.

Qualifications and Curriculum Authority for England (2000) Details of the key skills schemes and their implementation are available on the QCA Web site: www.qca.org.uk/keyskills

Part 2

Skills implementation – case examples

Introduction

Skills implementation can be achieved in many ways and this selection of chapters provides a range of illustrations.

The first group of case examples, in chapters 2–8, has been chosen to present a variety of institutional models of skills implementation. The institutions whose skills programmes provide the examples cited are:

- The University of Luton (the editors' home institution);
- Alverno College;
- Napier University;
- The University of South Australia;
- The University of Nottingham;
- Middlesex University;
- The University of Wollongong.

The institutions listed above have followed quite different approaches to skills provision. Different institutional priorities and practice have combined to shape the featured programmes.

The second group, in chapters 9–15, focuses on targeted initiatives, innovative approaches or special issues. Becka Currant and Pete Mitton report on the ways that student-led activities can contribute to skills development. Sue Drew indicates how current communications and information technology can be utilized in support of skills development. Stephen Fallows and Gordon Weller describe a skills programme for graduates. The Bowling Green State University 'Springboard' programme is described by Professor Milt Hakel and Eleanor McCreery. The use of case studies as a vehicle for skills development is described by members of the 'Context' project from the University of Leeds. Sue Bloy and Jean Williams illustrate the use of the QCA national skills framework in the development of personal skills assessment and development. Colleagues from the Curtin University of Technology describe their experience in support of lecturers who are implementing a skills programme.

The final group of contributions, in chapters 16–18, comprises three very different personal accounts. Donna McCarty is very supportive of skills initiatives but was undermined in her skills work by the concurrent initiation of other, more prestigious, activities that served to undermine the viability of her programme. Professor Alan Jenkins has been a skills enthusiast for many years, and his autobiographical account highlights many of the issues that his institution (Oxford Brookes) has considered in this area over the past decade. Finally, the possibly controversial contribution from Len Holmes is very challenging; he does not support the concept of a 'Skills Agenda' and sets out his personal alternative to the skills matters that are widely accepted as norms by the other contributors.

2

Embedding a skills programme for all students

Stephen Fallows and Christine Steven
University of Luton
UK

SUMMARY

This chapter describes the programme to embed a range of core skills (the retrieval and handling of information; communication and presentation; planning and problem solving; and social development and interaction) within each and every undergraduate programme of study at the University of Luton. The university's scheme involves the use of a very detailed skills template that describes skills development expectations at each level of undergraduate study. All modules in the university's Modular Credit Scheme have been mapped against the template to identify skills addressed in the module. Specific skills are not yet subject to individual assessment but all students leave the university with a transcript that recognizes their skills experience alongside their academic achievements.

THE UNIVERSITY OF LUTON'S SITUATION

Luton is the centre of the largest conurbation in south-east England outside London. It is a manufacturing town with traditional associations with the hat trade. Nowadays, Luton is the home town of several industrial enterprises, the largest being Vauxhall Motors, the UK arm of General Motors.

The University of Luton is England's most recently created university. It gained university status in 1993 following extensive review of the quality of its programmes and procedures by the Higher Education Quality Council acting on behalf of the Privy Council. However, the university has a history

17

that dates back to the 19th century; the institution grew through the 20th century and immediately prior to gaining university status was called the Luton College of Higher Education. Throughout its history, the university and its predecessor institutions grew by recognizing first of all the needs of the developing local manufacturing industries and more recently the national and international requirements for employable graduates. During the 1990s a number of organizations commented on the need for graduates to gain skills valued by employers whilst undertaking their programmes of higher education (Association of Graduate Recruiters (AGR), 1995; European Commission, 1995; National Committee of Inquiry into Higher Education (Dearing Committee), 1997; Secretary of State for Education and Employment, 1998).

The university has an overt focus on the quality of its teaching and has scored very well whenever external assessing panels have made judgements. Furthermore, the university recognizes that it is not sufficient for a graduate to leave the institution with detailed subject knowledge: today's graduates must also carry with them into the world of employment a range of transferable skills. It is the university's position that these skills are most appropriately gained alongside the formal academic curriculum.

DEVELOPING A SKILLS AGENDA

In many respects the University of Luton has always respected the need for students to be prepared for the work environment. Over the years, many programmes have led students from a specific named award towards work with a 'relevant' employer (for instance in electrical engineering or law). In the 1990s this position changed as the institution broadened its portfolio of programmes. At the same time it was recognized that many university graduates throughout the country, if not the majority, took up employment where the content of their degrees was irrelevant to the employer. For many employers, a university degree was becoming a mere indication of ability to operate at a particular academic level.

Through its involvement with the Enterprise in Higher Education initiative, the Luton College of Higher Education built upon and enhanced its links with employers, both local and national, and engaged with employer representatives in a debate concerning graduate attributes for the late 20th and early 21st century. The university's employer partners stressed that it was no longer sufficient for students to become knowledgeable in the subject matter of a named award; they must also be equipped for the transition into employment (Fallows, 1995).

As in other institutions (see Chapter 17), the consideration of a skills agenda was an important part of the work of the Luton Enterprise in Higher

Education team and a curriculum development conference held in February 1992 focused on options for skills development.

As long ago as 1994, the university's senior management took the strategic decision that steps should be taken to formally embed transferable skills into the curriculum for every student (The University of Luton, 1994). This decision fully accords with the declared mission of the university that makes reference to both 'high quality education' and 'vocational relevance'.

The 1994 decision was followed by a significant period of wide-ranging debate that included discussion at all levels of the institution. The objective in this debate was to determine the precise methodology for the implementation of a skills initiative. There was general agreement about the need for promotion of skills but there was a range of opinions about how the strategy might be operationalized in a manner that could include every student.

The university-wide debate led first of all to the decision that wherever possible, skills provision would be totally embedded within the delivery of the standard academic provision, and not totally separated out into skills modules. Next the university undertook the development of a detailed tabulation and description of the institution's skills expectations at each level of undergraduate provision.

Skills expectations

Figures 2.1, 2.2 and 2.3 detail the University of Luton's expectations in respect of skills acquisition through the students' time with the institution. The templates shown provide clear descriptions of what is expected of each student at each level of study. The descriptions are provided in three main groupings:

- The operational contexts. Here the emphasis is on a description of the general working environment to be experienced by the student. The approach is student-centred and progressive, with students taking greater responsibility for and ownership of their learning as they move towards graduation.
- Cognitive descriptors. These are intended to provide the student with an indication of what is expected of them at each level of study. There is an emphasis on progression towards achievement of an ability to work professionally and independently by graduation.
- Core skill descriptors. Here the student is provided with specific indication of the skills expectations.

Figure 2.1 University of Luton Modular Credit Scheme: Level 1 generic descriptors and core skills

	CHARACTERISTIC OF CONTEXT	RESPONSIBILITY	ETHICAL UNDERSTANDING
	At Level 1 the Learner:		
1. Operational Contexts	Should be working within defined contexts demanding the use of a specified range of standard techniques.	Should be learning in an environment where the work is directed, with limited autonomy, and within defined guidelines.	Should be aware of social and cultural diversity and ethical issues and be able to discuss these in relation to personal beliefs and values. In particular: – be sensitive to language and imagery – understand ethical issues relevant to the subject(s) of study – be aware of personal responsibilities and professional codes of conduct – work within the university guidelines on ethics.

	KNOWLEDGE & UNDERSTANDING	ANALYSIS	SYNTHESIS/ CREATIVITY	EVALUATION
	By the end of Level 1 the Learner:			
2. Cognitive Descriptors	Should have a given factual and/or conceptual knowledge base with emphasis on the nature of the field of study and appropriate terminology.	Should be able to analyse with guidance using given classifications/ principles.	Should be able to collect and characterise ideas and information in a predictable and standard format (eg in essay form, as a report, etc).	Should be able to evaluate the reliability of data using defined techniques and tutor guidance (where appropriate).

Figure 2.1 *(continued)*

	INFO. RETRIEVAL & HANDLING	COMMUNICATION & PRESENTATION	PLANNING & PROBLEM SOLVING	SOCIAL DEV. & INTERACTION
	By the end of Level 1 the Learner:			
	Should be able to seek, describe and interpret information. In particular:	Should be able to communicate effectively in context, both orally and on paper. In particular:	Should be able to apply given tools/methods accurately and carefully to a well-defined problem and draw appropriate conclusions. In particular:	Should be able to work with and meet obligations to others (tutors and/or other students). In particular:
3. Core Skills Descriptors	– identify and use a wide variety of primary sources, including electronic and print-based indices, citing sources appropriately **I1.1**	– distinguish between ideas, opinions and judgement in his/her own writing **C1.1**	– analyse problem situations, identifying and describing the nature of the problem **P1.1**	– demonstrate self-reliance by relating personal goals to planning and performance measurement, including completing work on time **S1.1**
	– describe, interpret and organize data establishing relevant information as necessary **I2.1**	– identify key themes from written work and oral presentations **C2.1**	– break a problem down into manageable parts, allocate priorities and identify suitable solution/draw appropriate conclusions **P2.1**	– relate to and cooperate with others in contributing to a group's achieving a defined goal **S2.1**
	– scan information under a time constraint for specific purposes **I3.1**	– express key themes in written work, recognizing the style, structure and level of written material in relation to its target audience **C3.1**	– implement and evaluate the solutions/conclusions **P3.1**	– recognize own strengths and weaknesses and give and receive constructive feedback. **S3.1**
	– use appropriate IT hardware (particularly microcomputer systems) safely, including power up, login/logout, protecting against accidental loss of data and obtaining hard copy **I4.1**	– write reports, notes and assessment material according to an approved standard, correcting grammar, spelling and syntax as necessary **C4.1**	– understand and apply numerical conventions, interpreting trends and data **P4.1**	
	– select and use appropriate packages (including word processors) making use of on-line help facilities **I5.1**	– give a short presentation using methods suitable for the target audience. **C5.1**	– communicate quantitative information effectively to the audience using an appropriate format (including charts, tabular data as necessary). **P5.1**	
	– use a spreadsheet package to handle data tables. **I6.1**			

Figure 2.2 University of Luton Modular Credit Scheme: Level 2 generic descriptors and core skills

	CHARACTERISTIC OF CONTEXT	RESPONSIBILITY	ETHICAL UNDERSTANDING
	At Level 2 the Learner:		
1. Operational Contexts	Should be working within simple but predictable or complex but predictable contexts demanding application of a wide range of techniques.	Should be learning in an environment where the work is managed within broad guidelines for defined activities.	Should be aware of the wider social and cultural diversity and ethical implications of the areas(s) of study and be able to debate issues in relation to more general ethical perspectives.

	KNOWLEDGE & UNDERSTANDING	ANALYSIS	SYNTHESIS/ CREATIVITY	EVALUATION
	By the end of LeveL 2 the Learner:			
2. Cognitive Descriptors	Should have a detailed knowledge of his/her discipline(s) and an awareness of a variety of ideas/contexts/frameworks which may apply to this.	Should be able to analyse a range of information with minimum guidance, apply major theories of the disciplines(s) and compare alternative methods/techniques for obtaining data.	Should be able to re-format/re-express a range of ideas/information towards a given purpose.	Should be able to select appropriate techniques of evaluation and evaluate the relevance and significance of the data collected.

Figure 2.2 *(continued)*

	INFO. RETRIEVAL & HANDLING	COMMUNICATION & PRESENTATION	PLANNING & PROBLEM SOLVING	SOCIAL DEV. & INTERACTION
	By the end of Level 2 the Learner:			
	Should be able to seek, describe and interpret information within the context of the discipline(s). In particular:	Should be able to communicate effectively in context, both orally and on paper. In particular:	Should be able to apply given tools/methods accurately and carefully to a well-defined problem and draw appropriate conclusions. In particular:	Should be able to work with and meet obligations to others (tutors and/or other students). In particular:
3. Core Skills Descriptors	– identify own information needs to support complex problem requirements **I1.3**	– produce a complex piece of work which demonstrates a grasp of vocabulary of the subject and deploys a range of skills of written expression appropriate to the subject **C1.3**	– decide on action plans and implement them effectively **P1.3**	– formulate effective strategies for achieving goals when working with others **S1.3**
	– complete an information search using a range of appropriate primary and secondary sources. Draw accurate conclusions independently using the subject methodology **I2.3**	– assess the quality of his or her own oral communication and identify areas for improvement **C2.3**	– manage time effectively in order to achieve intended goals **P2.3**	– participate effectively in the operation of a team and collaborate with members of the team. **S2.3**
	– analyse data, using appropriate techniques **I3.1**	– deliver a paper or presentation which succeeds in communicating a series of points effectively. **C3.3**	– clearly identify criteria for success and evaluate his or her own performance against those criteria **P3.3**	
	– use appropriate IT resources independently to support previously identified areas. **I4.3**		– produce creative and realistic solutions to complex problems. **P4.3**	

Note: The core skills descriptors are undifferentiated at Levels 2 and 3 and represent what is expected of the learner on completion of each level.

Figure 2.3 University of Luton Modular Credit Scheme: Level 3 generic descriptors and core skills

	CHARACTERISTIC OF CONTEXT	RESPONSIBILITY	ETHICAL UNDERSTANDING
	At Level 3 the Learner:		
1. Operational Contexts	Should be working within complex and unpredictable contexts demanding selection and application from a wide range of innovative or standard techniques.	Should be autonomous in planning and managing the learning process within broad guidelines.	Should be aware of personal responsibility and professional codes of conduct and be able to incorporate a critical ethical dimension into a major piece of work.

	KNOWLEDGE & UNDERSTANDING	ANALYSIS	SYNTHESIS/ CREATIVITY	EVALUATION
	By the end of Level 3 the Learner:			
2. Cognitive Descriptors	Should be able to demonstrate confident familiarity with the core knowledge base of his/her discipline(s) and an awareness of the provisional nature of knowledge.	Should be able to analyse new and/or abstract data and situations without guidance, using a wide range of techniques appropriate to the discipline(s).	With minimum guidance, should be able to transform abstract data and concepts towards a given purpose and be able to design novel solutions.	Should be able to critically review evidence supporting conclusions/ recommendations, including its reliability, validity and significance, and investigate contradictory information and/or identify reasons for the contradictions.

Figure 2.3 *(continued)*

	INFO. RETRIEVAL & HANDLING	COMMUNICATION & PRESENTATION	PLANNING & PROBLEM SOLVING	SOCIAL DEV. & INTERACTION
	By the end of Level 3 the Learner:			
	Should be able to seek, describe and interpret information within the context of the discipline(s). In particular:	Should be able to communicate effectively in context, both orally and on paper. In particular:	Should be able to apply given tools/methods accurately and carefully to a well-defined problem and draw appropriate conclusions. In particular:	Should be able to work with and meet obligations to others (tutors and/or other students). In particular:
	– identify own information needs to support complex problem requirements **I1.3**	– produce a complex piece of work which demonstrates a grasp of vocabulary of the subject and deploys a range of skills of written expression appropriate to the subject **C1.3**	– decide on action plans and implement them effectively **P1.3**	– formulate effective strategies for achieving goals when working with others **S1.3**
3. Core Skills Descriptors	– complete an information search using a range of appropriate primary and secondary sources. Draw accurate conclusions independently using the subject methodology **I2.3**	– assess the quality of his or her own oral communication and identify areas for improvement **C2.3**	– manage time effectively in order to achieve intended goals **P2.3**	– participate effectively in the operation of a team and collaborate with members of the team. **S2.3**
	– analyse data, using appropriate techniques **I3.3**	– deliver a paper or presentation which succeeds in communicating a series of points effectively. **C3.3**	– clearly identify criteria for success and evaluate his or her own performance against those criteria **P3.3**	
	– use appropriate IT resources independently to support previously identified areas. **I4.3**		– produce creative and realistic solutions to complex problems. **P4.3**	

The university has adopted a model that divides the core skills into four principal groups:

- information retrieval and handling;
- communication and presentation;
- planning and problem solving;
- social development and interaction.

Each of these four core skills groups is further divided through the indication of specific task-related expectations. At Level 1 a total of 19 skills descriptors are listed; for Levels 2 and 3, 13 skills descriptors are identified. Each skill-related task is given a code reference that identifies the skills descriptor and provides a useful shorthand for use in subsequent documentation.

The detailed identification of specific skills in this manner allows all lecturers to undertake a straightforward mapping of their individual modules against the expectations.

Once the skills descriptors had been agreed the university undertook a major four-stage programme to identify and highlight the skills being developed within the curriculum.

Stage 1: information gathering and skills mapping

Each of the modules offered within the university-wide modular credit scheme was subjected to thorough review to determine the existing skills development. In practice, much was already in place – for example, all degree-level programmes require information retrieval skills and certain communication skills, particularly in written format. Although much skills development was already taking place, this had not been formally recognized by the institution, by individual lecturers and, perhaps most importantly, by the students. This substantial exercise (the university offers over a thousand different modules) allowed for a mapping of current provision and hence the identification of any 'skills gaps' within individual named degree programmes.

The information gathering involved almost every member of the teaching staff and thus served as a further step in raising everyone's awareness of the skills initiative. Noting that much skills development was already in place helped to remove any last remaining pockets of resistance to the concept.

The intention in this exercise was to note that most modules include one or more skills elements: it was never the intention that all modules could address each one of the university's skills expectations.

Stage 2: validation

Once the information gathering and skills mapping exercise was completed, arrangements were put in place to plug the 'skills gaps' identified. For some programmes this has involved changes to the tasks undertaken within individual modules by students as either formative or summative exercises. Each module has been subjected to a revalidation procedure to formally recognize the skills elements. As observed above, this revalidation process had the extra function of strengthening the formal and informal institutional commitment to the skills initiative.

Today, as new modules are assessed for inclusion in the Modular Credit Scheme, consideration of the skills development is a central element in the validation process alongside the proposed academic content and intended assessment strategy. In practice, skills development forms a crucial component of the assessment strategy.

The information gathering, skills mapping and validation process took place over a three-year period as the skills initiative was progressively rolled out to all levels of the curriculum. Students entering the university in October 1996 experienced the initiative throughout their time there: those who studied on a full-time basis graduated in summer 1999.

Stage 3: module information

Following revalidation of each module, the information provided to students for making their personal study choices was revised. Each module has a module information form; these now draw specific attention to the skills that are developed or utilized whilst studying that module. In addition the course documentation provided to students following their registration on modules has been redrafted to highlight the skills being developed (the 'shorthand' codes referred to previously are used here) as well as the academic content descriptions. The statements of expected learning outcomes for each module now make overt reference to skill expectations as well as mainstream curriculum outcomes.

In practice, whilst it is expected that skills will be developed throughout the curriculum, it has become standard practice for particular skills-rich modules to be utilized at Levels 2 and 3. The Level 2 module is generally constructed to provide a preparation for the research project that will be undertaken at Level 3. For instance in biological and life sciences there is a core (compulsory) module entitled 'Skills for Life Sciences' which provides an opportunity to focus on the various skills required within this broad discipline. The research project double module at Level 3 provides students with a major opportunity to practise a range of skills from project management to report writing.

Stage 4: highlighting skills

Skills development is now brought to the attention of students whenever possible. This takes place most commonly with reference to assignment work, since most if not all assignments require the use of skills in the context of the academic curriculum (for instance: research and write a report, analyse certain data or work in a group to prepare an oral presentation). Many lecturers have revised their assessment strategy to ensure formal utilization of skills; others have been more adventurous and have adopted innovative teaching methodologies that have made skills provision a central element of the teaching and course experience. Four examples are given in an appendix at the end of this chapter.

Recording skills achievements

It has been an intention from the outset that all students, regardless of their primary academic discipline, would engage with and experience each and every one of the skills. This expectation is based on advice from employers who note that all graduate employees are likely to utilize the full range. In practice, the balance of emphasis differs between academic disciplines, with particular skills being given greater precedence in some disciplines than in others.

A key issue in the university's internal debates on skills has been whether skills should be formally assessed separately from the academic curriculum. The decision was taken that skills would contribute towards the general grade for a module but would not be given separate grades. Thus, for instance, the preparation of a report will require use of several skills: the student will have to deal with the necessary information, perhaps applying statistical tests; to prepare the written document; and to present this in an appropriate manner within the required deadlines. Similarly, for an oral presentation the student not only demonstrates subject knowledge but also uses a range of skills in the preparation and delivery of the presentation. In both of these instances, the higher-graded work will inevitably have utilized the skills to greater effect.

Although specific assessment of individual skills has been rejected, the university provides each graduate with a skills transcript as a formal record of engagement with the range of skills.

Furthermore, a key feature is the students' own recognition of the skills that they develop during their time with the university. Much skills development had always been present, but it was not formally recognized by the institution and hence students did not notice that it was taking place. Now that skills development is overt, the students recognize their personal skills development and hence gain the confidence to highlight this matter when making job applications.

A key element in the Luton skills initiative has been the parallel recognition of the need to promote the students' capabilities and responsibilities as independent learners. This ability is encouraged by the skills initiative and is in accord with the employer view that being a skilled independent learner is a valuable first step in the students' progression from education into employment. The universal promulgation of the skills initiative makes students much more conscious of their individual need to ensure that their personal experience of the university takes account of their intended progression into employment.

CONCLUDING COMMENTS

The Luton skills initiative has been driven enthusiastically by a strong managerial team who have attached their personal commitment to its development. This managerially driven push from the centre has ensured universal participation across all disciplines in a broadly standardized manner which can be logged against a detailed template of skills expectations that are published for each of the three undergraduate levels (see Figures 2.1, 2.2 and 2.3).

It is difficult to place an absolute measure of success onto an initiative such as this. We know that the students do gain the skills outlined and thus at local level we can claim success. However, the key purpose in undertaking the exercise is to provide students with abilities that will enable them to make a successful progression from education into employment and then to make progression appropriate to their abilities and ambitions. The first cohort to have experienced the skills initiative throughout their time with the university only graduated in summer 1999. The evidence suggests that Luton graduates have a good record in finding employment (HESA, annual publication). However, it is too early to consider the longer-term impact of the initiative on graduates' subsequent career progression: this will (undoubtedly) be a topic for future research.

APPENDIX

The following paragraphs provide illustration of ways in which four lecturers have adapted their teaching to embed particular skills elements[1].

- Kemal has restructured his science courses for built environment students to utilize 'experiential practicals' that place particular emphasis on the utilization of real-world data collected by the students themselves during their daily lives. The emphasis of the course has shifted from a theoretical discourse to analysis and interpretation. Results already show both raised academic achievement and improved student motivation (Ahmet and Fallows, 1998, 1999).

- Tom has developed case study exercises for his travel and tourism students in which group working skills are essential to completion of the set task since each student receives an incomplete set of information (as is generally the case in reality). The tasks set are not assessed but provide Tom with very useful formative information on the abilities of his students (Robinson, 1998).

- Lesley has introduced problem-based learning into her teaching. This approach is gaining increasing favour within professional disciplines that require both diagnostic skills and the ability to deal effectively with the diagnosis (most particularly within the wide range of health-related disciplines). The approach recognizes that, in many professional circumstances, problems can only be resolved through collaboration between individuals with different access to information, personal abilities and professional skills (Baillie, 1998).

- Christine used to deliver lectures on the theories of problem solving to her software-engineering students. She admits that the course did not inspire student interest. More recently, she has utilized a group exercise that provides her students with a collection of simple problems, taken from a variety of sources including popular puzzle books. The students are first of all asked to try to solve the problems and then asked to discuss *how* they addressed the problems. A subsequent session relates the group activity to the recognized academic theory. It seems that the solving of apparently irrelevant problems has not only provided an understanding of how to address problems, which is at the core of software engineering, but was also a valuable group working exercise in its own right (Steven and Fallows, 1998).

ENDNOTE

1. In all the examples cited the originator's true name has been used since each has indicated a willingness to be approached by colleagues wanting further information. Each of our colleagues may be contacted through the authors of this chapter.

REFERENCES

Ahmet, K and Fallows, S J (1998) *Science in Support of Professional Disciplines: An experiential approach*, paper to 6th International Conference on Experiential Learning, Tampare, Finland.

Ahmet, K and Fallows, S J (1999) Experiential learning through practicals, in *Inspiring Students: Case studies in motivating the learner*, eds S J Fallows and K Ahmet, Kogan Page, London, pp 7–16

Association of Graduate Recruiters (AGR) (1995) *Skills for Graduates in the 21st Century*, Association of Graduate Recruiters, Cambridge

Baillie, L (1998) *Problem Based Learning in Nurse Education* HELP! Higher Education: Learning and Practice, **3**, The University of Luton

European Commission (1995) *Teaching and Learning: Towards the learning society*, available on the Internet at www.cec.lu/en/comm/dg22/dg22.html

Fallows, S J (1995) *The Option of an Explicitly Vocational University Education*, paper to Society for Research in Higher Education Summer Conference on Changing the Student Experience, University of Central England, Birmingham

Higher Education Statistics Agency (HESA) (annual publication) *First Destinations of Students Leaving Higher Education Institutions*, HESA Services Ltd, Cheltenham.

National Committee of Inquiry into Higher Education (Dearing Committee) (1997) *Higher Education in the Learning Society*, The Stationery Office, London

Robinson, T (1998) *Sportor Limited: A flexible group exercise* HELP! Higher Education: Learning and Practice, **4**, The University of Luton

Secretary of State for Education and Employment (1998) *The Learning Age: A renaissance for a New Britain*, Command Paper Series, Cm 3790, The Stationery Office, London

Steven, C and Fallows, S J (1999) Skills in the curriculum: implementing a university-wide initiative in *Managing Learning Innovation: The challenges of the changing curriculum*, ed G Windle, Proceedings of a Society for Research in Higher Education Conference, pp 93–99, The University of Lincolnshire and Humberside, Lincoln

The University of Luton (1994) *Strategic Plan, 1993–98*, The University of Luton. (See also subsequent annual editions.)

3

Ability-based education

Kathleen O'Brien
Alverno College
USA

SUMMARY

What some might call employability skills or learning outcomes, the faculty
and staff at Alverno College call abilities. They see the abilities, as they have
identified them, as inherent in the practice of their disciplines, and they
place them at the heart of a liberal education, to be developed and demonstrated by students in an integrated manner across the curriculum.

THE INSTITUTION

Alverno, located in Milwaukee, Wisconsin, in the midwestern United States,
is a liberal arts college for women with a strong focus on preparing its students for professional careers. Currently it serves over 1900 degree students,
who attend classes either on weekdays or at weekends. Since 1973, students
seeking a degree participate in a curriculum centred on student abilities as
its outcome. These abilities are:

- communication (including analytic reading, writing, listening, speaking,
  quantitative literacy, computer literacy, and media literacy);
- analysis;
- global perspectives;
- problem solving;
- effective citizenship;
- valuing in a decision-making context;

- aesthetic responsiveness;
- social interaction.

Accountability for these student abilities is grounded in the values of the college. Some of the liberal learning values that Alverno faculty and staff made central to the operation of their curriculum are active self-sustained learning, individual developmental change, realization of human potential and self-assessment, application of knowledge integral to understanding, and achievement of competence and self-efficacy. These values underlie the mission of the college, a long-standing consensus that the learning of students is at the centre of the efforts of everyone at the institution. To that end the faculty and staff direct their shared commitment, their daily teaching and evaluating of students, and their administrative structures and operational systems.

HOW DID ALL THIS HAPPEN?

What prompted Alverno faculty to conceive of, design, and put into practice in 1973 an ability-based curriculum that has endured and is continually refined? In the late 1960s serious questions were arising throughout the country regarding the meaning and value of college and of a liberal education in particular. At Alverno these questions focused on the meaning of higher education for women at a time when women were redefining their place in society with a view to aspiring to and assuming socially responsible roles. How might the faculty and academic staff define an Alverno education in a way that would meet the needs of women and influence students to select the college from among all of the other educational opportunities that were available in Milwaukee?

Given the college's tradition of emphasis on the improvement of student learning, a new board of trustees and a new president initiated a self-examination, at the core of which was an exploration characterized by self-evaluation and a sense of renewal (Read and Sharkey, 1985). The president and dean took advantage of the time traditionally set aside for continuing dialogue on mission and curriculum and asked faculty to use that time to respond publicly, as departments, to a series of questions about the most significant dimensions of their respective disciplines for student learning. Among the most challenging questions was: 'What are you teaching that is so important that students cannot afford to pass up courses in your programme?'

The creation of the curriculum grew out of the resulting discussions over two years. Faculty discovered that several abilities kept surfacing as significant across the disciplines, whether in a context of individual disciplines or of an integration of them. The eight abilities that emerged represent the outcomes that faculty could say were essential to the education of their students, life-enhancing and life-sustaining from both a personal and a professional point of view. The fact that the identification of the abilities had its origin in the faculty's reflection on the nature of their disciplines as they are practised cannot be overstated. It assured the faculty's identification with and responsibility for the abilities as integral to the teaching of their disciplines, rather than something additional to what they already taught.

A SHARED COMMITMENT TO STUDENT LEARNING IN THE SHAPING OF A CURRICULUM

It is the goal of all at Alverno to see that students achieve the academic goals they set for themselves and that they are able to attain the standards of achievement required for degree completion. This is one expression of the college's mission. The curriculum is the central vehicle by which the college carries out this goal. The eight abilities became the framework by which a new curriculum was shaped between 1971 and 1973, when it was formally implemented. Shaping it meant reorganizing what was already taught to make explicit what students are expected to learn, with the disciplines providing distinctive contexts for the development and demonstration of abilities. The initial focus was to make clearer in each course and across the college the major outcomes of a liberal education. To accomplish that, faculty designed a scaffolding of six developmental levels or benchmarks for each ability. These inform the definition of the abilities to be integrated with content according to the conceptual and methodological requirements of each given area of study. (See Figure 3.1). The first four levels are incorporated into the core liberal arts courses for all students. Levels 5 and 6 are contextually defined, by the faculty of each major area of study for those abilities that are most relevant.

The integration of abilities and disciplinary content can be seen in Figure 3.2, which shows an increasingly specific contextualization of selected abilities.

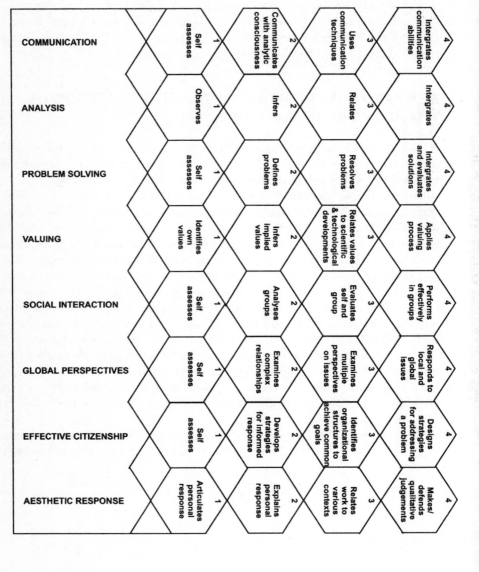

Figure 3.1 Conceptual and methodological requirements

The Social Science Major at Alverno College

Mission

Alverno College is an independent four-year liberal arts college serving women of all ages, races, and financial means. The student, her learning, and her personal and professional development are the central focus of everyone associated with Alverno.

Ability-based learning outcomes

Through the development of eight broad liberal arts abilities

Communication
analysis
problem solving
valuing in decision-making
social interaction
global perspectives
effective citizenship
aesthetic responsiveness

the Alverno student develops as an independent lifelong learner with

- a sense of responsibility for her own learning and the ability and desire to continue learning
- self-knowledge and the ability to assess her own performance critically and accurately
- an understanding of how to apply her knowledge and abilities in many different contexts.

Major outcomes

The student:

- Analyses the interdependence of peoples and societies in their ecological context. Analyses social arrangements cross-culturally and ecologically, compares diverse ways of life, and brings a global perspective to the discussion of social relations.
- Participates effectively in community life. Contributes to the well-being of her immediate environment by employing social scientific tools to make the best use of its organizations and institutions, creating new structures if necessary.
- Conducts social research. Effectively uses qualitative and quantitative research methodologies to pose questions and gather and interpret data.
- Exercises social imagination. Demonstrates creative thinking about how to resolve social problems, stimulates such creativity in others, and pursues the best of the old ways and seeks out the new in public discourse about today's issues.
- Articulates her social philosophy and refines it in dialogue with others. Uses the social science perspective to consider the ethical and moral aspects of social customs and public policies and creates effective criteria for evaluating her own positions on issues as a citizen. Applies her standards to critically examine various world views and develops her own positions in ongoing dialogue with others.

Example of individual social science course outcomes

"Comparative Social Institutions The Family" (6th semester)

The student:

- Comparatively analyses diverse family norms and values.
- Uses multiple theoretical perspectives in carrying out analyses.
- Conducts effective original research on contemporary family dynamics.
- Refines her ethical and political positions on some significant contemporary family issues.

Example of an assessment of individual course outcomes

The student uses ethnographic research methodology to study a family, incorporating disciplinary theories and frameworks to analyse the structure and dynamics of this family. She prepares a written research report and a written self-assessment of her performance, and gives a formal oral presentation of her findings to her peers to demonstrate her communication ability.

Criteria for successful performance

The student:

1. Chooses appropriate disciplinary theories, concepts, and frameworks to organize her work.
2. Discusses her research process, ethical aspects of this research, the problems she confronted, and how she overcame those problems.
3. Explicitly uses disciplinary theories and concepts to effectively analyse and present her data.
4. Clarifies her own beliefs and values about the family as an institution and distinguishes between her value system and that of the family she studies.
5. Meets the College's criteria for effective communication in advanced courses.

Figure 3.2 Integration of abilities and disciplinary content

A SHARED COMMITMENT TO STUDENT LEARNING IN HOW FACULTY TEACH AND ASSESS STUDENTS

Teaching

While it is true that the ability-based curriculum grew out of reflection on the nature of the disciplines, it is also the case that reflection on the abilities keeps affecting the way disciplines are conceptualized and taught. For example, faculty in the natural sciences emphasize the use of concepts as tools for problem solving, so that students are constantly using their knowledge in the laboratory and in the classroom to solve problems. The central role of interactive ability in the professions today has increasingly informed the kind of pedagogical strategies faculties use to teach students in those fields. In order to achieve that, faculty have had to give serious attention to the meaning of those abilities in their field, often drawing on insights from ability departments that were formed to take responsibility for the conceptualization of the abilities. In other words, faculty in all departments have thought about teaching their disciplines and professions through the lens of the abilities and have developed pedagogical practices grounded in their growing understanding of the abilities most central to their fields.

In addition to addressing the unique abilities that are most germane to each discipline, faculty take responsibility for teaching abilities across the disciplines. All faculty, for example, are committed to assisting students with their analytic abilities and their ability to communicate in both written and spoken form. This commitment means that faculty in all disciplines provide opportunities for practise of these abilities and give students feedback on how they can improve. It is standard for faculty in the music department, for example, to discuss with each other ways of helping their students learn to write as a way of learning about music itself. It is part of usual discourse in the philosophy department that the members of the department work together to design ways that students might demonstrate their understanding of an argument by presenting it to fellow class members and responding to their questions. The psychology department has designed a senior seminar in which students not only write a research paper but also present it in a formal setting to other students and faculty. These are only a few examples, but they illustrate how faculty take responsibility for the teaching of writing and speaking in ways that inform how they teach their disciplines. It should be noted here that faculty see this as another dimension of helping students practise the discipline in useful ways, not as a distraction from the study of the discipline.

The faculty are also well aware of the developmental nature of learning and thus carefully consider not only how to teach for abilities across the curriculum, but also how to teach in ways appropriate to the level of the student. The developmental levels of the abilities reflect this notion, but this kind of development happens because the framework informs the way the faculty approach everything from individual class sessions, to course design, to planning a programme of study. This means, for example, that when conceiving the plan for a course or programme of study Alverno faculty consider not just what the students will study, but also the sequence of learning experiences that will help the students progress in their understanding and use of a discipline or an integration of disciplines.

At the beginning of a course, students may need questions and suggestions to help them learn how to read a chemistry text or a novel, or how to observe movement in dance or listen to a piece of music. With this in mind, faculty across the disciplines design worksheets that students use in their reading or listening or observation. As the students become more sophisticated, they are able to do those kinds of analyses independently, but teaching involves creating the processes that get them to that point. Although faculty have schedule and course plans in mind at the beginning of a semester, they frequently modify those plans if students seem to need more time to work with a concept or ability. It is also common for Alverno faculty to enter a class session with a particular agenda and discover that it is best to follow the thread of a conversation or a significant question that actually requires breaking from the agenda.

Alverno faculty stress that learning does not happen in a strict linear fashion. The curriculum, programmes, courses, and learning experiences they have designed and implemented provide a pedagogical developmental structure, but they are not taught as if each student proceeds in a straight line from one step to the next. It is important to emphasize in the midst of our concern for development that we continue to modify our design based on what seems to be best for each student and each group of students.

Assessing

Because inherent in the development of abilities is the *use* of knowledge – understanding, as Gardner defines it (1999) – the faculty at Alverno saw that evaluating student achievement would mean evaluating performance. Students would need to show that they could think, that they could communicate, that they could create meaning interactively. Faculty and academic staff therefore developed a concept they put into practice that they initially called 'assessment' and gradually – because of the ambiguous expansion of meaning of that term in the United States – came to call 'student assessment-as-learning', a particular kind of performance assessment that is incorporated across the curriculum. They define it as 'a process integral to learning that involves observation, analysis, and judgement of each student's performance on the basis of explicit criteria, with resulting feedback to the student.' (Alverno College Faculty, 1994, cf Harvey and Knight, 1996).

The faculty and academic staff determined the essential characteristics of student assessment by working through their principles of learning. If learning is to be integrative/experiential, assessment must judge performance. If learning is to be self-aware, assessment must include self-assessment as well as public expected outcomes and developmental criteria (cf Loacker, Cromwell, and O'Brien, 1986; Sadler, 1989). If learning is to be active/interactive, assessment must include feedback and elements of externality as well as performance. If learning is to be developmental, assessment must be cumulative and expansive. Finally, if learning is to be transferable, assessment must be multiple in mode and context and relate to life outside college.

Assessment in the liberal arts core of the curriculum

Assessment begins for Alverno students before the start of classes. A diagnostic communication placement assessment elicits performances in analytic reading, writing, quantitative literacy, and computer literacy. Beginning with students' first semester, the general education courses they take provide them with the opportunity to demonstrate, as well as develop, each of the eight abilities at the core of the curriculum. In registering for a course, students in effect commit themselves to develop the levels of ability that the instructor has specified for that course. All courses include performance assessments, some as individual simulations and some as processes or projects throughout a course. These assessments all include explicit criteria and feedback on the basis of those criteria. This system of assessment assures multiplicity; the exact number of assessments depends on the nature of the course and the discretion of the individual instructor.

Further assurance of multiplicity of modes of assessment comes from the assessments students take outside their courses. Several times throughout their academic programme, students take comprehensive outside-class assessments that provide an opportunity to integrate their knowledge and abilities.

Assessment in major studies

For each major area of study, assessment continues in all courses. The number and kind of assessments that students take outside their courses depend on the nature of the major as it has been defined by the faculty of a given department, and may include research projects, process and reflective portfolios, or student teaching. Each major department has set forth its plan for student assessment so that students can get an overall picture of the process by which they will demonstrate their developing abilities. The plan tells students how assessment works in their individual courses, including the kinds of performance that might be required. For example, the plan suggests that assessments, depending on course goals and instructor style, might ask them to write an article ready for publication. Or assessments might entail an instructor observing their process in solving a scientific problem. Or an assessment might require them to design a financial plan for a small business to be presented to and assessed by a bank officer off-campus.

Department plans also tell students what cumulative assessments they might have at some points outside of class time. The latter range from extended simulations to student presentations of required portfolios.

The relationships between the institutionally required abilities, the contextualized abilities for students in a given academic department, the outcomes of a specific given course, and the criteria for a sample assessment from that course can be seen in Figure 3.2. The chart emphasizes the importance of the abilities in relating to and informing assessment and learning experiences throughout the curriculum and how they are consistently integrated with the content of a field of study (cf. Ewell, 1997, and Cowan, 1998).

Student assessment-as-learning enables students to participate in continuous evaluation of their progress in developing the abilities they must demonstrate in order to graduate. Alverno's recent development of a diagnostic digital portfolio has made accessible what students need to do more consistently and thoroughly. The portfolio is a software package that enables students to analyse their own learning sequentially and iteratively in a way that reveals learning patterns and characteristics related to the learner's strengths and to areas in particular need of development. It matches student performance against faculty-designed benchmarks to record developmental changes at key points as well as over time.

This system assists students to monitor their own learning in a developmental fashion and enhances the faculty's ability to teach students how to self-assess – the fundamental ability all students need to learn as they progress from beginning to intermediate to advanced levels.

A SHARED COMMITMENT TO STUDENT LEARNING IN EVALUATION OF PROGRAMMES AND INSTITUTIONAL IMPACT

So does it work? This became the question most frequently asked early in the history of instituting this outcome-oriented curriculum even when no students had yet graduated. Clearly, the faculty had to commit themselves to an extensive process of programme evaluation on a number of levels. To do this, the college established an Office of Educational Research and Evaluation and a Research and Evaluation Council composed of faculty and academic administrators from across the college. These groups, working with the entire faculty and the Council on Student Assessment, focused evaluation efforts on a series of faculty-generated questions: Do students achieve as a result of the curriculum? Compared to what standards? To the level faculty expect?

These and other questions led to a series of studies using a longitudinal design throughout the latter half of the 1970s and into the 1980s. We found that Alverno graduates do measure up. The majority are effective performers, clear thinkers and problem solvers in novel situations, articulate communicators in settings where the message is the means to achievement, initiators when the barriers seem impassable, and skilled interpersonally when teamwork is demanded. Most importantly to the faculty, they act with integrity even when there are strong pressures to do otherwise (cf Barnett, 2000). These conclusions and others are detailed in a just published book, *Learning That Lasts* (Mentkowski, 2000) in which we set forth our evaluation strategies and research methodology within the context of evaluation in higher education.

Continuing evaluation strategies

Besides our longitudinal research and because of our commitment to continuous improvement, faculty employ a number of ongoing evaluation strategies: evaluation of general education and the major field, validation of performance assessment, and practitioner-based enquiry studies. These are also more fully described in *Learning That Lasts* and are briefly noted here.

Evaluation of general education and the major field
In working with faculty in major fields, the Office of Educational Research and Evaluation designed a process unique to each major but that is informed by a common general framework. Relying on faculty-designed outcomes of the major field, professional or disciplinary standards, and other public expectations, faculty determine the Alverno questions and criteria that shape the study design.

Strategies for evaluating general education and the major fields include inter- and intra-individual pattern analyses of student performance throughout the curriculum using data generated from faculty-designed external measures, including portfolio assessment and external data sources and comparison. To ensure integration of these efforts with other research efforts, some of the same approaches are also used, such as the Behavioral Event Interview, the Learning Style Inventory, and the Perry Scheme of Intellectual and Ethical Development.

Validation of performance assessment
Evaluating and validating ability-based performance assessment for us means validating the process as well as individual instruments. While both

the assessment process and the instruments change, the process is more stable over time. Evaluation of the degree to which faculty-designed instruments meet the principles and elements of the assessment process becomes an instrument validation strategy, just as establishing the validity of the assessment process becomes a curriculum validation strategy.

The Assessment Council, in collaboration with the Office of Educational Research and Evaluation, takes responsibility for scheduling reviews of those instruments and assessment processes. A series of strategies for reviewing instruments focuses on the relation to guidelines for instruments, student performance, quality of assessor training, and inter-assessor agreement. The Office of Research and Evaluation has developed a workable definition of contextual validity and strategies for validating faculty-designed performance assessment measures and the performance assessment process.

Practitioner-based enquiry studies

Alverno faculty and staff have worked together to create a theoretical and practice base for research related to the improvement of teaching and assessment. In the course of this work we have clarified research questions to be examined and have defined the meaning of practitioner-based enquiry.

Faculty and staff work individually or in groups to conduct projects within courses or departments or across the curriculum for the purpose of improving designs and implementation of teaching and learning activities. Some examples of practitioner-based enquiry studies include student background and learning styles, developmental considerations in teaching writing, improving integrated language practice, development of intermediate students, innovations in mathematics instruction, and the making of educators.

A SHARED COMMITMENT TO STUDENT LEARNING IN DEVELOPING STRUCTURE AND SYSTEMS

To ensure the continual development of the educational programme, the Alverno faculty and staff designed an administrative structure that would provide for the effective use of the results of their reflective practice in:

- defining teaching and learning;
- revising ability sequences;
- reconceptualizing majors;
- designing, implementing, and evaluating student, programme, and institutional assessment.

Theoretical Framework
Mission of the College

Educational Theory, Principles and Assumptions	Eight Abilities, Major Outcomes

Reconceptualized teaching, learning and assessment: principles, assumptions, and practice
    Coherent Curriculum (including integration of college, major and course outcomes)
    Student Learning (including redesign and use of syllabi, texts)
    Student Performance Assessment
Reconceptualized faculty's scholarship of teaching
Reconceptualized assessment of institutional effectiveness	

What has changed and continues to change, and what needs to be sustained in order to implement the mission, theory and principles?

Changes to college structure	*Changes to resources and supports*
NEW	Academic Calendar
Ability Departments parallel to Discipline Departments	Friday afternoon meeting/workshops
Assessment Council	All-college Institutes: August,
Assessment Center	January, May
Office of Educational Research and Evaluation	On-going workshops for new faculty
Research and Evaluation Committee	Faculty promotion, rank and criteria
	Physical environment
RETHOUGHT	Use of technology
Career Development Office	Partnerships with community
Internships and Experiential Learning Office	External Assessors
Student Services	Internship Mentors
Instructional Services Center	Advising
Computer Center	New Student Seminar
Multimedia Center	Pre-professional Seminar
	Professional advisors

Figure 3.3   Components of the educational programme at Alverno College

As Figure 3.3 suggests, initial and continuing changes in structures as well as in practice are informed by an articulated theoretical framework. Key to how structures would contribute to an operational system were the developing of a matrix organization of discipline and ability departments and an academic calendar to support faculty and staff collaborative work. New councils, committees, and offices were added because of the assessment focus. For student assessment-as-learning, a council made up of faculty and staff was organized to ensure the quality of the student assessment process and an assessment centre to assist the faculty in administering complex, outside-class assessments. For programme and institutional assessment, an office of educational research and evaluation, with a separate advisory committee, was created to research and evaluate the value, validity, and effectiveness of the educational programme and to research student outcomes for a better understanding of learning and development in and after college.

The combined system that these structures represent permits, and in fact encourages, a dynamic process of development with a stable framework that can flex in response to the needs of students in a contemporary and future world.

ONGOING COMMITMENT

The challenge to colleges like Alverno is to keep bringing what it has learned and continues to learn about the education of students into a world being transformed by technology. Administrators at Alverno claim that their best learning comes from working with their students. They value the expansion of that learning from the questions and insights of colleagues in higher education and professional schools, as well as elementary and secondary school educators: scholar-practitioners in North America and in other continents with whom they seek continuing dialogue.

REFERENCES

Alverno College Faculty (1994) *Student Assessment-as-Learning at Alverno College*, Alverno College Institute, Milwaukee, Wisconsin

Barnett, R (2000) *Realizing the University in an Age of Supercomplexity*, SRHE and Open University Press, Buckingham

Cowan, J (1998) *On Becoming an Innovative University Teacher: Reflection in action*, SRHE and Open University Press, Buckingham

Ewell, P T (1997) Organizing for learning: a new imperative, *AAHE Bulletin*, **50**, pp 3–6

Gardner, H (1999) *The Disciplined Mind*, Simon & Schuster, New York

Harvey, L and Knight, P (1996) *Transforming Higher Education*, SRHE and Open University Press, Buckingham

Loacker, G, Cromwell, L and O'Brien, K (1986) Assessment in higher education: to serve the learner, Report No. OR 86-301, in *Assessment in Higher Education: Issues and Contexts*, ed C Adelman, US Department of Education, Washington, DC

Mentkowski, M and Associates (2000) *Learning That Lasts: Integrating, learning, performance, and development in college and beyond*, Jossey-Bass, San Francisco

Read, J and Sharkey, S R (1985) Alverno College: toward a community of learning, in *Opportunity in Adversity*, eds J S Green and A Levine, Jossey-Bass, San Francisco

Sadler, D R (1989) Formative assessment and the design of instructional systems, *Instructional Science*, **18**, pp 119–144

4

Evolution of skills development initiatives

Phyllis Laybourn, Nancy Falchikov, Judy Goldfinch and Jenny Westwood
Napier University
UK

BACKGROUND

Napier University is one of the largest higher education establishments in Scotland, with about 12,000 students of whom about 10,000 are studying at undergraduate level. The history of key skills at the university is a long one. Largely associated with vocational degrees, the institution has a strong tradition of working closely with employers, producing students with generic skills for the workplace and equipped for wide-ranging capability and learning. The unfolding of this history provides a fascinating case study and illustrates the complexities associated with carrying the ideal of a strong commitment to key skills through to universal acceptance and implementation. Amongst the many issues that have beset developments over the past decade, four major ones are worthy of emphasis:

● to what extent generic skills are truly transferable;
● whether it is better to embed key skills within the subject discipline or teach them as a stand-alone unit;
● where the balance should lie between regulatory imposition and freedom to exercise professional judgement;
● the importance of genuine staff consultation in policy decisions.

This chapter will firstly outline the main phases in development of employability skills at Napier over the past ten years. It will then examine in more detail several aspects of these developments by:

- discussing some of the issues associated with the delivery of generic skills development programmes;
- describing the implementation and evaluation of the university-wide first year key skills 'ToolKit' initiative;
- highlighting some alternative methods of developing key skills at higher levels of study (eg the Learning and Skills Development in Partnership with Employers (LANDSKAPE) project, Goldfinch *et al*, 1999);
- describing the current strategy for the mapping and enhancement of key skills across all years of the curriculum.

We shall start by considering the issue of transferability of generic skills.

ARE GENERIC OR TRANSFERABLE SKILLS TRULY TRANSFERABLE?

It is sometimes assumed (but infrequently demonstrated) that, once learned, generic or personal transferable skills will transfer from the context in which they were acquired to another. Courses in any skill deemed essential to the educated, Carter (1993) argued, tend to rest on assumptions that they can be 'decontextualized', and that students will be able to apply them to other domains, 'including their lives'. However, this may not happen in practice. While there is a well-established research literature in psychology concerned with the transfer of training, often focusing on laboratory experiments, there appears to be very little empirical evidence concerning the transferability of generic skills.

However, debates surrounding the transferability of generic skills, while important as aids to reflection on our part, and no doubt stimulating to the protagonists, should not divert us from the main concern of much generic skills training and development: helping and supporting students as they enter higher education.

THE HISTORY OF GENERIC SKILLS DEVELOPMENT AT NAPIER

In 1992, while transforming degree provision into a modular structure, Napier University took the bold and ground-breaking step of building in a regulatory requirement that 'enterprise skills' be explicitly written into each module descriptor.

This style of embedded model did not, however, last long. Two years later, the modular system at Napier was revised. In the face of widespread criticism of too little staff consultation in the design and implementation of the first version of the modular scheme, the university responded by putting the revision process more firmly in the hands of academic staff. Among the many changes that were made, the definition, description, teaching and assessment of what were now named 'generic skills' was left to the discretion of programme teams. This step might be perceived as a downgrading of 'key skills'. Was this the sacrificial lamb, appeasing the more general complaint that the modular system presented a more rigid, bureaucratic constraint on professional freedom? More positively, the change provided programme teams with greater power to incorporate skills in ways best suited to the given subject discipline.

By 1997, concerns about the students' skills base and progression rates led to the commissioning of a working party to once again define skills for effective learning and wider ranging employability called the 'Toolkit' (See Table 4.1).

Table 4.1   1997 list of Toolkit skills, as used in the evaluation

Study skills	Communica-tion skills	IT skills	Library/ information skills	Quantitative skills
• Time management • Taking notes • Identifying resources • Group working	• Spelling and grammar • Essay writing • Giving presentations • Using the telephone	• Using a PC or MAC • Using a word processor • Using e-mail • Using a spreadsheet	• Finding information using keywords • Finding current information • Searching the WWW • Compiling a bibliography	• Arithmetic • Simple equations • Simple statistics (averages, percentages) • Interpreting graphical data

Having done this, programme teams were then required to deliver either a stand-alone or an embedded model in the first year of their programme. This phase of development was characterized by being staff led and involving wide-ranging consultation and by showing a genuine commitment to review and evaluation.

In recent years, the strong commitment to the teaching of 'key skills' has led once more to an examination of skills development across the entire degree programme: defining key skills; mapping them within degree programmes; and enhancing their provision. The impetus for this has been boosted by the production of the university's Strategy for Learning, Teaching and Assessment (LTA). The strategy makes a commitment to 'the conscious development of employability skills across all levels of programmes' (Napier University, 1999). In the closing days of the old millennium, a process for change was set in motion which at first glance appears to aim roughly back to where we were in 1992. However, back then it was a case of too much too soon. The key difference today is that the balance has shifted more appropriately towards allowing the expertise of staff to drive the process. Thus, staff are engaged more meaningfully in the process and everyone profits from the transference of good practice across the university. However, before we proceed further, it may be profitable to consider another of the issues identified above: that of whether stand-alone or embedded delivery is likely to be most effective.

EMBEDDING VERSUS STAND-ALONE OR PURPOSE-BUILT MODULE CONTROVERSY

While there is surprising consensus within higher education about the desirability of helping students develop generic, transferable skills, there is less agreement about how this may be best achieved. Many strategies for generic skills development employ an embedded approach where generic skills are developed within specialist courses or modules. Research reports describe the embedding within specialist subject teaching of a variety of generic skills: application of theory to practice and reflection (Falchikov and Macleod, 1996); critical reasoning and thinking (Shelpak, Curry-Jackson and Moore, 1992); critical feedback (Falchikov, 1996); oral communication and team working (Devine *et al*, 1994); library skills (Madge, 1995); listening skills (Falchikov, 1995); keyboard competence, time management, group interaction and personal presentation (Hall, 1995). Specialist modules, courses or areas used as vehicles for the development of generic skills are very varied, ranging from business studies to soil science. However, the majority of contexts are in the social sciences. Unsurprisingly, several of these reports expressed the view that embedding generic skills development was preferable to developing these skills in stand-alone modules.

The single most frequently encountered area of generic skills development is in the area of Information Technology (IT). For example, Watson (1997) argued that the use of IT is more 'naturally embedded' throughout the curriculum than many skills. Within the area of IT skills, there seems to be a consensus that embedding skills development within a course is preferable to the stand-alone model. There is even a meagre amount of evidence to support this view (eg Bull and Zakrzewski, 1997).

While evaluations of IT skills initiatives have suggested that embedded delivery is most likely to meet with success, some problems and questions remain. For example, few if any direct comparisons of stand-alone and embedded or integrated deliveries are to be found. We do not know whether development of other generic skills resembles development of IT skills. Moreover, in some studies the mode of delivery variable is confused with the variable relating to voluntary or compulsory take up.

THE TOOLKIT EVALUATION RESEARCH PROJECT

The ToolKit evaluation research project at Napier University provided the opportunity to carry out a rigorous evaluation of different modes of delivery of generic skills development. The evaluation involved the following steps:

1. 'Before' measures of skills levels were taken.
2. A survey of strategies selected by each department within the university was carried out.
3. A questionnaire survey went to all staff involved in the design and delivery of ToolKit skills modules (or ToolKit outcomes within other parts of the curriculum).
4. Focus group interviews with staff were carried out.
5. Focus group interviews with random samples of Year 1 students from a range of departments were carried out.
6. A questionnaire survey was made of all staff involved in teaching Year 1 students.
7. A questionnaire survey of all Year 1 students was carried out.
8. 'After' measures of skills levels were taken.

The 'before' and 'after' skills levels were measured by a test, partly based on one developed and used at Nottingham Trent University, and including self-reports (eg on the frequency of the student's experience of working as a part of a group); confidence logs (eg the student's confidence in giving a talk to a group of 20 people); and some objective elements (eg a spelling and grammar test and questions on basic quantitative skills). A group of students from each faculty took the tests, once at the beginning of their first semester at university, and again at the beginning of their second semester in order to measure any changes over the semester in which they had received their first generic skills training. A class of first year students from another university, with no explicit skills training, was also given the tests, to act as a control.

RESULTS OF THE TOOLKIT EVALUATION STUDY

Questionnaire data

Questionnaires were completed by 643 students and 77 staff. The stand-alone model had been adopted by 11 departments in the university, while the embedded model had been adopted by 16 departments. Both students and staff expressed a preference for the embedded over the stand-alone model, though significantly more of these were those who had experienced the embedded model (see Table 4.2).

Table 4.2   Student and staff preferences for embedded versus stand-alone delivery

Students	Preferred embedded delivery	Preferred stand-alone delivery
Experienced embedded delivery	64%	36%
Experienced stand-alone delivery	55%	45%
Overall	60%	40%

Staff	Preferred embedded delivery	Preferred stand-alone delivery
Experienced embedded delivery	76%	24%
Experienced stand-alone delivery	40%	60%
Overall	55%	45%

Reasons for preferring the embedded model mostly concerned students seeing the relevance of the skills to their subject area, whereas a preference for the stand-alone model often mentioned the problems of allocating marks to the skills in an embedded model. A stand-alone model was felt to prevent the skills from getting sidelined, and to make students more aware of them, but could cause problems with student motivation.

In general, if students were aware of having been taught a skill, they also reported an improvement. Students who had experienced the stand-alone model were considerably more aware that they had been taught the skills in all skill areas, and also felt less need for further improvement in some of these (library/information skills and quantitative skills) than students from groups where skills development was embedded.

There were few other differences between the two groups in terms of their perceptions of skills improvement or need for further development.

'Before' and 'After' comparisons

The results from the 'Before' test indicated little difference between the faculties in study skills, nor between the Napier students and the control group. The Science faculty students scored lowest on communication skills and on library/information skills, with the Arts and Social Studies students scoring highest of the Napier students in both these areas. However, Science faculty students scored significantly higher than other Napier students did in quantitative skills. The control group scored significantly higher than the Napier students in library/information skills and IT skills. (The latter had been anticipated, as the members of the control group were registered for a BSc degree in Computer Science). In other areas the control group scores were generally similar to the higher Napier scores.

Over the first semester, Napier students showed some improvement in at least seven of the nine skill sub-areas tested, compared to improvements in only four areas for the control group and indeed some deterioration in another four. No pattern of superiority of improvement resulted from one or other of the modes of delivery. All groups, on average, reported increased experience with IT and more training in giving presentations. The Napier students had generally improved their study skills significantly more than the control group. In addition, they felt more confident in their communication skills than controls, and had had more practice at making presentations. However, two Napier groups appeared to have deteriorated in their spelling and grammar skills.

In summary, while the embedded model is more popular with both staff and students than the stand-alone model, both models seem to be effective in raising student skill levels as judged by the test used in this study.

WHAT NEXT?

As illustrated above, the introduction of ToolKit as a Level 1 experience has been a useful enhancement to the curriculum for Napier students and has contributed to improvements in their ability to cope with the demands of higher education. However, it was recognized as being only a starting point in the development of skills necessary to produce both the 'adaptive' and 'transformative' graduates of the future (Harvey *et al*, 1997). There was an agreed need within the university to build on ToolKit skills, to further develop them and to widen them to include skills and attributes required to equip students for employment. This viewpoint is captured in Napier's LTA strategy, which includes a commitment to: 'the conscious development of employability skills across all levels of programmes' (Napier University, 1999) as part of its responsibility to help the university to meet its vision of being 'focused on students and helping them to realize their full potential' and being 'the lifelong university in South East Scotland' (Napier University, Strategic Plan 1999–2003).

Napier has many staff actively engaged in enhancement activities, many of which build on work begun under the Enterprise in Higher Education initiative. Examples of these include the university's accreditation opportunities for work placement, part-time work, volunteer and student tutoring activities, the Learning and Skills Development in Partnership with Employers (LANDSKAPE) project, its Careers Network with employers, and use of live projects, alongside a number of other innovative programme design, delivery and assessment practices. Harnessing such expertise was acknowledged, by Napier's Employability Skills Group, as critical. Such action was supported by research showing that any skills development initiative is most likely to be effective 'within a holistic and effectively managed change programme' and that 'whilst piecemeal measures may appear positive, they are unlikely to produce effective skills provision' (Drummond *et al*, 1999). Key staff involved in these activities were encouraged to contribute to a lively internal debate which took account of the external one. As a consequence, an outline plan of activities was drawn up.

EMPLOYABILITY SKILLS AND ATTRIBUTES MODEL

The first task was to agree a model that reflected the skills and attributes being labelled as 'employability skills' (see Figure 4.1).

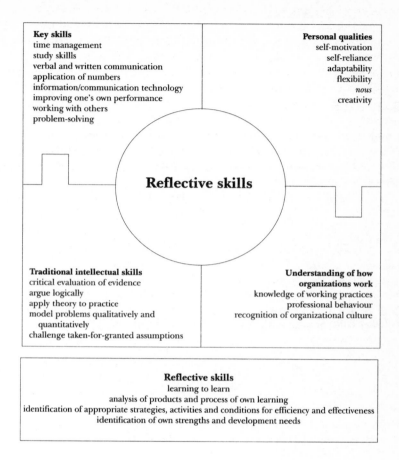

Key skills
time management
study skillls
verbal and written communication
application of numbers
information/communication technology
improving one's own performance
working with others
problem-solving

Personal qualities
self-motivation
self-reliance
adaptability
flexibility
nous
creativity

Reflective skills

Traditional intellectual skills
critical evaluation of evidence
argue logically
apply theory to practice
model problems qualitatively and
    quantitatively
challenge taken-for-granted assumptions

**Understanding of how
organizations work**
knowledge of working practices
professional behaviour
recognition of organizational culture

Reflective skills
learning to learn
analysis of products and process of own learning
identification of appropriate strategies, activities and conditions for efficiency and effectiveness
identification of own strengths and development needs

Figure 4.1   Napier University's employability skills and attributes model

The purpose of such a model was to provide a focus for dialogue with staff, students and employers alike that could inform curriculum planning, implementation and review and establish priorities as well as capture the essence of the agreement. It was deliberately presented simply to aid rather than distract from such discussions.

As this book is going to press, the first of a series of staff development events is about to begin – The Employability Skills Roadshow. This is to be followed by information briefings to faculty and departmental teams and by workshop activities within subject-specific areas to consider how such skills can be realistically yet effectively and visibly built into the curriculum.

As you can imagine, we like to be kept busy!

ACKNOWLEDGEMENT

We wish to thank Sandra Foubister for her work on the ToolKit evaluation study.

REFERENCES

Bull, J and Zakrzewski, S (1997) Implementing learning technologies: a university-wide approach, in Embedding technology into teaching: achieving institutional change, eds J Martin and H Beetham, *Active Learning*, **6**, pp 15–19

Carter, D (1993) Critical thinking for writers: transferable skills or discipline specific strategies?', *Composition Studies/Freshman English News*, **21** (1), pp 86–93

Devine, M et al (1994) *School for skills: A national survey of the development through TVEI of personal and transferable skills*, Technical and Vocational Initiative, Scottish Council for Research in Education, Edinburgh

Drummond, I et al (1999) *Managing Curriculum Change in Higher Education: Realising good practice in key skills development*, University of Newcastle

Falchikov, N (1995) Peer feedback marking: developing peer assessment, *Innovations in Education and Training International*, **32** (2), pp 175–187

Falchikov, N (1996) Improving learning through critical peer feedback and reflection, *Higher Education Research and Development*, **19**, pp 214–218

Falchikov, N and Macleod, L (1996) Using psychology in the community: developing transferable skills, *Psychology Teaching Review*, **5** (2), pp 63–74

Goldfinch, J *et al* (1999) Improving group working skills in undergraduates through employer involvement, *Assessment & Evaluation in Higher Education*, **24** (1), pp 41–51

Hall, T (1995) Birmingham's prelim project: transferable skills in foreign language teaching, *Language Learning Journal*, **11**, March, pp 43–46

Harvey, L et al (1997) *Graduates' Work: Organisational change and students' attributes*, Centre for Research into Quality, Birmingham

Madge, C (1995) More than books: use of a problem-solving exercise to explore university library resources, *Journal of Geography in Higher Education*, **19** (1), pp 69–82

Napier University (1999) *Strategic Plan 1999–2003*, Napier University, Edinburgh

Shelpak, N A, Curry-Jackson, A and Moore, V L (1992) Critical thinking in introductory sociology classes: a program of implementation and evaluation, *Teaching Sociology*, **20** (1), January, pp 18–27

Watson, B (1997) Supporting the integration of IT into the curriculum at the University of Durham, in Embedding technology into teaching: achieving institutional change, eds J Martin and H Beetham, *Active Learning*, **6**, pp 36–37

5

Implementing graduate skills at an Australian university

Ted Nunan, Rigmor George and Holly McCausland
University of South Australia
Australia

SUMMARY

The University of South Australia has adopted as institutional policy a statement of seven graduate qualities as the outcomes it seeks for its graduates. The qualities provide an integrating framework for reforming the university's courses, teaching and learning activities, assessment and the activities of a portfolio of complementary learning support services. This case study outlines a range of initiatives that provide powerful examples of the transformative potential of the framework.

INTRODUCTION

The University of South Australia is in the process of changing its teaching and learning practices to ensure that its students develop a set of seven graduate qualities that incorporate a range of key skills. The range of initiatives presented here demonstrate that the central direction, support and coordination offered by a powerful framework of graduate qualities can support the interrelated and pervasive changes to teaching, learning and assessment that together constitute significant educational reform.

THE AUSTRALIAN HIGHER EDUCATION CONTEXT FOR GRADUATE SKILLS

Various investigations in the late 1980s and early 1990s were concerned to match the outcomes of education with Australia's wider economic context and needs (Coaldrake and Stedman, 1998). These investigations proposed that education should declare and develop 'competencies' in graduates through its curriculum. Universities aggressively opposed this idea – competencies were seen as reductionist and did not convey the complexity and sophistication of outcomes that arose from the university experience.

The move to specify the qualities or attributes of graduates was heralded in a government report, *Achieving Quality* (Higher Education Council, 1992), which put the position that one aspect of the quality of a university was whether its graduates achieve particular attributes. Commenting on this position, Peter Coaldrake pointed out that progress in the area of graduate attributes has been slow:

> Many universities in Australia have now at least articulated the generic and professional attributes that their graduates ought to possess on graduation. Progress on translating these into practice has been slow. One barrier to progress is posed by academic territorialism and financial incentives for 'owning' student load, factors that encourage courses to be developed around institutional structures and professional or departmental preferences rather than graduate attributes.
>
> (Coaldrake, 1998: 12)

An important aspect of quality assurance for university teaching has become a process of measuring whether graduates have achieved the skills and attributes that institutions claim their graduates have attained. Government has recently set in train two mechanisms for such quality assurance. First, it requires that the plans for institutional quality assurance 'as a minimum requirement... are expected to include a description of graduate attributes' that they seek to develop (Department of Education, Training and Youth Affairs, 1999). Second, it has commissioned the development of a graduate skills assessment instrument. The usual process of commissioning research and evaluation studies and funding development grants (Bowden *et al*, 1998; Bowden *et al*, 2000; A C Nielsen, 2000) was instrumental in preparing the ground for these mechanisms.

A focus on graduate skills is part of a government programme of 'educational reform through accountability'. From the viewpoint of the contractor (government) the stated graduate attributes are outcomes that contractees (institutions) are expected to produce through their processes. Further, customers (students) should have the right to gauge whether their supplier (institution) has delivered what was promised. Thus institutions should cite the qualities that they expect from their graduates. It is then up to the institutions and individual students to substantiate claims that such qualities, attributes or skills are indeed developed.

This context has been the backdrop against which the University of South Australia has worked since 1992 to determine the characteristics of its graduates. From this followed changes to ensure that the qualities identified are systematically developed through its courses.

GRADUATE QUALITIES AT THE UNIVERSITY OF SOUTH AUSTRALIA

The university's submission to a 1994 national quality audit set out a staged process for the period 1992 to 2003 by which it proposed to change its teaching and learning environment and determine the characteristics of effective undergraduate and postgraduate courses. A chancellor's working group was formed to explore the desired qualities of a University of South Australia graduate. In December 1995, after extensive consultation with the university community, Professor Denise Bradley (then deputy vice-chancellor) formulated a set of seven qualities of a graduate of the University of South Australia. An implementation framework that would carry the university through to December 1999 was also developed. The Academic Board and the University Council accepted the set of qualities and the framework in May 1996.

The University of South Australia has determined that every one of its graduates will be:

- able to operate effectively with and upon a body of knowledge of sufficient depth to begin professional practice;
- prepared for lifelong learning in pursuit of ongoing personal development and excellence in professional practice;
- an effective problem solver, capable of applying logical, critical and creative thinking to a range of problems;
- able to work both autonomously and collaboratively as a professional;
- committed to ethical action and social responsibility as a professional and as a citizen;
- able to communicate effectively in professional practice and as a member of the community;
- able to demonstrate international perspectives as a professional and as a citizen.

Within this set of seven qualities, the dimensions of 'body of knowledge' and employability attributes (ie working autonomously and collaboratively, problem solving, and effective communication) are integrated with significant social, ethical and international dimensions to form a set of qualities that apply to both professional life and citizenship (Bradley, 2000). Further, the university sought to avoid reductionist notions linked to the term 'skills' by using more complex statements of the characteristics of a graduate. These statements include issues of scope, context, and application. It is this integration and balance (Nunan, 1999a) that both defines and differentiates graduates of the University of South Australia. Significantly, the university conceptualized the development of such qualities as 'built-in' to all components of all of its courses and not as 'bolt-on' optional extras to existing course arrangements.

All higher education institutions would claim that the university experience produces 'learning that lasts' in the form of core or generic skills. However, the approach taken at the University of South Australia since 1996 has been to put in place a whole of institution process to bring about the development of a set of qualities which encompass such skills. The provision of frameworks that provide direction, support and coordination was central to the university's strategy for successful and managed implementation of graduate qualities (Drummond, Nixon and Wiltshire, 1998).

While implementation has been driven by policy, initiatives that develop graduate qualities within contexts of the classroom, distance education and Internet-based learning are rewarded. There are few other Australian examples of policy-led development and implementation in this area.

CHANGING PRACTICES AT THE UNIVERSITY OF SOUTH AUSTRALIA

What is described here are a number of initiatives that are indicative of the range of activities to develop graduate qualities within the University, namely:

- changing courses to develop graduate qualities;
- a lifelong learning strategy;
- internationalization as a curriculum outcome;
- developing more inclusive curricula;
- reconceptualizing student support;
- a communication skills strategy for students from non-English-speaking backgrounds;
- students recording their achievements in terms of the graduate qualities.

While each of these initiatives involves providing learning opportunities for students to develop graduate qualities and associated skills, the qualities framework has also acted as a catalyst for complementary improvements in the teaching and learning environment. Concern with how students develop qualities has renewed a focus on student-centredness in the university's learning environment.

What is significant about the seven focuses of activity is that they are all interrelated and can be seen as outworkings of the university's position about the centrality of graduate qualities for effective teaching, learning and assessment. In what follows we have used interchangeably such terms as 'qualities', 'attributes' and 'skills' for those core or generic outcomes expected of graduates. We acknowledge that there is a considerable literature on distinctions between these terms and have already used distinctions between skills and qualities in our preceding discussion (Bennett, Dunne and Carre, 1999). However, common usage by staff and students makes little of distinctions and for ease of description we will do so likewise. The descriptions of each of the areas of activity are necessarily brief – the reference list indicates sources that give a more extensive description and analysis.

Changing courses to develop graduate qualities

The ways that courses are constructed have undergone major change. Policy and administrative requirements in relation to course documentation and approval processes have been undertaken around graduate qualities. It is now a requirement of all courses that the course aims are elaborated and contextualized statements of the university's set of graduate qualities. Further, the teaching, learning and assessment arrangements of each subject of a course are selected to provide opportunities for the development of the qualities. Subject descriptions are required to inform students of the relative weighting given to the development of particular qualities in terms of the amount of student effort expected.

A lifelong learning strategy

In a world characterized by rapid change, the educational opportunities that relate to new and renewed forms of work are critical to economic and social well-being. The notion of lifelong learning is a response to this need and encompasses cradle-to-grave learning opportunities in formal and informal settings in planned or opportunistic ways.

The University of South Australia has developed a strategic approach to lifelong learning (George *et al*, 2000) that is grounded in the graduate qualities and as such is seen as integral to the curriculum. That is, when any teaching and learning occurs within a course, using whatever processes are appropriate to the field of study, students will be developing information literacy in preparation for lifelong learning. To this extent, a student cannot be seen as competent in the field without the appropriate levels of information literacy associated with that field.

The strategic initiative has three interrelated dimensions: a comprehensive and yet accessible means of understanding the concept of lifelong learning through a statement of the characteristics of the lifelong learner; a comprehensive resource to be used in the design and delivery of lifelong learning within subjects and courses and examples of how this has been done within specific fields; and a tool for auditing subjects and courses.

The lifelong learning strategy has brought together professionals from a portfolio of learning support services – the library, information technology services and professional development – in a collaboration to support a changed and changing learning environment.

Internationalization as a curriculum outcome

Globalization increasingly requires professionals to be able to live and work effectively at home and abroad in contexts where cross-cultural awareness and understanding and international perspectives are essential.

The University of South Australia has formally accepted a framework for internationalization that includes, as a central component, the last graduate quality in the list above, which is concerned with developing international perspectives (Leask, 1999a). All courses develop 'international perspectives' as a graduate outcome and as a consequence the content and delivery processes of courses are changing to achieve this (Leask, 1999b). The interpretation of international perspectives goes beyond the acquisition of skills and knowledge to the development of values and cross-cultural awareness and relates them to course matters. In addition to this there is a constellation of other organizational and programme strategies and practices including study pathways, staff and student exchanges and international student markets.

Developing more inclusive curricula

If we take seriously the claim that graduate students should be able to demonstrate particular levels of achievement in core skills, qualities or attributes, then we would expect that in a mass higher education system all students should have the opportunity to develop and achieve such skills. That is, our educational outcomes and processes should be such that no student or group of students is inherently disadvantaged in relation to other students or groups because of the curriculum or educational processes in delivering the curriculum.

The university's mission is to provide education in ways that are inclusive and has located its approach to developing inclusive curriculum within the graduate qualities. Generic indicators, developed to illustrate each of the graduate qualities, were reframed on inclusivity principles – in effect, generic indicators have been transformed into inclusivity indicators. Such an approach positions inclusivity as mainstream curriculum development by linking it to teaching, learning and assessment strategies (Nunan, George and McCausland, 2000a).

Reconceptualizing student support

Another significant area of policy-led development is in the reconceptualization of student support services (Hicks and George, 1998). A focus on graduate qualities has meant that the means of supporting students has become dependent upon curriculum decisions. Student support staff now focus on influencing such decisions so that when subjects are redeveloped support is embedded as a step in the primary delivery of subjects. This constitutes a significant shift from service delivery through parallel sessions or in catch-up activities when students fail. Support staff work in collaboration with the teachers and such collaboration contributes significantly to the professional development of academic teachers.

Supporting students through indirect rather than direct means can be seen as much more effective. In addition, there has been an increasing emphasis on the provision of both generic and subject-specific online resources that support students. This is consistent with the goal of autonomous learning in the fourth graduate quality and has increased the client base through improved access and flexibility.

The shift in services and practices has been significant. The approach harnesses the expertise and experience of academic student support staff to achieve systemic change identified at the institutional level (Nunan, George and McCausland, 2000b). Rather than dealing with relatively small numbers of students in ways that are often idiosyncratic, the approach links the activity of staff to institutionally identified outcomes and provides support for both staff and students in achieving these.

A communication skills strategy for students from non-English-speaking backgrounds

A major issue in some courses at the University of South Australia is the high proportion of students from non-English-speaking backgrounds. This can present considerable difficulty within the teaching of subjects and also has implications for graduating students in gaining appropriate professional registration in order to be able to practise. The graduate quality concerned with communicating effectively in professional practice provides the basis for a course-wide language strategy which benefits all students in the course but which has particular outcomes for students from non-English-speaking backgrounds. The strategy is a collaborative venture between the course-based academics, learning advisers and professional development staff.

The strategy identifies the language and communication qualities expected by stakeholders. Curriculum mapping is undertaken and the course analysed for the opportunities within subjects where the qualities can be developed and assessed most effectively. Students with language proficiency difficulties are identified in the first semester of their first year and particular strategies, including group sessions, are put in place for them. To support both staff and students in the learning and assessment tasks, materials are developed for both staff and students.

Experience with this approach has revealed the following advantages:

- Language expectations are related to the professional performance of the graduate.
- Learning and assessment are developmental and supported for all students.
- All students benefit because they are supported in the development of their professional communication.
- Students with particular language needs are supported within the assessment framework, rather than being loaded with a further burden of remedial exercises.

Students recording their achievements in terms of the graduate qualities

The qualities of a graduate are concerned with what students learn through their university studies. The qualities may well be learnt, rehearsed, and developed elsewhere as well, but the act of linking qualities with graduation sets the expectation that university studies have a significant role in developing them. From an institutional perspective, this is achieved through overtly promoting the set of graduate qualities through processes that shape the curriculum and the teaching and learning arrangements within the university. From a student perspective, the qualities gain particular meaning and power when they are used to reach personal goals.

Students recording and reflecting on activities relating to the qualities is one mechanism to increase their awareness of, and agency in managing, their development of qualities. Such 'mapping' can reveal 'gaps in the record' or highlight where experiences have not yet provided the desired level of development. Students may then seek out opportunities to strengthen their achievements and fill the gaps. Such a record, while having a formative function in directing subsequent actions, can also have a summative function in that the records of achievements can be selected and tailored as evidence for essential criteria in job applications.

A student recording of achievement of graduate qualities pilot project (the ROA project) is part of the university's wider programme of implementation of graduate qualities. The project is being trialled with staff and up to 500 students of the university's School of International Business (Nunan, 1999b). The project will develop tools and processes that will become resources for implementation across the institution.

Graduate skills – their future at the University of South Australia

The graduate qualities are becoming part of the language and culture of the institution as these initiatives meet, overlap and spark new initiatives. The University of South Australia has taken a particular approach to crafting its teaching and learning environment to bring about changes that are in the interests of students, governed by equity and inclusiveness considerations, yet sensitive to the need to produce high-quality graduates in the competitive environments of higher education and job markets (Nunan and McCausland, 1998). The initiatives described are part of the process of changing the fundamental culture of the institution. The frameworks and mechanisms described only have importance if they are used by staff and students to guide and question their practices. Frameworks and processes must be subject to continual use, valuation and renewal if they are to become part of institutional culture. The momentum achieved through the initiatives described here provide the impetus for continuing change.

REFERENCES

A C Nielsen Research Services (2000) *Employer satisfaction with graduate skills*, Evaluations and Investigations Program, Higher Education Division, Department of Education, Training and Youth Affairs, Canberra

Bennett, N, Dunne, E and Carre, C (1999) Patterns of core and generic skill provision in higher education, *Higher Education*, **37**, pp 71–93

Bowden, J *et al* (1998) *Defining, developing and assessing generic capabilities of ATN graduates*, funding submission to Department of Education, Training and Youth Affairs, Canberra

Bowden, J *et al* (2000) *Five universities – one vision: generic capabilities of ATN university graduates*, Draft report, pp 1–33, Teaching and Learning Committee, Australian Technology Network, Melbourne, Australia

Bradley, D (2000) The citizen of the new century, *On line opinion*, Feb/March 2000, www.onlineopinion.com.au/feb00/bradley.htm

Coaldrake, P (1998) *Reflections on the repositioning of the government's approach to higher education*, Keynote address, Reworking the University Conference, pp 1–17, Griffith University, Brisbane, Australia

Coaldrake, P and Stedman, L (1998) *On the Brink: Australia's universities confronting their future*, p 59, University of Queensland Press, St Lucia

Department of Education, Training and Youth Affairs (1999) *The quality of Australian higher education 1999*, Higher Education Division, Department of Education, Training and Youth Affairs, Canberra

Drummond, I, Nixon, I and Wiltshire, J (1998) Personal transferable skills in higher education: the problems of implementing good practice, *Quality Assurance in Education*, **6** (1), pp 19–27

George, R *et al* (2000) *Information literacy – an institution wide strategy*, paper accepted for Lifelong Learning: Development of Generic Skills in Higher Education international conference, July, Central Queensland University, Rockhampton

Hicks, M and George, R (1998) *Approaches to improving student learning at the University of South Australia*, HERDSA Annual conference Transformation in Higher Education, Auckland, New Zealand, www.cce.auckland.ac.nz/herdsa98/HTML/LearnSup/HICKSM.HTM

Higher Education Council, National Board of Employment, Education and Training (1992) *Achieving quality*, AGPS, Canberra

Leask, B (1999a) *Bridging the gap: internationalising university curricula*, National Liaison Committee for International Students in Australia, Sydney

Leask, B (1999b) *Internationalisation of the curriculum: key challenges and strategies*, Australian International Education Conference, International Development Program Education Australia, Perth

Nunan, T (1999a) *Redefining worthwhile knowledge in higher education*, paper for the Australian Association for Research in Education/New Zealand Association for Research in Education Conference 1999, Global issues and local effects: the challenge for educational research, Melbourne

Nunan, T (1999b) *Graduate qualities, employment, and mass higher education*. Paper delivered at HERDSA conference Cornerstones: What do we value in higher education? Melbourne, www.herdsa.org.au/vic/cornerstones/authorframeset.htm

Nunan, T, George, R and McCausland, H (2000a) Inclusive education in universities: why it is important and how it might be achieved, *International Journal of Inclusive Education*, **4** (1), pp 63–88

Nunan, T, George, R and McCausland, H (2000b) Rethinking the ways in which teaching and learning are supported, *Journal of Higher Education Policy and Management*, **22** (1), pp 85–98

Nunan, T and McCausland, H (1998) *Changing institutional cultures: creating learner centred environments*, pp 105–112 contributed papers, 24th International Conference: Improving University Learning and Teaching, Griffith University, Brisbane

6

Embedding key skills in a traditional university

Mary Chapple and Harry Tolley
University of Nottingham
UK

SUMMARY

The project that provides the focus for this case study was one of a number of key skills projects awarded funding by the Department for Education and Employment (DfEE). The case study begins with a brief sketch of the ethos of the university. An overview of the purposes and characteristics of the development work of the project are then outlined and the lessons that can been learnt about embedding key skills within a higher education institution of this kind is provided.

INTRODUCTION

A team based in the Teaching Enhancement Office (TEO) of the University of Nottingham carried out the two-year (1998–2000) Embedding Key Skills in a Traditional University Project. Eight schools and divisions – departments of the university – representing a range of academic and professional vocational and non-vocational courses participated in the project.

The university: background and context

The university is a 'traditional university' that is committed to achieving excellence both in research and in teaching and learning. This is demonstrated by the results it has achieved in the both the research assessment exercise (RAE) and Quality Assurance Agency (QAA) assessment of teaching quality. It is a large, complex multi-campus institution that is dynamic, rapidly changing and expanding. Programmes of study at both undergraduate and postgraduate levels across the full range of academic disciplines attract large numbers of well-qualified applicants from home and abroad, many of whom are intellectually ready for higher education and bring a variety of skills with them. This inevitably has an impact on staff perceptions of the need for embedding key skills within the curriculum.

The university: organizational setting

The university's academic work is organized on the basis of divisions that are grouped into schools and faculties. Within this organizational structure there is an established tradition of substantial autonomy with regard to academic matters, and distinctive departmental cultures have evolved. In common with other pre-1992 universities whose claim to excellence may once have rested on the quality of their research portfolio, there is an ongoing tension between the competing demands of teaching and research. This has a strong influence on the way in which some academic staff react to what they perceive to be externally imposed curriculum and teaching initiatives.

The university's approach to developing a culture conducive to encouraging innovation and excellence in teaching and learning is to work with departments from within. Rather than employing professional experts to promote good teaching and develop new ideas it draws on the experience, enthusiasm and creativity of working academic staff who are seconded from their departments on a part time basis to the TEO. The role of these academics is to undertake cross-disciplinary activity and to spread good practice through the university, with the TEO acting as a source of information and funding, and as a network for exchanging new ideas and sharing best practice.

Key skills at the university

The development of skills relevant to employment and future learning is an integral part of the university's Teaching and Learning Strategy and it is a general requirement that all modules be written in terms of the transferable skills to be developed. As a consequence of this remit all schools have made a move towards integrating skills development into their teaching, although institutional practice is varied and difficult to quantify.

The Careers Advisory Service and the Students' Union are involved in providing opportunities for students to develop key skills alongside the curriculum and are seeking to work ever more closely with academic departments. There are also several stand-alone key skills opportunities operating across the university. The University Basic Information Technology Skills

(BITS) course and the development of literacy courses are just two examples of these.

The Centre for Developing and Evaluating Lifelong Learning (CDELL) based in the School of Education has a number of ongoing and recently completed externally funded national research projects related to key skills initiatives in higher education.

The Personal and Academic Records for Students in Higher Education (PARSHE) Project started at the university in 1995. Since then the initiative has been extended to promote personal and academic records (PARs) in five UK universities. As a consequence many schools across the university have introduced electronic or paper-based PARs into their personal tutor systems.

THE EMBEDDING KEY SKILLS IN A TRADITIONAL UNIVERSITY PROJECT

The project had two main aims. One was to develop mechanisms for embedding key skills within a range of undergraduate and postgraduate courses in a traditional university so that they could be disseminated to other courses. The other was to establish ways in which the assessment and recording of key skill competencies can be included within existing institutional, personal and academic recording systems.

Outline of the project

The project extended over a period of two years and was organized in four overlapping stages. In the Preparation stage, the main focus was on selecting the key skills to be developed and on devising strategies and tools for developing, assessing and recording key skills. In the Implementation stage, the key skills procedures and materials were piloted. In the Dissemination and Evaluation stages, the success of these strategies and tools was evaluated and the outcomes were disseminated across the university and to other universities. The duration of each stage of the project was adapted to take account of the differing timescales and nature and requirements of the individual departments.

CHARACTERISTICS OF THE DEVELOPMENT WORK UNDERTAKEN

In a large and complex higher education institution such as this one embedding key skills in the curriculum is a difficult exercise in planning and the management of change. It was clear from the start that if key skills provision were to be successfully embedded within the curriculum of the participating departments a variety of different approaches would be required. Some of these measures adopted are given below.

Participating departments

The departments that participated in the project were drawn from across the university:

- Biological Sciences;
- Education;
- English Studies;
- General Practice;
- Mathematical Sciences;
- Nursing;
- Physiotherapy;
- Social Sciences and Social Policy.

They were all selected because they had performed well in their teaching quality assessment and because work had already started on developing and implementing transferable skills and/or PARs into their curriculum. It was anticipated that the progress, solutions, obstacles and successes of each department would be disseminated to colleagues and peers, with the aim of encouraging a demonstration effect that would provide an impetus and bridge for change across the university.

Departmental leaders as change agents

A key element of the project's strategy for embedding key skills within the curriculum was the appointment of departmental leaders, working academics who would act as change agents and would monitor and coordinate key skills development within their individual departments. These individuals were seconded to the project on a part-time basis. This approach was consistent with the university's strategy of developing teaching innovations from within, rather than imposing it from outside.

Staff training and development

A programme of staff development seminars and workshops with international and national key skills experts was run to introduce departmental leaders to the concept of key skills and the different approaches that existed for developing students' key skills. This programme was not intended to produce a set of ideal strategies; rather it aimed to stimulate debate on what key skills are, how they might be developed and assessed, and how they might be implemented within individual departments.

A problem-centred approach

At the beginning of the project each of the departments was at very different stages of development in respect of key skills. For instance, the School of Education, with previous experience of developing key skills in its courses and with externally imposed requirements from the Teacher Training Agency (TTA), was in a very different position from those subject-based departments that were delivering academic courses to undergraduate students.

There was also considerable variation in the context within which the key skills programmes were being developed. For example, the Biological Sciences, Physiotherapy and English Studies departments were working with single cohorts of students based in one teaching centre and being taught by a small group of academic staff. In contrast, the Nursing department was seeking to develop key skills in modules that were being delivered across five education centres spread across a large geographical area to part-time students on a variety of programmes. Similarly, the situation in the General Practice department was also extremely complex as they were seeking to develop students' communication skills during a four-week placement within a general practice setting. Thus they were faced not only with developing students' key skills within the classroom, but also with the logistics of preparing and supporting large numbers of part-time tutors, many of whom were medical practitioners with no formal academic or teaching experience. For these reasons the development work initiated by the departmental leaders was 'problem-centred'. In other words, the starting point for innovation in each of the departments was a perceived need for course improvement rather than a desire to incorporate key skills into the curriculum per se. These needs can be seen in Table 6.1. It was anticipated that this approach would generate motivation and commitment amongst those individuals who were actually delivering the programme and would provide them with a sense of purpose and direction.

Table 6.1   The problems that provided the starting point for key skills development

Department	Initial problem	Key skills
Biological Sciences	Improving written communication skills of Year 1 and Year 2 students	Communication
Education	Meeting the key skills requirements of the TTA (Teacher Training Agency) for PGCE (Postgraduate Certificate in Education) students	Application of numbers Communication Information technology
English Studies	Developing oral presentation and team working skills of Year 1 students	Communication Working with others
General Practice	Improving oral communication skills of Year 4 Medical Students in the context of doctor–patient consultations	Communication Improving own learning and performance
Mathematical Sciences	Improving oral presentation and team working skills of Year 1 and Year 3 students	Communication Working with others
Nursing	Improving oral and written communication skills and learning to learn skills of Post Registration Nurses	Communication Improving own learning and performance
Physiotherapy	Improving the information technology skills of Year 1 students	Information technology Working with others
Social Sciences and Social Policy	Developing greater learner autonomy in Year 1 students	Communication Improving own learning and performance Working with others

Developing key skills that were 'naturally occurring'

On commencement of the project there were many discussions about the nature and terminology of key skills. It became clear very early in the project that the different disciplines valued and embodied each of the key skills to a different extent. For instance team-working skills were more highly valued in the Physiotherapy and Nursing departments, where they were considered essential, than in the School of Mathematical Sciences, where they were thought to be of limited relevance. Also, there were obviously wide differences of specialization and sophistication in the nature and use of some skills between disciplines. For example, the range of relatively specialist textually descriptive written communication skills developed in English Studies courses would not normally have been included in a written communication skills programme for Social Science students. Moreover, an adequate communication skills course that was considered to be appropriate for biological scientists was thought to be unlikely to equip medical students with the skills they required to communicate with patients and to maintain clinical records. Therefore, no attempt was made to map the full range of key skills, as explicated in the Qualifications and Curriculum Authority (QCA) specifications, onto existing courses. Rather, in each case the starting point for the development process was the selection of those key skills that were 'naturally occurring' within the subject discipline and which the academic staff judged to be of value and importance to students in that discipline. This had the advantage that skills development took place in a meaningful context and the students were able to engage with the material and make it their own. The key skills selected by each department can be seen in Table 6.1.

Developing approaches that were sensitive to individual contexts

Owing to the differences and diversity existing within the departments, it was clearly not going to be fruitful to impose one master plan for key skills development across all departments. Therefore, the departmental leaders interpreted and adapted the development programme to their individual contexts, whilst remaining focused on the project's aims and objectives. Some of the approaches that they adopted are itemized below:

- The nature and purpose of the planned innovation, and the scale, timing and pace of the development were tailored to their specific circumstances.

- In order to ensure coherence and progression throughout the course, skills audits were carried out so that key skills provision was integrated into the curriculum where the subject matter and modular outcomes lent themselves most effectively to the development of specific key skills.

- Departments developed their own key skills materials and strategies and customized centrally and externally produced resources to meet their particular needs.

● Students' key skills acquisition was integrated into existing assessment strategies and criteria. In this way tutors were encouraged to provide regular and ongoing feedback to students on their key skills development and students were encouraged to value key skills development.

● Existing student feedback mechanisms, such as questionnaires and end-of-module reviews, were amended to solicit feedback about the new key skills provision from students. The Independent Evaluator also obtained feedback on the new practices from staff and students. The results of these exercises were used to revise the development programme and to demonstrate good practice to sceptical colleagues and students of the legitimacy and practicality of the department's key skills programme.

This flexible approach to key skills development enabled all of the departments to start the process of embedding key skills in the curriculum in ways that took account of their own academic or professional discipline, student population, ethos and need.

KEY LESSONS LEARNED

Several lessons can be learnt from the experiences of the participating departments within this project.

Impact on the wider curriculum

Despite their different origins and intentions, all of the attempts to embed key skills into the curriculum have inevitably involved a shift towards a more student-centred style of teaching and learning. Consequently, although the stated aim may have been to develop a particular skill, the resultant process of learning has required students to engage more deeply with the relevant subject matter. Evidence of this can be seen in this observation made by a student who was talking about a learning activity designed to develop oral presentation skills:

> The last mathematical model we had to deal with involved a swimmer and was more open-ended and difficult. The test was to try and incorporate the maths at the proper level into the presentation. It made you think… I was confused at first, but had to resolve the difficulties by thinking hard about them.
>
> (Mathematics student in a focus group)

This quote seems to suggest that the communication skills being developed were being complemented by the growth of subject knowledge and understanding and cannot be separated from it.

The advantages of encouraging students to adopt 'deep' approaches to their learning through the tasks they are set for assessment purposes and the feedback they receive have been summarized by Entwistle (1992) and Gibbs (1994). Similarly, students were invariably involved in developing a wider range of skills, such as improving their own learning and performance, working with others and solving problems, whilst in the process of acquiring other key skills. These skills will not only help them to cope more effectively with future learning, but they are highly valued by employers (Association of Graduate Careers Advisory Services (AGCAS) 1999).

Supporting students' key skills development

The experience of this project suggests that the incorporation of key skills into the curriculum of a university of this kind can be done in ways that have a beneficial effect on student learning. However, it is also equally evident that in order for this to occur, a number of elements in the students' learning environment needed to be brought into constructive alignment:

- All individuals who are delivering the programme need to recognize the importance of key skills in the curriculum and inform themselves on the processes involved.
- Appropriate forms of tutorial support must be provided, to give students formative feedback on their key skills performance, and to encourage them to reflect upon their own learning and develop action plans.
- Assessment methods need to be adapted to accommodate key skills in ways that provide coherence and progression, that encourage students to adopt a 'deep' approach to their learning, and that provide students with feedback on the effectiveness of their learning.
- PARs or progress files have an important role to play as a means of encouraging students to evaluate and plan their own learning and to track the development of their key skills, including those acquired through extra-curricular activities.

The cumulative effect of such changes will not only reinforce the students' immediate key skills development, but in the longer term will nurture their ability to accept greater responsibility for the direction and management of their own learning. This should give them a number of lasting advantages, including the ability to cope with the need for continuing professional development once they have entered employment and with the demands of lifelong learning. A student in a focus group summed this up: 'We are acquiring these skills so that we can keep developing ourselves in the future and keep abreast of changing technology and new knowledge and information as it emerges.'

These measures should also help to ensure that the students are capable of transferring what they have learned in one situation to another one: they should be helped to overcome the 'situatedness' of their cognition (Lave, 1990). This requires that students are challenged and supported in a manner that ensures their 'learning goes beyond what the situation calls for' and leads them towards an understanding of 'deep principles' (Bereiter, 1997). If learning occurs in this way the chances of students being capable of transferring their so-called 'transferable skills' should be increased.

CONCLUSIONS

This project has discovered that embedding key skills within the curriculum of a large and complex higher education institution is a far from easy process. Time and considerable effort are required to ensure that key skills become fully integrated into all aspects of teaching, learning and assessment. Irrespective of this, within the short time span of this project the eight participating departments have all demonstrated the potential that key skills has for adding value to the learning experiences of students. A foundation has been laid on which future developments can be built across the university as a whole.

REFERENCES

Association of Graduate Careers Advisory Services (AGCAS) (1999) *Higher Education Careers Services and the Development of Employability Skills: A position paper*, written by M E Thorne, University of Nottingham
Bereiter, C (1997) Situated Cognition and how to Overcome it, in *Situated Cognition: Social, semiotic and psychological perspectives*, eds D Kirshener and J Whitson, Lawrence Erlbaum Associates, Mahwash, New Jersey
Entwistle, N (1992) *The Impact of Teaching on Learning Outcomes in Higher Education*, Committee of Vice-Chancellors and Principals (Staff Development Unit), Sheffield
Gibbs, G (1994) *Improving Student Learning: Theory and practice*, Oxford Centre for Staff Development, Oxford
Lave, J (1990) *Cultural Psychology: Essays on comparative and human development*, Cambridge University Press, Cambridge

7

Creating incurable learners: building learner autonomy through key skills

Judith Harding
Middlesex University
UK

SUMMARY

Implementing a key skills module in a large multi-campus institution involves at least two main considerations: *that* it happens and *how* it happens. The first is relatively simple: a central executive decision, explored by a task group and approved by an academic board, decrees that it shall happen. The second, how it happens, is more complex and problematic. It requires careful handling. However well intentioned, such a decision may be perceived as a threat to the coherence of subject areas and to academic control of learning contexts. Its imposition can be experienced as loss – of ownership, of choice, and, in cases where effective modules have already been developed and are seen to work well, of a sense of local inventiveness not being valued.

This chapter reflects on the two-year process of introducing a cross-university key skills module. It is, in a sense, a postcard from the middle of the reflective cycle; more will be learnt as the system becomes fully operational. Unexpected developmental effects, as well as predictable reservations, emerged. As the reflective process encourages us to recognize, both kinds of effects can change the way in which we adjust future planning. In particular, the development of a template module, adaptable to different subject needs and drawing imaginatively on unusual sources, has led to new ways of thinking about skills in general. Extensive consultation with staff and students has reinforced a conviction that focusing on key skills in relation to personal frameworks and the processes of research can offer ways of building broader learner autonomy.

BACKGROUND

A task group, formed by the executive to consider the role of skills in the curriculum, met during the academic year 1998–99. This group, consisting largely of senior managers who had little direct contact with students, decided to require skills modules in all programmes. In structurally foregrounding the importance of skills by requiring dedicated modules in all programmes, this group was responding to a variety of influences: the Dearing Report, research on employer needs, government skills initiatives and the experience of other institutions (National Committee of Inquiry into Higher Education (Dearing Committee), 1997). The decision also rested on some doubt that claims by some areas that skills were already embedded in subject modules were as substantial as they might have wished. Concluding their deliberations, the group identified a set of key skills based on consultation with other institutions. This list described six areas to be addressed at three levels:

- career management (to become, as a result of consultation, 'personal and career development');
- effective learning;
- communication;
- teamwork;
- numeracy;
- information technology.

In the following academic year an implementation group was charged with making this plan a reality. The university's Centre for Learning Development (CLD), given a lead role, encouraged a shift in membership to include more on-the-ground experience. Enthusiasts who had been working with first-year students and who had designed skills initiatives in their own areas were included, as were students and student support staff. In general this group had a greater awareness of students' experiences as well as possible consequences of implementation.

Discussions with staff in the individual schools showed that the original grid of learning outcomes contained unnecessary repetition and blurring of requirements over three levels. It was agreed to refine the statements of learning outcomes, concentrating on those designated for Level 1, and to suggest evidence to show the level of specificity needed. Some areas already had modules in place that could be modified, while others needed to design new ones. Plans for the template module were proposed. It was also agreed that 'personal development' might be more appropriate than 'career management'; this eventually took the compromise form of 'personal and career development' to accommodate both the local interests in career issues and the driver of employer needs for focus on skills.

Over the next two months, the CLD team refined the learning outcome statements, reviewed existing materials, supported the development of new modules within the schools, and discussed plans for the template module with stakeholders. Drawing on recent pedagogical research and the experience of thinking about these skills with staff and students, the team designed the broad shape of a template module to address not only the specific needs of the areas identified by the Academic Board, but also some broader, and perhaps more crucial, issues of attitudes and approaches. Supporting materials and a resource bank of sequenced contact activities were begun and trialling with staff and students planned. A series of academic development events for staff who would be working on key skills modules would offer opportunities for staff to share their ideas across the institution as well as to take advantage of the reviews of existing and new materials and approaches.

During this development phase, it became clear that the success of any of this implementation rests on enthusiastic ownership and support of subject-specific staff who have high credibility with students. Students, and other staff, need persuading that this is not a time-wasting soft option, but can be a worthwhile, interesting and important experience, central to students' academic and workplace futures; conditions for such an experience need to be in place through careful design and implementation of the module. Ideally, contact staff must be excellent communicators who care about students' development and can channel enthusiasm for the project into thinking imaginatively about it, even when it may sound initially like the imposition of an additional burden for everyone involved.

THE TEMPLATE MODULE

The following description of the ideas informing the template module was circulated to staff involved in developing the school-based modules, along with drafts of the revised learning outcomes and suggested evidence. An important factor in breaking down staff resistance and building cooperation was the decision to let each school develop its own subject-specific variations of the module rather than being fixed to a common central formula. The template module was intended to stimulate thinking about the task in general and to suggest alternative ways of presenting the notion of skills in relation to issues of research, reflection and autonomy. After an initial section charting the background, listing the specific skills, and stating the need for such a module were the following five sections. These are entitled:

● The module: assumptions and starting points.

- Research as relating.
- Questioning (?), connecting (&) and telling (!).
- Image and metaphor.
- Employability.

The module: assumptions and starting points

In thinking about the shape of a module that could address the identified key areas for development, it was felt crucial to begin with the live experience that students bring with them, whether academic, work or social. Anyone who has survived to the age of considering entering university has developed a considerable range of skills in all the identified areas, though it may not be readily apparent how these operate in an academic setting. It is important to value what students do bring with them, and to encourage them to value their existing skills by exploring and specifying what those skills might look like in an academic setting. It is crucial to avoid patronizing but it is also necessary to provide sufficient challenge for those who come well prepared.

For this reason, we have thought of the module in three broad sections. One relates to the person, their history and experience of using skills in a non-academic setting. The second relates to that person's role as a student in the context of the university and the way those 'life' skills can be adapted to the needs and responsibilities of the new situation. The third deals with the adaptability of those skills to the needs of working and researching in a specific academic subject.

Research as relating

These three areas can also be thought of as a sequence of activities relating to any kind of investigation – research – in which a person moves from finding out, through connecting, to communicating. First one discovers one's interests, drives and motivations. Then one thinks individually and with others about what has been found out and how the various parts relate to one another in patterns and constructs. Finally one makes public what has been discovered and related. These three stages of curiosity, connecting and communicating give a broad framework in which to develop, through repeated revisiting of each skill area in its application to a central core project over the whole semester, the essential fuel that can make it all work: confidence, imagination, flexibility, and ability to challenge assumptions and ask good questions. These are precisely the skills that many employers claim they are looking for more than specific academic knowledge.

This framework of investigation, whether of personal history or of an academic research topic, is a pattern that emphasizes the idea of relating, in all its senses. The rather cold and clinical enumeration of key skills, placed in the context of the richer complex of activities that academics value as the stages in research, takes on a new sense of life. These are not skills to be delivered but tools and processes to be used in the overall aims of finding out, putting together, and telling someone about it.

This makes the activity of learning to use them a bit like an archaeological investigation, a kaleidoscope or a theatrical performance, or like travel. In travelling, there are choices: the safety and predictability of the package tour, the more independent self-catering holiday, or the adventurous and challenging backpacking exploration of an unknown and possibly danger-ous but beautiful mountainous terrain. Acquiring the tools needed for this latter autonomous journey is a matter of developing a backpack adequate enough to support possible needs and emergencies, and light and compact enough not to be an additional burden. It's a Swiss Army knife, with a rudi-mentary map that can only be completed as the journey proceeds, a mental camera and a set of postcards to write home. At the end of the experience, the traveller should be able to write an individualized travel guide to prepare for further journeys and know what pitfalls and dangerous valleys to avoid as well as the most scenic routes.

(The idea of relating is the fourth step in both Biggs's SOLO taxonomy (Biggs, 1999) and Marton and Saljo's Conceptions of Learning (Marton and Saljo, 1997); it is the key idea in moving from the point of having no idea whatever, through knowing one or two things, through being able to make an unconnected list, to the point of being able to see how things fit together and how they interrelate and relate to other concepts, to a final stage of being able to hypothesize about how things might be if they were otherwise.)

Our original working title for this module was 'Researching your Learning'. Gradually we have begun to think of it as more a course in asking questions rather than being given answers: it focuses on the need and curios-ity, the incessant asking of why and how, that is as much at the heart of the researcher's motivation as it is of the insatiable (and often irritating) search-ing of a three-year-old. We have considered the title 'What would happen if...?' but may find it useful to incorporate the term 'self-reliant learner'. Our aim overall, whatever the title, is to create the conditions for encouraging autonomous, reflective 'incurable learners'. The name QUEST has emerged as an appropriate designation that condenses the ideas of questioning, the metaphor of adventurous travel, and the notion of research.

Questioning (?), connecting (&) and telling (!)

The actual structure of each contact session will suggest a central topic in which specific activities will address and require applications of each skill in order to accomplish the task. This means that each area will be revisited and practised in a number of different contexts, rather than having individual sessions treating one skill at a time. This structure reinforces the point that they are all connected, and that their value is in their use, rather than their possession. The unopened Swiss Army knife remains only a set of possibilities. A particular emphasis in the activities will be on the processes of reading, paraphrasing and restating, understanding, comparing and evaluating the content and structures of written material to underpin the processes of writing by asking questions about its processes. Another emphasis will be to identify the things that get in the way by specifically addressing the issues of boredom, confusion and fear.

Image and metaphor

In thinking with others about the requirements and possibilities of this template module, several images kept returning. One was the image of turning the camel of the task of implementation into a well-formed horse of what the module might actually be in practice. These horses might look quite different according to what subject area designed or modified them: circus horse, police horse, race horse, etc. This led to thinking about the key skills module itself as a kind of Trojan horse, marching into the programme looking like something rather frightening, but once there, opening up to reveal the unicorn, whose powerful properties could unlock possibilities and carry through some of the more complex, less directly measurable but equally important skills and approaches. The combination of this image with one that has often surfaced in our discussions of a single tool that can be used in many different ways led to the intriguing and playful image of the Swiss Army unicorn. This has made us think about how important the use of visual and verbal metaphor is in developing alternative ways of thinking about complex issues and of finding many ways of explaining them to different audiences. Searching for metaphors has helped us focus on the problem, has broken down some of the resistance among staff for the project as a whole, as they see that it has the possibilities for carrying some of the key concepts of their subject areas. It has been a revealing tool to discover the levels of flexibility and imaginative thinking in staff groups. It has introduced the idea of the ability to make something initially forbidding and boring into something interesting simply by the way it is thought about becoming an important skill in itself. This is why a subtext in the whole module and its supporting materials will be the encouragement of the use of metaphor and visual image as a way of understanding and presenting complex material.

Employability

Behind this development lies the 'keyest' of concepts, and demonstrably that of most interest to students, that of employability. Research suggests that, in this era of serial and portfolio careers, what employers really want are the 'unicorn' concepts – flexibility, imagination, ability to ask good questions, to hypothesize what a situation might be like under other circumstances, and all our 'C' words – creativity, confidence, challenge, curiosity, connecting, and communication – which are also at the heart of research. By starting with the assumption that the module has a direct relationship to all of the students' life, their prior experience, their present life outside the university setting, and their future work and learning life, there is a reason and a need for them to value the tools it will ask them to learn to use. This links with the ethos of work-based learning, where reflection on past and current experience becomes the heart of assessing one's own learning. This module offers an opportunity to bring together many strands of university activity in an exercise in joined-up thinking whose aim is to encourage our students' awareness of their own possibilities and creative thinking about their past experience.

EFFECT OF THE TEMPLATE MODULE

Because it drew on unusual resources (the philosophy with children movement, popular understandings of science, local learner autonomy debates, and the visual arts as well as strands of current higher education pedagogical theory) and alternative approaches to thinking about skills, there was a feeling that the template module might be taken up quite enthusiastically. In fact, the response was remarkably polarized. Some areas, primarily those whose discipline had more natural inclination to the interpersonal and the creative, warmed to the ideas more and wished to use its pattern and ideas almost unchanged. Others responded coolly, or ignored it.

Surprisingly, the net effect was motivational, but not quite in the way anticipated. The implied imminent threat of a centrally imposed module, however interesting, had the effect of mobilizing teams that had not really addressed the task seriously before. Suddenly there was evidence of rapid progress in local initiatives to develop modules that addressed local needs in the framework of specified learning outcomes. It was particularly important, and somewhat difficult to convey, that all skills modules needed to share common learning outcomes, no matter what subject specific elements were added, so that any student transferring areas could not be asked to repeat it. They needed to be mutually recognized and mutually inclusive.

As well as providing a pattern to react against as much as to adopt, the template module became developmental in several ways. It introduced some theoretical ideas to a wider audience. The need to consider the agreed learning outcomes led staff to reconsider their attitudes to assessment. Like the externally imposed requirements of subject reviews and teaching quality assessments, it provided a forum and a need for rethinking curriculum design issues and the way in which aims and outcomes are distinguished and explained to students. It raised, in the effort to define skills in relationship to particular subject areas and to engage in the 'embedded-generic' debate, wider issues of learner autonomy. It offered another opportunity to persuade staff committed to traditional lecture-seminar patterns to think about the implications of use versus delivery. It has required staff to plan together in new ways. Though the template module may never have a life as an operational module, its ideas are informing the support sessions for staff working on the new module.

STUDENT RESPONSE

Confirmation that these ideas might prove persuasive to students came from their responses in a short series of cross-university focus groups. Working with two groups in three intensive two-hour sessions, CLD staff surveyed their views on skills, and introduced a range of exercises, materials and approaches based on the questioning–connecting–telling pattern and the idea of starting from their own experiential frameworks.

Though the responses of this thoughtful and articulate group (that included all years as well as post-graduate students) may not have reflected the full range of student attitude, they suggested that these approaches were on the right track. The students felt strongly that initial intensive face-to-face contact that respected their intelligence and individuality was crucial to persuade them that having a dedicated skills module would be useful, and would develop their ability to work independently later on. The module needed to be group- rather than lecture-based, with lecturers included in the discussions and sharing their own experiences of learning and confronting obstacles. It needed to be enjoyable, but never patronizing. Materials must *look* as well as *be* interesting. Processes needed to be visual, interactive, imaginative and energetic. They needed to concentrate on reading, understanding, thinking and challenging received views. Management language should be avoided. Lecturers need to listen. Students need to feel listened to.

The students welcomed the idea that any skills module should, above all, be designed around the need to use and relate the agreed skills defined in the learning outcomes in a personally meaningful and interesting subject-based real-life project. They identified the danger that some students, unless they can see the point, might react cynically, especially where staff were unconvinced and unenthusiastic. Whoever worked with this module, they felt, needed to believe in its value and find ways of making it meaningful and vivid to themselves as well as a wide range of students.

Leaflets designed to inform incoming students about the new skills requirement responded to an executive concern to focus on employers' needs and employability. Its design, however, is based on the trio of symbols representing the questioning–connecting–communicating processes. The question mark, ampersand and exclamation mark have evolved into a logo that represents the central concepts of autonomous research and learning that need to inform the skills modules, whatever their local framing.

CONCLUSIONS

Much has been learnt during this process. While it may still be a matter of debate whether the centrally determined requirement of a universal skill provision is the most useful approach to improving student skills, it is clear that keeping a substantial measure of local control is crucial to securing any sense of ownership of the project. It is now clear, too, that far more consultation with students and staff who work directly with first-year students could be helpful in the initial planning stages. Local administrative and advisory staff who understand the practical consequences of varying student programmes, progression and assessment mechanisms, as well as local learning resources staff, need to be included in early discussions.

As a developmental exercise, much has been accomplished that could not have been explicitly planned. The fact of having to address a genuine (though perhaps less than welcome) real-life need encouraged groups of academic and support staff to work productively together. The process of redesigning provision made discussion of pedagogical issues necessary. Comparing the different forms of modules emerging across the university has increased awareness of differences in subject needs and campus contexts. It has shown that rejection of a well-thought through model can have positive effects in mobilizing autonomous local team initiatives. It is becoming clear that the module will offer an effective way of extending the induction process and provide a comprehensive means of monitoring initial student experience.

As staff felt more ownership they began to make their own contributions to the general presentation of the module. One favourite that has now come into general use and seemed to tie many ideas together was the student counsellor's observation that if we rearranged the order of numeracy and information technology in the original list, the named skills formed the acronym 'pectin' – a slightly unusual word which after a few minutes most people recognize as the substance that makes jam set, that makes things gel. Useful as a simple mnemonic to call up the list, it is also a reminder that there can be a sense in skills implementation of some larger idea binding it all together, connecting skills and experience in a more organic way.

More lessons will be learnt as the progress of implementation of a variety of module patterns is tracked. Whatever adjustments need to be made in the future (as the skills provision is extended to second and third years in line with the original task group's decision) it is clear that any skill development rests, like the Freierian need to say, on the need to be used in real and meaningful applications (Freire, 1998). Creating autonomous 'incurable learners' needs to draw on the attitudes and enthusiasms of academic researchers who can share those skills with students. And perhaps the most useful skill of all, as the students pointed out, is the ability to make, on their own, something that looks difficult and boring into something personal, interesting and creative.

ACKNOWLEDGEMENTS

Contributions to the project were made by CLD members: Professor Barry Jackson, who led the implementation team; Michelle Haynes, who collaborated with the author on refining the agreed learning outcomes, discussing early versions of the template module, and facilitating the student consultation sessions; and Kyriaki Anagnostopoulou, who designed the graphic presentation grid.

REFERENCES

Biggs, J (1999) *Teaching for Quality Learning at University*, SRHE/Open University Press, Buckingham

Freire, P (1998) *Pedagogy of the Oppressed*, revised edition, Continuum Publishing, New York

Marton, F and Saljo, R (1997) Approaches to learning, in *The Experience of Learning*, eds F Marton et al, Scottish Academic Press, Edinburgh

National Committee of Inquiry into Higher Education (Dearing Committee) (1997) *Higher Education in the Learning Society*, The Stationery Office, London

8

Tertiary literacies: integrating generic skills into the curriculum

Catherine Milne
University of Wollongong
Australia

SUMMARY

At the University of Wollongong any consideration of the integration of generic or transferable skills must start with an examination of the relationship between generic skills and graduate attributes. It is from this relationship that the university's notion of tertiary literacies is constructed. Graduate attributes can be described as capabilities students develop at university that go beyond content. This chapter is an account of how the University of Wollongong's notion of quality higher education led to the explication of a clear relationship between generic skills and graduate attributes and its incorporation into curriculum development.

As early as 1990 the University of Wollongong identified some of the attributes of its graduates by including a list of skills expected of all graduates in its mission statement. At this stage, these skills were a first attempt by the university to identify skills that graduates should possess as a result of their studies.

In 1992, the Higher Education Council in Australia linked generic skills with graduate attributes. It identified generic skills as a component of one of three graduate attributes. Its perspective was premised on the notion that attributes were the outcomes that 'graduates should acquire if exposed to a high-quality higher education system including all its processes' (Higher Education Council, 1992: 19). The Council argued that there was a need for universities to 'round out' the 'whole person', producing graduates with certain skills, attributes and values. These skills would be transferable to the extent that once acquired in one context students could apply them in a different context. Generic skills were also called transferable skills. The Council was adamant that not all the attributes are quantifiable and they do not immediately lead to employment, but they stressed the need for quality higher education institutions to make the mechanisms for achieving these attributes as transparent as possible.

ATTRIBUTES OF A WOLLONGONG GRADUATE

Even before the publication of the Higher Education Council's monograph (1992), staff at the University of Wollongong had developed a set of graduate attributes that were consistent with the university's mission and vision (University of Wollongong, 1992).

These attributes were articulated as *The attributes of a Wollongong graduate* and served to define 'graduateness' within the university (Wright, 1996). The attributes of a Wollongong graduate identified specific capabilities that graduates should develop during their course of study at the university. There was awareness that the ability to use these attributes prepared graduates more effectively for the workplace and for lifelong learning (Wright *et al*, 1997). There was acceptance that for these attributes to be more than platitudes they needed to form part of a wider teaching and learning strategy at the university. The university had already started to link the attainment of graduate attributes to quality higher education. The steps for quality would include the following:

1. Involvement of the stakeholders in identification of the attributes of a Wollongong graduate.
2. Development of a strategy to make attributes explicit in the curriculum.
3. Generation of evidence that students are able to learn these attributes.
4. Implementation of programmes to achieve continuous development.

INVOLVING THE STAKEHOLDERS

In order to address the question of whether these attributes were reasonable, stakeholders were involved in a consultative process to revise and articulate the attributes of a Wollongong graduate. Firstly, major employers of the university's graduates were surveyed to find out which attributes they valued. For employers, coherent and extensive knowledge in a discipline was most highly rated. However, they also valued the ability to write clearly and fluently, the capacity for cooperation and teamwork, problem solving and decision-making ability, and the capacity to change and adapt. In 1993, major employers, academic staff, graduates and students were involved in developing a shared set of graduate attributes. These attributes were selected because they were considered to support learning throughout life and in the workforce. The current attributes (1997–2005) are very similar to the original attributes although they are not divided into competencies and attributes and they are expressed more actively, providing a firmer basis for teaching, learning and assessment.

To claim that our graduates experienced quality higher education the graduate attributes needed to become part of a strategy for the development of quality higher education. Part of this strategy included acknowledgement of the role of graduate attributes in preparing students for lifelong learning and employability; that quality required a focus on outcomes rather than objectives, and that attributes developed in the context of a discipline but that the skills involved were transferable.

INTEGRATING GRADUATE ATTRIBUTES INTO THE ORGANIZATIONAL STRUCTURES OF THE UNIVERSITY

With the incorporation of the articulated attributes into university policy the next step was their integration into curriculum planning and development. This step was informed by the belief that if attributes are enabling character- istics then they need to be taught. In the past, programme developers, sub- ject developers and educators had not been asked to be explicit about how the attributes of a Wollongong graduate were developed in their programme or subject. Also, social and cultural developments were indicating that grad- uates would need to have the skills to be able to continue learning when they left university.

These developments included: the shift to an information society; increas- ing globalization; the knowledge and technology explosion (encouraging universities to think of learning smart rather than trying to learn the lot); a shift in the types of careers available; and changes in the workplace such as increasing automation.

Graduates could be expected to have the skills that they needed to engage in self-directed learning, postgraduate study or professional development associated with employment (Candy, Crebert and O'Leary, 1994). The notion of a lifelong learner implied that certain skills would be valued at the undergraduate level including:

● information and computer literacy;
● understanding how knowledge is constructed within the discipline and the limits of that discipline;
● skills to reason critically;

- organizational skills;
- the learner's awareness of his or her preferred learning style.

Initially, efforts towards curriculum reform were uneven and tended to be restricted to the enthusiastic few. For example, by 1997 Learning Development was working with staff from some departments to develop programmes in which generic skills, appropriate to student learning within the discipline, were sequenced and specified. There was a realization that the attributes needed to be 'unpacked' and that skills associated with each attribute needed to be identified if this reform were to be taken further. In order to establish a strategy that assisted staff to integrate graduate attributes, two working parties were established, the Comprehensive Information Literacies Working Party in 1995 and the Generic Skills Working Party in 1997. There already existed awareness that generic skills and graduate attributes were linked but the university had yet to specify which skills were linked with which attribute (Milne, 2000).

The outcomes of these working parties included:

- a description of generic skills as 'those skills which are achievable, worthwhile and essential for all undergraduate students regardless of their course of study' (Wright *et al*, 1997):
- identification of specific generic skill indicators for each graduate attribute;
- an endorsement of the context-dependent nature of generic skills and their transferability to different situations;
- a curriculum strategy that proposed a curriculum-integrated approach and developmental programme for the teaching of generic skills, supported by a familiarization unit that would introduce beginning undergraduates to the information environment of the university and to some basic computer and information skills;
- the need for generic skills to be taught explicitly by being identified in subject descriptions, learning outcomes and assessments.

These outcomes provided a framework for curriculum development. However, the two working parties had adopted different broad terms for the skills, capabilities and understandings that constituted their area of investigation and there was concern that discussion of information literacies and generic skills could confuse staff. For example, staff asked questions such as, what is the relationship between information literacies and generic skills? Are the skills outlined in the Comprehensive Information Literacies Report more accessible because they are less cognitive than other generic skills? Where do academic skills or tertiary literacy skills sit within generic skills?

At the same time as these working parties were deliberating, the attributes of a Wollongong graduate were revised for inclusion in the University Strategic Plan for 1997–2005. Attributes were specified as given in Table 8.1.

Table 8.1 Attributes of a University of Wollongong graduate

ATTRIBUTES OF A WOLLONGONG GRADUATE

(University Strategic Plan 1997–2005)

- A commitment to continued and independent learning, intellectual development, critical analysis and creativity.
- A coherent and extensive knowledge in a discipline, appropriate ethical standards and, where appropriate, defined professional skills.
- Self-confidence combined with oral and written skills of a high level.
- A capacity for, and understanding of, teamwork.
- An ability to logically analyse issues, consider different options and viewpoints and implement decisions.
- An appreciation and valuing of cultural and intellectual diversity and ability to function in a multi-cultural or global environment.
- A basic understanding of information literacy and specific skills in acquiring, organizing and presenting information, particularly through computer-based activity.
- A desire to continually seek improved solutions and to initiate, and participate in, organization and social change.
- An acknowledgment and acceptance of individual responsibilities and obligations and of the assertion of the rights of the individual and the community.

EMERGENCE OF TERTIARY LITERACIES

An umbrella term, 'tertiary literacies', was proposed to remove any confusion about generic skills and information literacies. In this case, literacy is described as having the skills or being literate with regard to a particular area of knowledge and experience. Thus, literacies encompass the skills and understandings of a graduate attribute within a context and discipline area. This definition provided a framework for the integration of information literacies and generic skills under specific graduate attributes. Towards the end of 1997, the Tertiary Literacies Working Party was established. It proposed the Tertiary Literacies Inventory that brought together the attributes of a Wollongong graduate and the recommendations of both the Comprehensive Information Literacies Working Party and the Generic Skills Working Party. As it developed this inventory, the working party emphasized that the skills listed under each attribute functioned as indicators of that attribute. The list of skills was not designed to be limiting or complete because there might be skills or sub-skills indicative of an attribute but not specified by the working party.

To ensure that tertiary literacies were incorporated into programmes of study, they are identified as an essential component of New Subject Proposals that are presented by faculties for approval of the governing body of the university. At workshops, seminars and meetings emphasis is placed on the need to incorporate tertiary literacies into the curriculum and to explicitly identify the tertiary literacies that are important to the subject.

The learning outcomes and assessment tasks for specific subjects include an exposition of tertiary literacies involved. This means the subject developer has thought about which tertiary literacies they need to teach students so students can learn them and, therefore, complete the requirements of the subject. These learning outcomes and assessment tasks are included in subject outlines. This means that the tertiary literacies that are developed in the subject are presented explicitly, thereby making this information available to stakeholders, in particular to students.

Within the teaching/learning of a specific subject the application of tertiary literacies is modelled by teachers, students are provided with the opportunity to practise these literacies, feedback about their facility with these tertiary literacies is provided to students and these literacies are assessed within the subject. There is awareness amongst staff that students need opportunities to practise these tertiary literacies during their classes.

IMPLEMENTATION IN THE DEPARTMENT OF BIOLOGICAL SCIENCES

The assessment of tertiary literacies is a thorny issue. As subject developers and educators begin to reflect on the tertiary literacies that students need to be successful in their subject, they begin to realize that they sometimes make unwarranted assumptions about the skills that students possess before they begin their subject.

The Department of Biological Sciences conducted an assessment audit in order to gain a better understanding of the assessment tasks expected of students. Two of their concerns related to the teaching/learning of skills: whether there was a variety of assessment tasks required of students or they were required to demonstrate the same skills for each subject; and the relationship between the timing of instruction in the tertiary literacy skills needed to be successful at an assessment task and the timing of the task, that is, did the instruction come before the assessment?

The first assessment audit was conducted of the first year subjects in the Biological Sciences programme. Examining the types of assessment used can indicate coursework requirements, as subject coordinators ask themselves and their colleagues to identify the skills that students need to complete the assessment tasks and where these skills are taught in the subject.

The outcomes

The audit allowed Biological Sciences to examine the major streams in Biology, initially at the first year level, to ensure that key generic skills in areas such as oral and written communication are taught prior to assessment; and to ensure that students have the opportunity to consolidate their skills development by iteration but not to the point of overworking certain skills.

In 1997, a collaborative team consisting of members from Learning Development and Biological Sciences was established. It formulated an integrated skills development strategy initially within the first-year programme. The tertiary literacy skills that were emphasized were those associated with providing students with opportunities to learn skills that they needed to be successful in the subject and to progress through the programme. These skills included study skills, appropriate reading of a range of scientific genres and making notes of those readings, writing scientific reports and developing interpersonal skills.

The assessment task that assessed students' ability to write scientific reports assesses both students' general literacy and their ability to communicate in the biological field. Peer marking is used so students have access to other student scientific report models and so they are aware of how literacy criteria are used to assess their reports. Feedback is provided to students after they submit a draft version of the assignment and after peer marking. This process involves:

- active learning, as students work in groups to analyse and annotate reports;
- instruction using modelling of desired skills;
- instruction using feedback, so that students can identify their weaknesses;
- iteration, providing students with the opportunity to develop their skills and with the knowledge that would allow them to resubmit a report more closely approximating the model reports.

Although the assessment audit is still in its infancy and has yet to be completed for second- and third-year subjects, as it develops it provides more detailed information for subject coordinators as they evaluate the subjects that they teach. It provides a mechanism for highlighting the skills that are integral to each of the subjects but which need to be made more explicit so that students become aware of the skills that they need and are assisted to develop these skills. The process of developing an integrated skills programme highlights the advantages of a collaborative approach to such a strategy.

LEARNING THE ATTRIBUTES OF A WOLLONGONG GRADUATE

Faculties such as Education and Commerce are involved in a process of auditing, mapping and profiling of graduate attributes in order to assess the integration of tertiary literacies into programmes of study that are offered within each faculty. For example, the Faculty of Education offers undergraduate programmes in early childhood education, primary education and physical and health education. The process of auditing, mapping and profiling allows the faculty to evaluate the integration between the skills and knowledge presented in subjects that constitute each programme and the graduate attributes of the university (Temmerman and Wright, 2000).

Auditing involves examination of components of subject outlines such as aims, learning outcomes, subject descriptions, and assessment tasks, for reference to graduate attributes. Skill indicators, presented below each attribute in the Tertiary Literacies Inventory, served as guides for the sorts of skill statements in the subject outlines or descriptions that indicated a link to a graduate attribute. Mapping occurs at the programme or course level and involves making links between subjects and attributes via the skill indicators in the Tertiary Literacies Inventory. Such mapping is usually presented in a summary table of the subjects in the programme. Once the mapping is complete, a profile for each graduate attribute within a programme can be presented pictorially. These profiles provide evidence of the distribution of graduate attributes within programs, the connectivity between learning outcomes and assessment tasks within subjects, and whether graduate attributes are presented developmentally within a programme.

This process of auditing, mapping and profiling forms part of a quality assurance cycle and serves to assist the faculty in the following ways:

- It helps to answer the question: Are we, the faculty, doing what we say we are doing?

- It provides the faculty with a mechanism for demonstrating where students have opportunities to develop graduate attributes and the extent to which these opportunities are available.

- It provides evidence of the faculty's commitment to the attributes of a Wollongong graduate (the sociograms that are developed as a result of the profiling can indicate where in a programme there are gaps in skills, and where, perhaps, specific skills are overemphasized).

- It furnishes information that can be used for further curriculum planning. Once the evaluation of subjects using auditing, mapping and profiling is complete, it informs the planning process that then informs the implementation of subjects.

Commerce and Education offer professional degrees. These degrees tend to be highly structured and to offer a relatively narrow range of subject choices to students. Other faculties such as the Faculty of Arts are also involved in mapping and profiling their subjects but they have adopted a slightly different approach because of the numerous ways that students can become Arts graduates. Arts Faculty staff began their analysis by distinguishing the attributes of an Arts graduate. The next step required 'unpacking' these attributes to identify the specific skills that students need to demonstrate these attributes. For example, critical analysis was broken down into its constituent skills and it was presented developmentally over three years so that students would learn to think critically in a more sophisticated way over the years from Year 1 to Year 3. Finally, the evaluation stage required links to be made between these attributes and the attributes of a Wollongong graduate (Albury *et al*, 1999).

FOSTERING DEVELOPMENT

The advantages of these approaches to the evaluation of integration of graduate attributes are that they are being conducted at the departmental or faculty level. This requires a collaborative team effort and involves staff in learning more about structuring curricula. These approaches also provide information that can be invaluable for future curriculum planning.

However, for this integration of tertiary literacies to be fostered there need to be opportunities for staff to learn more and to have access to professional development, there need to be staff incentives, and there need to be standards that are applied campus-wide. At the University of Wollongong the following processes have been introduced:

- professional development programmes involving staff in developing curricula, writing learning outcomes and assessment tasks, and identifying and assessing skills;

● Outstanding Contribution to Teaching and Learning Awards (OCTL Awards), which recognize quality, innovation and commitment in teaching;

● establishment of Learning and Teaching Research so staff can gain recognition for their research in the area of teaching and learning in higher education;

● appointment of a Tertiary Literacies Officer to assist staff in the integration of tertiary literacies and in the measurement of that integration.

CONCLUSION

There is still some distance to travel along the pathway of tertiary literacies integration for the University of Wollongong. However, the four-step approach adopted here provides a strategy for fostering curriculum integration of the transferable skills needed for lifelong learning and for employability. These steps are:

1. Involving the stakeholders so that there is a shared understanding of the graduate attributes and of their value to prospective graduates.
2. Linking attributes to skills so that teaching staff have access to a framework for implementing and assessing the curriculum integration of graduate attributes.
3. Using auditing, mapping and profiling of tertiary literacies to provide evidence of the level of integration, allowing informed planning of curriculum development.
4. Providing support for staff that fosters continued evaluation and action in subject development, teaching and learning.

The benefits of this approach are twofold. Firstly, it involves teams of staff from a specific programme of study in the process of curriculum reform so that the effort is collaborative. Secondly, it provides a framework for developing a curriculum-integrated approach to teaching the attributes of a Wollongong graduate. Such an approach places the University of Wollongong at the forefront of curriculum development in this area. This strategy for the integration of skills is established so that we can be confident that we are providing students with the opportunity to learn these skills. In this programme they develop the skills and understandings that they need to be confident of their ability to apply skills flexibly, to respond effectively to the demands of employment and to be capable of continuing their learning when they leave university.

ACKNOWLEDGEMENT

I would like to thank Brenda Weekes and Lynne Wright who provided invaluable information on the early history of graduate attributes at the University of Wollongong.

REFERENCES

Albury, R *et al* (1999) Passing through the pain barrier: making a flexibly delivered degree, in *Cornerstones, Proceedings of the HERDSA conference*, Melbourne, Australia. URL: www.herdsa.org.au/vic/cornerstones/

Candy, P C, Crebert, G and O'Leary, J (1994) *Developing Lifelong Learners Through Undergraduate Education*, Australian Government Printing Service, Canberra

Higher Education Council (1992) *Achieving Quality*, National Board of Employment, Education and Training, Canberra

Milne, C (2000) Developing an instructional description of generic skills, in *Proceedings of the Lifelong Learning Conference*, Yeppoon, Central Queensland, in press

Temmerman, N and Wright, L (2000) Approaches to integrating tertiary literacies into curricula at the University of Wollongong, in *Proceedings of the Lifelong Learning Conference*, Yeppoon, Central Queensland, in press

University of Wollongong (1992) *Towards 2000 Strategic Plan*, University of Wollongong

Wright, L et al (1997) *Generic Skills Working Party Final Report and Recommendations*, University of Wollongong

Wright, P (1996) What are graduates? Clarifying the attributes of 'graduateness', paper published in DeLiberations, URL: www.lgu.ac.uk/deliberations/graduates/starter.html

9

Skills development through student-led activities

Becka Currant and Pete Mitton
University of Bradford
UK

SUMMARY

When children of different age groups are taught in a single room, it is normal for the older children to assist in the teaching of the younger children. This chapter describes how this principle can be used within a modern higher educational establishment. Student course representatives acquire the skills they require for their role by participating in training provided by experienced students. These experienced students provide both training and facilitation to aid their colleagues' learning. A description is given of some of the concerns that need to be addressed in establishing this training. It is proposed that for effective learning a community must be created in which all participants are equally important.

INTRODUCTION

The realization that students leaving further and higher education establishments should possess a range of transferable key skills has led to many changes in the courses offered by these institutions. The main approach has been to educate students in these skills either within the established course structure or alternatively within a separate module that concentrates on these skills. At the University of Bradford an extra-curricular approach has been taken where students take the lead in providing an environment in which students can acquire the requisite skills.

This chapter provides a short introduction to the approach taken at Bradford and discusses a brief history of the development of these ideas, the courses and opportunities offered, and future directions.

HISTORY

Within any academic organization it is important, for the course to improve, that student feedback is listened to and acted upon. However, for this to happen it is important for the student course representatives to have the necessary skills to canvass their fellow students' opinions, to communicate those opinions to academic staff, to suggest improvements to courses and to report back to students on their actions.

Many institutions have training courses for their course representatives run by either the institution or student union staff. However, making the use of the past experiences of other course representatives is comparatively rare.

Ten years ago the university's staff development department ran a course for academic staff on alternative forms of course delivery. The course included small-group work that was facilitated by the course organizers. Experiential learning was emphasized and it was felt that the course would also have relevance for students.

The course was re-run for student course representatives with members of staff development and academic staff facilitating the students' learning experience (Sayers *et al*, 1995). The students' response was very encouraging. In particular, a number of students expressed an interest in developing the skills they had acquired during the course.

The programme of course representative training has developed over the years with the contribution of the students in course delivery increasing every year. The stage has now been reached where the majority of the course is presented and facilitated by students with the assistance of the student development coordinator (SDC). The SDC post, a full-time position within the careers service, was created after the success of the early courses. The first two holders of the post were Bradford students who had developed their skills during the course representative training sessions.

After the first year of the course students took the role of facilitators for the small-group work. In later years students also took on the role of leading the sessions by presenting the material and picking out key learning points from the exercises.

However, it was realized that for students to fulfil these roles effectively additional training was needed. To address these issues additional training was provided in facilitation skills and later in training skills.

When the opportunity came to produce a booklet informing students of the possibilities for key skills development during their time at university, it was natural to continue the student-led approach.

Finally, the provision of key skills training has not and should not be restricted solely to course representatives. Student facilitators have now been trained to present material to other students in the form of 'The Alternative Degree'.

THE COURSE REPRESENTATIVE TRAINING

The most visible form of student-led self-directed learning is still the course representative training. The training consists of three evening sessions, each run twice, followed by a residential weekend. The training is available to all course representatives within the university. It is disappointing that only between a quarter and a third of the eligible students attend the courses; they are voluntary courses, and whether or not a student attends seems to be determined by his or her department's enthusiasm for its students to attend, and whether or not students from that department are already involved within the student development team. The university's engineering, physical science, health and social science specialities are all represented.

The evening sessions and residential weekend consist of a series of small-group exercises that allow the members to become aware of the skills required to work as an effective team. Debriefing every major exercise increases the participants' awareness by encouraging them to reflect on their individual performance and the effect it has on other members of the team. A commonly used debriefing technique is a three-stage feedback model:

- What went well?
- What could be improved?
- What specifically, if anything, would you do differently next time?

The emphasis is on the positive aspects of the exercise.

Two students lead each session, taking turns to present theoretical material and to introduce the exercises. They are also responsible for identifying key learning points from the exercises.

The student facilitator's role is to assist in this process by observing the group dynamics and ensuring that the group effectively debrief each session. The facilitators may also suggest energizers if appropriate.

The SDC or a more experienced student will act as support to both the facilitators and the leaders. Ideally, he or she should not have to present any material to the participants. However, if complex questions are asked or other difficulties occur the SDC or other student is available to intervene. His or her primary role is to act as a safety net to give the student leaders and facilitators confidence.

Theory is introduced either before the exercise, with the participants asked to consider the theory during the exercise, or alternatively after the exercise, to explain what has occurred. The theory sessions are kept as short as possible whilst conveying all the important information. Handouts reinforce the theory.

The course varies from year to year dependent on the previous year's experiences. What follows is intended to be a broad outline of the course content; it does not represent any particular year's course.

Evening session 1

This session concentrates on group working and problem-solving skills. A brainstorming exercise encourages the participants to think laterally. They are given an everyday object and have to come up with as many possible uses as possible within a given time period.

A plenary session allows the groups to feed back their ideas to the other participants. A typical learning outcome would be that the best uses are often not the first.

The IDEAL (Bransford and Stein, 1984) problem-solving methodology is introduced:

- Identify the problem.
- Define the problem.
- Examine possible solutions.
- Act upon your preferred solution.
- Look at the effects of your actions.

The groups are given a problem and asked to use the IDEAL model to come up with a solution. During debriefing the effectiveness of the methodology is considered.

A further exercise will concentrate on group dynamics and the participants will be introduced to Belbin's team roles (Belbin, 1993). The facilitators will explain their own most preferred roles and the secondary roles they sometimes fill. The Belbin questionnaire is not given out, although it may be requested, as it has been found that if participants become aware of their primary role at this stage they tend to stick within that role.

Evening session 2

This concentrates on communication skills, learning skills and further group work skills. The importance of active listening is introduced and a suitable exercise is set. The participants are asked to consider a development of the three-stage feedback model and use it as a way of communicating feedback to departments:

● Tell them what they are doing well.
● Tell them what could be improved.
● Suggest ways of improving the course.

Again the emphasis is on the positive.

An introduction is also provided to Adair's idea of Action Centred Leadership (1973) concerning the importance of the following when evaluating the performance of a team:

● team;
● task;
● individual.

This may also be used as a debriefing tool. Participants are introduced to Kolb's learning cycle (Kolb, 1976, 1984) and Honey and Mumford's learning styles (Honey and Mumford, 1982).

The exercises in the first two weeks are generally non-academic. The plenary session is used to ask students how they can introduce the ideas within an academic environment.

Evening session 3

The final session takes the form of a mock staff–student liaison committee meeting. The student leaders and facilitators play the role of the staff and the participants are the students. The task is for the students to raise issues about the poor performance of a member of staff and also to ask for funding for a course representatives' residential weekend.

The session is facilitated and debriefed as before.

Clapham – the residential weekend

At the residential weekend members of the academic and non-academic staff join the student participants. On occasions people from outside the university have attended the sessions. Groups are formed for the weekend that typically include one or two staff members and five or six students. Each group is assigned a student facilitator for the weekend.

On the Friday evening the groups get to know each other. The groups brief those participants who have not attended the evening sessions. The exercises encourage lateral thinking skills. It is emphasized to the participants that it is often their own preconceptions about a problem that prevent a solution being found.

The Saturday morning activity consists of a number of simple concurrent exercises that require the groups to function despite not being in a single physical location: this makes communication between the teams' members difficult. Planning the exercises is paramount. Points are awarded for completion and presentation of solutions but no mention of winners and losers is made.

Most years, at some stage in these exercises a team, or teams, realizes that cooperation is allowed and the problem is then how to manage communication within the larger group. To summarize, chaos normally ensues...

An extensive debrief of the session occurs after lunch. The difficulty of the combined exercises has normally led to plenty of soul-searching within each group on why they have not performed as well as they would have liked. During this session they identify what they consider to be the strengths of the group and also areas that they would like to improve.

Each group then selects a partner group whose strengths match areas in their own group they would like to improve and vice versa. For the rest of the day these pairs discuss what each would like to improve and the task for each team is to devise an exercise that will allow the other to improve in the areas identified.

On Sunday morning the teams carry out each other's exercise and debrief the experience. Changes in a group's performance can most clearly be identified during the design of the exercise and the carrying out of the other team's exercise. Again an extensive debrief occurs, drawing out the key learning points for each group and individual. A plenary session allows the groups to share their experiences and the weekend ends with individuals' experiences expressed as haikus.

This description has only scratched the surface of the subtleties of the weekend.

The course representative training does not produce students who have all the skills identified earlier for them to be effective. But it is a start. For the students to acquire the skills, they must practise the ideas presented in the training and reflect on the effect their actions have on others. Feedback from students indicates that it can be a year or two before they realize the benefits of the seeds planted during the training. Students returning from placement years often remark that they found the training very useful in business.

Final year students remark that their performance at assessment centres is improved. Lecturers remark that students who have been on the course present problems in more positive and constructive ways. The ethos of the weekend is to provide structured learning within a supportive and fun environment.

Members of staff report that what they are most surprised by is the amount of enthusiasm and effort the students are willing to invest in the training.

The key learning point here is that if the students enjoy the experience and the presenters have enthusiasm, the learning experience is amplified.

FACILITATOR TRAINING

For course representative training to be effectively carried out by students it is essential that they receive training in how to be good facilitators. The university's staff development unit has provided this training for four years.

Would-be facilitators are encouraged to reflect on their own experiences at being facilitated and to consider the different styles of facilitation that they have observed. They are encouraged to develop a personal style whilst obeying the one golden rule of facilitation to 'keep your paws off their learning'.

The staff development unit has a great deal of experience in facilitation and they are able to provide the aspirants with a theoretical background. At the end of the course students are encouraged to identify those skills that they need to improve to become good facilitators and to keep learning logs of how they achieve those skills.

STEPPING STONES TO SUCCESS

The University of Bradford received funding from the Department for Education and Employment (DfEE) to increase key skills provision within the university. One contribution of the SDC was to produce a booklet identifying those activities that students could participate in that would allow them to gain key skills outside of the university curriculum. Examples of such areas are participation in the running of student union clubs and societies, representing other students' interests as course or student union representatives and contributing to the student radio station or magazine.

The preparation of the booklet was an ideal opportunity for students to acquire key skills. A number of students who had not previously been active in any of the areas identified above were recruited to provide material. They were responsible for the basic research on what material to include and for gathering suitable illustrations, comments from students currently involved and the contact details for each area identified. These students were also responsible for assuring that the contents conformed to a house style and for the overall layout of the booklet.

The booklet was produced and distributed to all first and final year students at the university. It is envisaged that the material will be updated annually using the same approach.

TRAINING THE TRAINER FOR THE ALTERNATIVE DEGREE

The SDC and a number of students identified the need for key skills training to be available to all students in the university. A plan was developed for the creation of a seven-week course, 'The Alternative Degree', that would provide the skills that students may not have identified they needed until they arrived at university. The individual sessions covered:

- team working;
- study skills;
- self-evaluation;
- time management;
- presentation skills;
- examination skills;
- stress management.

The timetable for this course was that it should begin early in the second semester after students had taken their first semester examinations. By this time they should have identified how prepared they were for university life.

Trained students would deliver the course. However, the experiential approach used for the course representative training was not appropriate for most of the course. A more directive approach was needed, whilst retaining the enthusiasm and commitment displayed during the course representative training.

To give the students the necessary skills an external trainer of trainers was brought in to deliver a weekend of training. The external trainer was one of a number of former Bradford students who have used the skills gained in facilitating and leading the course representative training to gain employment.

The training took the participants through the whole process of designing, delivering and assessing a course of learning.

THE FUTURE

A review is currently taking place to decide how to develop the courses and learn from advances made in training/education/learning in both the academic and business fields.

A reunion weekend was held to discover what insights previous participants in the training could offer. The participants suggested that the course had prepared them for a number of challenges that they had found in employment but also identified other challenges, particularly interpersonal, that they were not prepared for upon graduation.

The major failing of the methodology, which must be addressed by the review, is the lack of hard assessment of the benefits of the course. Currently a typical student will attend the course representative training as a participant in the first year, a facilitator in their second and assist in the presentation and planning of material during their final year. Approximately 50 per cent of participants in course representative training are involved at a later stage. As it is believed that the benefits are long term, the assessment must also be long term. A comparison between future employment of students who have participated in the student development scheme and a representative control group would be beneficial.

The anecdotal evidence is strong and positive. However, increasing use is being made of written feedback on the courses and this will be used in the annual redesign of the course.

CONCLUSION

Learning should be fun. Committed, enthusiastic practitioners should facilitate that learning. At the University of Bradford the students who have contributed their time and efforts to helping other students have ensured that the learning provided by the student development team meets those criteria.

The students feel an involvement in the process of learning that is lacking in traditional education. Figure 9.1 gives a summary of the current annual programme.

The number of students who are being given training in key skills development through student-led self-directed learning is increasing annually. However, the numbers are currently a very small percentage of the total student population.

The scheme has introduced a number of staff and students to alternative forms of learning. These methods are geared more closely to modern educational needs in that they encourage students to take responsibility for their own learning. To gain maximum benefit for all, the institution should foster a true community of learning, where both staff and students are equal, and respected, contributors.

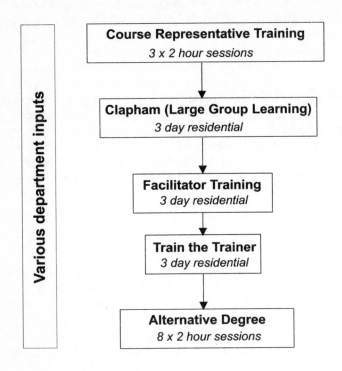

Figure 9.1   Outline of current annual programme

REFERENCES

Adair, John (1973) *Action-Centred Leadership*, McGraw-Hill, London

Belbin, Meredith (1993) *Team Roles at Work*, Butterworth-Heinemann, Oxford

Bransford, J D and Stein, B S (1984) *The Ideal Problem Solver*, W H Freeman, New York

Honey, P and Mumford, A (1982) *The Manual of Learning Styles*, Peter Honey, Maidenhead

Kolb, J (1976) *Learning Style Inventory, Technical Manual*, McBer and Company, Boston

Kolb, J (1984) *Experiential Learning, Experience as the source of learning and development*, Prentice-Hall, London

Sayers, P *et al* (1995) Creating an Environment for Peer Learning – the Bradford experience of course rep training, *Innovations in Education and Training International*, **33** (3), pp 171–77

10

Use of the Web to support development of key skills

Sue Drew
Sheffield Hallam University
UK

SUMMARY

This chapter is based on the experiences of the Key to Key Skills Project, funded by the Teaching and Learning Technology Programme of the Higher Education Funding Council for England (HEFCE). The chapter introduces the project and the system it developed and describes its context. It then considers the students' perspective, issues for staff, the institution and developers, and looks at particular issues related to supporting key skills on the Web.

INTRODUCTION

The author managed the Key to Key Skills Project, 1998–2000, funded by the Teaching and Learning Technology Programme of the HEFCE. The project made a Web-based system developed at Leeds Metropolitan University (LMU) portable to other institutions, implementing it firstly at Sheffield Hallam University (SHU) and then at the University of Plymouth (www.shu.ac.uk/keytokey/). The project was led by the Learning and Teaching Institute (LTI) of Sheffield Hallam University. The system supports students' key skills development.

This chapter draws on the project's experience to consider some of the main issues in delivering support for key skills over an intranet, focusing in particular on the perspectives of:

- students;
- teaching staff;
- the institution;
- the system developers.

The system was thoroughly evaluated at the three institutions, with in total 26 courses and 1500 students, and the project is still collating evaluative information. A mixture of evaluation tools was used: a student questionnaire, observations, focus groups with students, and interviews with staff. While the same system was evaluated, its content varied. At LMU it was their 'Skills for Learning' material with the SHU 'Skill Checks' inserted, at SHU it was 'Key Skills On-Line', developed alongside the TLTP Project (LTI, 2000), and at Plymouth the content was the Writing Skills section of the SHU system. The SHU Skill Checks are self-assessments sitting at the start of themes and guiding students to help in the system. Both the LMU and SHU content has on-screen guidance and references to further support (eg published materials).

The author takes a particular view of key skills in developing support materials (Drew and Bingham, 1997; Drew and Gibson, 1998), namely that 'skill' is being able to behave effectively for a specific context (Schon, 1987; Elliott, 1991), in a way that takes account of one's own goals and abilities. This implies being able to use a range of strategies and techniques, to pick up clues about a context, to make judgements, and to maximize your strengths and limit the possible effects of your weaknesses. It consists of sophisticated processes involving values and feelings and cognitive skills. Materials should encourage:

- self-awareness, and the related skills of seeking and using feedback and of reflection;
- familiarization with techniques and strategies, involving practice;
- analysis of contexts;
- independent judgement.

CONTEXT

SHU and LMU are situated in northern industrial cities, 40 miles apart. SHU has 17,700 full-time equivalent students and LMU has 15,000. The University of Plymouth is in a major port city in the south-west of England and has 18,000 full-time equivalent students. All three universities are ex-polytechnics with many vocational courses and are multi-site. All are committed to the development of key skills in students, and face supporting this with large numbers of students, with tightening resources and with increasing concerns for costs and the quality of provision.

THE STUDENTS' PERSPECTIVE

The project evaluation indicated that students liked the concept of a Web-based system to support their key skills. It was 'modern', using it helped the students develop IT skills, it collected support for a range of skills into a 'one-stop shop', and they could access it when they needed it. They also wanted off-campus access.

The students found the system and its navigation tools easy to use, and students with no prior experience of using computers quickly learnt to use it, but instructions needed to be crystal clear. For example, some students did not understand 'continue' on the first button to enter the system (it was changed to 'start'). Not all students were familiar with Internet conventions and did not know to click on words underlined and highlighted as links (instructions to do so were inserted). Where there were problems with logging on, students were much more critical of the system than otherwise. These technical issues were the students' first focus and problems here affected their view of the content.

However, given no logging-on problems or navigation difficulties the students' main concern was with the content:

- Students needed to understand the relevance of the system to their needs. Where a tutor did not make clear the reason for direction to the system there was confusion and reduced interest.

- Students wanted to find the information they needed quickly. The pages were reorganized and a search engine added.

- Students tended to use the on-screen guidance rather than the further resources they were pointed towards. At LMU when students were directed to material in the Learning Centre many preferred on-line downloadable guidance. At SHU each section of the system had on-screen guidance and details of further resources, but most students used only the on-screen guidance.

- Students tended to want paper copies of material. Some at SHU preferred the paper-based Skill Packs on which some of the contents were based (Drew and Bingham, 1997; Pettigrew and Elliott, 1999), as they are usable in any situation, without computer access. However, this did not mean that the students did not want the system (they did) but that a mix of types of support is important (the author is concerned at SHU to encourage the ongoing usage of the Skill Packs alongside the system).

- Computer guidance was seen as more personal than that on paper (even where one was derived from the other!). Seeking skills support from a computer could be less threatening than approaching a tutor to admit a shortcoming or need.

- Students liked the concept of the Skill Checks with its self-awareness focus, although they needed clearer criteria for self-evaluation and a more varied approach. The Results page was critical. The original concept was that institutions with different content from SHU could slot a Skill Check into their system and link it to their content. This proved difficult at LMU, where existing content did not match the Skill Check questions, and students were more critical of the Skill Checks than at SHU, where they linked more effectively into the content. Students wanted the Results page to lead them to more specific help than in the initial prototypes. Some students were cautious about honesty in completing the Skill Checks, for fear that staff might see their replies, and the amended versions make clear that staff do not have access to their responses, although they may ask them to submit a copy of a completed Skill Check for coursework (the implication being that students can then decide on their level of honesty).

- The system's appearance was seen as very important. SHU students disliked the colour, all students disliked too much unbroken text on screen, and all liked interaction.

- Text on screen seemed to be used differently from text on paper. Students skimmed and scanned, and where they wanted to read in depth they printed the material. There are implications here for design and also for costs. At SHU a shift from the paper-based Skill Packs provided by courses towards use of the system could mean a shift in printing costs to the students (and also a shift in use of resources from the university's print unit to networked printers).

ISSUES FOR STAFF

Four models of use were identified by the Project:

- optional: students were told of the system;
- directed: students were directed to a particular part of the system;
- partially integrated: students were required to use part of the system for a course or assessed task;
- fully integrated: students had class sessions based on the system and used several parts of it in course or assessed tasks.

Where the optional model was used few students used the system. A few more did so with the directed model. Students were most likely to use it with the partially or fully integrated models, and more likely to use parts of it in addition to those required by the tutor several parts of it with the latter. It was not effective to tell students about the system in a general induction or in an overall introduction to Learning Centre facilities, but it was useful to demonstrate the system in class, and it was most useful if students had a task in class helping them to explore the system's features.

Within SHU and LMU the project wishes to increase general awareness of the system by staff and students (eg by locating it visibly on university Web pages, providing information in staff/student materials), but it is more concerned to encourage those models of use that encourage usage. The project findings support the view of the team that it is not adequate to provide skills support for students outside the curriculum. Ways in which the system has been embedded in the curriculum include:

- setting exercises for students using part of the system, eg correcting a list of references using the guidance on referencing;

- having students consider a section of the system before discussing it in small groups, eg group work ground rules;

- having students complete a Skill Check and provide a printout of the Results page with an action plan (but see the above comments about student honesty – this strategy may be more effective in introducing students to the processes of reflection and action planning than in providing staff with accurate student self-assessments);

- having students use the system to collect evidence of their work (eg the 'Scratch Pad' allows them to save notes and there are templates for completion).

ISSUES FOR THE INSTITUTION

This section draws mainly on experience at SHU. Institutional issues closely relate to the models of use, since where the system is used on an optional basis only, there are fewer 'quality' issues than where the models of use adopted are fully or partially integrated.

If the system is used by students as part of assessed work, then the institution must ensure that students can access it. Increasing numbers of students have home Internet access, but not enough for the institution to assume such provision, and there must be enough on-campus provision for students to access the system when needed. If the system is formally introduced by tutors and used for class tasks, then teaching rooms with computers are needed.

SHU's new Learning Centre at its city centre site opened in 1996 and has over 400 computers for students' use. SHU has two further sites, the Learning Centre at the second having 64 computers and that at the third having 16. In addition to Learning Centre computers there are computer suites, each usually with 25 computers. All the computers mentioned so far, a total of 1055, are managed by a central computing support department (Corporate Information Systems – CIS). In addition the schools in the university have their own computer rooms, with currently about 988 computers in total.

Embedded in the above information are a number of issues. One is that CIS computer provision varies between sites. The third site mentioned above has problems in expanding its computer provision because of space and it was difficult to pilot the system there with anything other than an optional model. There are few computers in its Learning Centre, and its CIS computer suites are heavily booked for classes (the School of Cultural Studies on the site is strongly committed to IT skills development).

The other two sites have good provision by UK standards, but most of it is heavily used for class sessions from 9.00 am to 5.00 pm, also the busiest time in the Learning Centre. In the Learning Centre many students use computers to word process assignments, leaving few available for other purposes, and a number of computers are reserved for computer-based learning, bookable in block by staff. The second site referred to above has recently tried all-night opening in a computer suite, so successfully that it is continuing the experiment. The university is cautious about investing in many more computers and computer accommodation if its existing provision is underused outside the traditional hours. However, extending this provision relies on a number of factors such as security (for all-night working), staffing (technical and academic support), and encouraging staff and students to move away from traditional working hours.

The system developed by the project had to be appropriate for the machine and software specifications in the university. However, almost half the university's computers are not managed by CIS, but by schools (departments). It was easy for the project to communicate with CIS, but it proved difficult to get an up-to-date list of school IT managers and to obtain responses from them. The situation was resolved during the lifetime of the project when CIS agreed with all schools that they would adopt the same 'desktop'.

The system was piloted on-campus only and soon the project was receiving requests for it to be available off-campus to full-time students at home, students on placement, and to part-time or distance-learning students. There is an increasing focus within the university on flexibility of mode and on work-based learning, and a blurring between full-time and part-time modes. As the contents of the system are copyright, a security system allowing access but limiting it to SHU students and staff became essential.

What are the implications of the above? One is that those wishing to implement such systems must communicate fully with those responsible for institutional computing infrastructures. Another is that partial or fully integrated models can only be used where there is adequate teaching space for demonstration and practice and adequate individual access. At SHU, where provision is on the whole good but where there are still difficulties, this means not moving wholesale across all courses to these models of use. It also means encouraging cooperation between the academic staff using these models and those managing the resources – in SHU's case this has meant involving information specialists ('librarians'), who have worked closely with the academic staff. One successful strategy at SHU has been to create a Computer-Based Learning Implementation Group, with membership from CIS, the Learning Centre and the LTI to identify issues, where possible to deal with them, to establish new procedures, and to feed back issues and suggestions for their resolution.

Further institutional issues relate to 'quality' and the curriculum. SHU has no formal key skills policy and as yet no formally adopted key skills framework (there may be one in the near future), although there is extensive practice at all levels. The SHU system is based upon the QCA national framework (QCA 1999) and its five levels, but this was the author's choice rather than that of the institution. So, one issue for an institution is what framework and levels should the system use? Should this be agreed at institutional level? The flexibility built into the system allows institutions to insert their own skill themes based on their own frameworks.

If the system is widely used it will affect institutional standards, particularly where the fully or partially integrated models are used. Indeed, students and staff, rather unnervingly from this author's viewpoint, see it as representing the university's position and standards. The author checked out the content that clearly impinges on university policies (eg statements on plagiarism), but what else may have 'sneaked through'? If an institution uses content developed elsewhere will somebody check to ensure there is no conflict with the institution's policies and standards? At SHU the project has met with the Head of Quality to review these issues and has begun discussions on guidance about the system for course planning or validation teams.

ISSUES FOR DEVELOPERS

There were two main sets of issues for the project's development work, the first relating to the portability of the system to other institutions and the second to the content of the system.

In term of portability it was difficult to discover the norm for software, browsers, browser set-ups and hardware in higher education institutions.

The project looked at provision within the three partners and received help from two other higher education institutions (Ripon and York St John and the Crewe and Alsager Faculty of Manchester Metropolitan University), which carried out trial installations of the system. It also used the knowledge of technical team members about the current scene (there was a 'blip' when an enthusiastic courseware designer used new software that was not generally available). There is a trade-off: ensuring the system will run versus innovation.

Many institutions have their own skills material and the 'not invented here' syndrome is strong. Other institutions can insert their own content into the project's system using only word-processing skills, and can customize it. (They can also buy the SHU contents.) It was therefore not possible to produce an 'off-the-peg' system, but rather one which, whilst easy to install, requires computing expertise to do so. The installation had to be as easy and quick as possible (it took 20 minutes at Ripon and York St John) with very clear guidance notes. Again there is a trade-off: customizability versus ease of installation.

The main findings from the evaluation have already been used to amend the SHU contents. The following seem particularly important:

- Clear views on how skills are developed (these may be similar to or different from the views held by this author) are crucial to produce Web-based skills materials. At SHU the views underpinning the contents of the system draw on the skills literature such as that on transfer. This indicates a lack of clear research evidence for transfer but suggests some of the conditions that may facilitate it, such as recognizing common elements and sharing a cultural understanding of what is required (Neath 1998). They also draw on the experience of writing and evaluating paper-based Skill Packs, which are process based and encourage self-awareness. It is also crucial to understand what the software can do and a team approach where technical members have a 'can-do' approach is particularly valuable.

- On-screen instructions must be clear and simple. The author (non-technical) held, and initially lost, debates with courseware designers who thought their instructions were clear (eg icons with no words) or necessary (eg hedged to cover all eventualities), only to have her naïve view corroborated when observing students using the system.

- Self-assessments must be designed integrally with the contents. The project team is now very cautious about stand-alone 'diagnostics' which do not lead to support.

- The on-screen guidance must be made attractive (eg through its layout, use of colour, and by avoiding unbroken blocks of text). It should also be concise and punchy.

- Interaction needs to be built into the system to encourage engagement.

- The on-screen guidance needs to provide support without requiring the user to leave the computer to go to further resources, although external resources can be supplementary.

SUPPORTING KEY SKILLS ON THE WEB – PARTICULAR ISSUES

Many of the issues in this chapter apply to any Web-based learning materials, but the Key to Key Skills Project highlighted them because of its extent: few other topics are relevant to every student in a university at all levels from undergraduate to postgraduate, and even to staff. Key skills also provide particular challenges. How can the computer support skills development and where are its limitations? The system:

- seems particularly useful for interactive activities encouraging self-awareness and reflection;
- can, through interaction, encourage students to analyse the needs of a context in which they must use a skill;
- can aid planning (eg planning to use skills and to take action to improve) and recording (eg evidence of skills use);
- can suggest techniques and strategies;
- can provide an opportunity to practise some skills (eg IT, information skills), but not others (eg oral presentation);
- can build confidence by giving access to advice, techniques, and strategies at a time when they are needed (this is possibly why students want search engines to help them go directly to items, and why computer access and logging-on time are critical);
- is perceived by students as personalized support, possibly because it is more capable of personal adaptation than paper-based material (eg you decide on the order in which to access items). However, it is solitary and students also wanted interaction with peers and tutors.

CONCLUSION

The project highlighted the importance of thinking through carefully how to structure and present Web support materials, of allowing for technical infrastructures and institutional contexts, and of encouraging integration into the curriculum. It also emphasized the importance of acting on feedback from users and of a team approach, drawing together varied expertise, in producing such systems.

REFERENCES

Drew, S and Bingham, R (1997) *The Student Skills Guide*, Gower, Aldershot

Drew, S and Gibson, R (1998) *The Student Guide to Making Oral Presentations*, Gower CD ROM, Aldershot

Elliott, J (1991) *Action Research for Educational Change*, Open University Press, Buckingham

Key to Key Skills Project Web Site, www.shu.ac.uk/keytokey/

LTI, Sheffield Hallam University (2000) *Key Skills On-Line. Intranet support for students*, Gower CD ROM, Aldershot

Neath, M (1998) *The Development and Transfer of Undergraduate Group Work Skills* (PhD thesis), Sheffield Hallam University

Pettigrew, M and Elliott, D (1999) *Student IT Skills*, Gower, Aldershot

QCA (Qualifications, Curriculum and Assessment Authority) (1999) *Key Skill Units. Levels 1–5*, QCA, London

Schon, D A (1987) *Educating the Reflective Practitioner*, Jossey Bass, San Francisco

11

A graduate apprenticeship scheme

Stephen Fallows and Gordon Weller
University of Luton
UK

SUMMARY

The University of Luton has piloted and developed a Graduate Apprentice-ship Scheme. This is a programme for the new graduate that involves a mix of work placements and skills development workshops. Placements are with small and medium sized enterprises (SMEs) and voluntary groups. The workshops lead to professional qualifications including National Vocational Qualifications (NVQs). Participating employers are encouraged to utilize the scheme as a low-risk means of evaluating graduates prior to formal employ-ment. Project evaluation is discussed in the context of graduate expectations, under-employment, employer expectations, acceptance of NVQs and life-long learning.

INTRODUCTION

Many new graduates experience difficulties in securing employment at what they consider to be an appropriate level immediately after leaving university. Many begin their working life in positions that do not require graduate achievement. It is common for graduates to take between two and three years to establish themselves in graduate level employment (Connor *et al*, 1997; Elias *et al*, 1999). This applies widely and not only to those whose discipline has no obvious link to a particular job. Often those with vocationally related degrees find that the possession of current technical expertise is insufficient to overcome the lack of practical on-the-job experience.

This chapter describes a series of initiatives at the University of Luton since the mid-1990s. Collectively, these initiatives will be referred to as the

Luton Graduate Apprenticeship Scheme. (The term 'Graduate Apprenticeship' has been taken up by the Department for Education and Employment (DfEE) (DfEE, 1998a) for a series of National Training Organization sectoral pilot schemes which adopt many of the principles pioneered at the University of Luton.)

THE LUTON GRADUATE APPRENTICESHIP SCHEME

Traditional apprentices provide the model that has been adapted by the university. Employers recruit young people as apprentices to learn a trade whilst working alongside experienced staff. The apprentice arrives with little or no prior experience and receives practical on-the-job experience, often in conjunction with college-based training. Apprenticeship programmes recognize that this transition phase, ahead of permanent employment, allows the apprentice to absorb the organizational and work culture whilst undergoing job-specific training. The transitional nature of apprenticeships is long established and provides both employer and apprentice with the opportunity to withdraw if required after a defined period of time.

At craft, technician and junior management levels, the traditional apprenticeship has recently been updated through the introduction of the 'modern apprenticeship' under the aegis of the DfEE.

The University of Luton application of the apprenticeship model at graduate level has proved to be a novel extension of the concept, yielding the 'graduate apprentice'. The Luton Graduate Apprenticeship Scheme began in 1996 as a development project funded by the DfEE. The broad aims set by government were to use graduate skills effectively, and to overcome barriers to graduate employment.

The university interpreted this to yield the following local aims:

- to provide opportunities for local unemployed recent graduates to undertake workplace experience, with the possibility of progression into permanent employment;
- to provide work-based training for graduate apprentices, individually negotiated between the employer, the graduate apprentice and the university tutor;
- to develop a network of SMEs willing to participate in the scheme.

The Luton Graduate Apprenticeship Scheme focuses on employers who might consider employing a new graduate but have concerns about the lack of work experience. It encourages employers to consider a wider range of applicants than might otherwise be the case. Essentially the programme provides participants with a structured approach that offers three main services:

- brokerage: matching employer needs to a selection of graduates;
- skills audit: linking key skills required by the employer to a personal development plan for each graduate;
- monitoring and support for the graduate by a university tutor, to maintain links between the employer and the university.

The scheme has the strong support of local employer representatives who have advised on how the university might best meet the needs of employing organizations, especially smaller firms and voluntary groups.

Since 1996, the Luton Graduate Apprenticeship Scheme has undergone significant development, evolution and expansion. From 1997 to 1998, the Government Office for the Eastern Region (GOER) provided finance from its Higher Education Regional Development Fund to refocus the university's support for the graduate apprentices to achieve recognition with respect to higher level key skills. Key skills were incorporated into a comprehensive professional development programme, leading over a year of evening workshops to the EDEXEL Capability Award (EDEXEL, 2000). (Previously, the Luton Graduate Apprenticeship Scheme had provided only a non-certificated skills programme.)

Since 1998, the university has begun to mainstream the concept with graduate apprentices formally recognized as part-time students. This latest evolution has resulted in notable expansion of participant numbers and formal incorporation of the scheme into the university's strategic plans (University of Luton, 1998).

Most recently (December 1999), the University of Luton's pioneering work has again been recognized by the DfEE. This has led to the award of funding to support the active dissemination of the methodology to other higher education institutions.

For the first two years of the scheme, 1996–97 (DfEE-funded) and 1997–98 (GOER-funded), participant numbers were limited to 37 and 36 respectively; however, in both years over 150 graduates attended the programme of skills workshops whilst also seeking employment. The development of the scheme is more fully described in two final project reports (Weller 1998a and 1998b).

A NEW ROLE FOR THE UNIVERSITY

The concept that underpins the scheme is new to higher education. In the traditional model, a university has no responsibility for work-related training and development after the student has completed a degree programme, and similarly an employer has no responsibility for graduate training before employment. The process of change generated through Enterprise in Higher Education has allowed the graduate apprenticeship scheme to emerge as an effective continuation strategy to maintain and enhance partnerships with employers; these relationships are particularly important (Hawkins and Winter, 1997). The focus on SMEs reflects these organizations' demands that new employees are ready for work; larger organizations may be able to offer graduate training programmes, but these are neither feasible nor affordable for smaller organizations.

The Luton Graduate Apprenticeship Scheme provides professional development in higher level key skills, supported by university-based workshops provided specifically for this group. The schedule of workshops is given in Table 11.1.

Table 11.1   Schedule of skills workshops

Part 1:   July to September

Workshops on the following themes:

- Careers guidance and management
- Interview techniques
- CV preparation
- Job-seeking skills
- Introduction to key skills and work-based learning
- Introduction to maintaining a profile of personal and professional development
- Understanding organizations in the small-business sector
- Customer service: the internal and external customer

Part 2:   October to March

Workshops on the following themes:

- Improving own learning and performance*
- Working with others*
- Communication*
- Problem solving
- Use of information technology
- Application of number
- Understanding equal opportunities
- Health and safety in the workplace
- The new professional/practitioner role

Skills marked * are given particular attention following feedback from employers.

Participants in the scheme are all recent graduates and are drawn from a range of disciplines. The scheme is not limited to Luton graduates but rather is restricted to those able to travel to the university to participate in the programme. Participating graduates are recruited through careers advisory services, local media and through liaison with local Job Centres.

Participating employers have been recruited through leaflets distributed via business-related organizations such as the Training and Enterprise Council, Chambers of Commerce and the Federation of Small Businesses. The programme team has also made presentations to several business meetings. In addition, the scheme has included members of the local business community on its steering committee and advisory groups.

This provision is a part of the university's broader commitment to skill development and employment related education. Other major elements of the university's portfolio of activities include:

- All undergraduates engage with a range of key skills during their studies (see Chapter 2).

- The Careers Service offers a career development module; this gives students the opportunity to study the current employment situation and to develop a personal action plan for employment. The service has recently been engaged in an Integrated Employability Project (IEP), funded by the East of England Development Agency, which builds on the experience of the Luton Graduate Apprenticeship Scheme to offer an enhanced career development module, a job search database and a graduate jobs fair.

- A work-based learning module is available to all undergraduates; this allows them to undertake structured learning in the workplace. This module has been subject to development over a period of years and now involves a progressive triangulation of learning activities (Bailey, Fallows and Weller, 1999).

The Luton Graduate Apprenticeship Scheme uses work-based learning to enable graduates to develop their employability skills in order to contribute directly to the work of their placement organization. The scheme was given government support in recognition of the needs of SMEs and therefore the majority of placements are with SMEs. The remainder of placements are with voluntary organizations; thus placements can be paid or unpaid, depending on the abilities and requirements of the collaborating organization. It is intended that placements will be for a period of one year and this is generally the case; however, there is flexibility. Participants often move onto the permanent workforce before the formal end of placement.

Each apprenticeship placement involves negotiation of an individual learning agreement signed by the employer, graduate and university tutor.

SUPPORT FOR SMEs

The Luton Graduate Apprenticeship Scheme provides a brokerage service to link the participating SMEs with likely candidates for the placements offered. The potential employer discusses the intended placement with a university tutor who pre-selects likely candidates from graduates registered with the scheme.

Feedback from employers has identified the following benefits:

- Saving on employment agency fees and/or advertising charges.
- As part of the university pre-selection process, candidates are interviewed before details are sent to the employer, thus reducing the number of employer interviews.
- Employers may conduct interviews on university premises, with university staff making the necessary arrangements.
- Regular monitoring and review visits to the workplace by a university tutor ensure that the apprenticeship placement is progressing as planned for all parties.
- Employers may visit the university to browse through CVs of registered graduates.

These benefits go some way to resolving concerns held by SMEs new to graduate employment, as reported by Harvey, Moon and Geall (1997).

EVALUATION

The service provided by the Luton Graduate Apprenticeship Scheme has been subject to close evaluation. This has been conducted in accordance with principles outlined by the DfEE (1996, 1998b). The process has been described in more detail elsewhere (Fallows, 1998).

The local evaluation of each phase in the scheme's development has taken a formative emphasis; that is, the findings have principally been collected in a manner and at times chosen to assist in forward planning and evolution. The evaluation has sought feedback primarily from the scheme's main client groups: graduates and employers.

GRADUATE EXPECTATIONS AND REFLECTIONS

The evaluation feedback from new graduates has been gathered from structured questionnaires and through focus group meetings.

Questionnaires

These are administered as workshop exercises early in each year's programme of activities. Administration in this manner allows data collection to serve a second purpose since it provides a very successful learning activity. Over the years, the outcomes have been remarkably consistent. One exercise investigates participants' expectations from the scheme and for their future. Not unexpectedly, the immediate expectations have been work experience, assistance with clarification of career direction, improved confidence, knowledge of employer expectations and, undoubtedly the most important expectation, a job.

Longer-term aspirations can be summed up in the words of one participant as the desire to be 'on the way to a good standard of living with a progressive career and to be set up and independent'.

A second exercise has required participants to indicate agreement with a series of statements using a five-point Likert scale. Over the years the exercise has been modified and it is not appropriate to provide a numerical summation of results from the different groups. However, the outcomes include:

- consistently strong agreement that today's graduates must be flexible when seeking employment;

- strong agreement with the notion that graduates would benefit if potential employers were involved in the development of university courses;

- recognition that most employers are as interested in a range of personal skills as the subject studied for the degree (and more so in many cases);

- recognition that SMEs are likely to be increasingly important as employers of graduates (but it should be remembered that the scheme has an SME focus);

- evidence that NVQs were not particularly highly rated as key qualifications for graduates.

The above comments confirm many of the outcomes of the study for the Association of Graduate Careers Advisory Services by the University of Warwick Institute for Employment Research (Purcell and Pitcher, 1996).

Focus groups

The following points represent some of the main findings from the focus groups.

- Some graduates find their break with university life very unsettling, and suggest that there should be some way to maintain the link with the university on a social and a personal or professional development basis. (This is especially true for those who have yet to secure employment.)

● There is a general lack of 'after-sales service' for higher education; on completion of the degree most universities make little further provision for preparation for work. There may be Careers Service support for those who have already graduated but the primary focus of such activity is on those completing their final year of study.

● The need for 'after-sales care' in the form of skills workshops and preparatory courses with a placement service available for graduates (such as in this scheme) is generalizable. The metaphor of a finishing school for graduates has been used.

● Participants indicate that continued involvement is not a one-way exercise; graduates would like to 'give something back to the university'. For example, some of the graduates who have completed a graduate apprenticeship have suggested that they would like to help to promote employability skills development to undergraduates.

EMPLOYER EXPECTATIONS AND OUTCOMES

The views of participating employers have been regarded as especially important throughout the scheme's evolution.

Employers have provided views on the skills required of graduates when they enter employment. Skills identified by our small cohorts of SME-based employers accord with those suggested in surveys of more established graduate employers (see for example the Association of Graduate Recruiters (1995, 1999)). Overwhelmingly, employers regard good communication skills and personal skills, such as the ability to work effectively with others, to be of paramount importance.

The second employer exercise identified questions that SMEs address when considering participating in the scheme and again when taking the key placement decisions with respect to a graduate apprentice:

● Is the graduate able to mix well and fit in with the existing team?

● Is the graduate confident, willing, flexible and able to organize him- or herself?

● Does the graduate have the technical and cognitive ability to contribute to the work of the organization?

Employer surveys also reviewed the NVQ Key Skills as a basis for ranking skills by importance to the organization. Employers considered all the listed skills are important but gave particular emphasis to:

- communication;
- working with others;
- improving own learning and performance.

Employers commented that whilst it would be desirable for each graduate to have these skills on arrival, there was opportunity (through the Luton Graduate Apprenticeship Scheme) for early development of the missing elements.

CONCLUSION

The Luton Graduate Apprenticeship Scheme notes that many graduates do not initially consider smaller organizations. However, the scheme has enabled many new graduates to take up jobs with small firms. There have been many successes, with lessons to be learnt by each of the main stakeholders: the graduates, the employers and the university. These lessons have contributed to the mature model now in operation.

Graduate expectations

Throughout the operation of the Luton Graduate Apprenticeship Scheme there has been an observation that graduate expectations of employment prospects are excessive, sometimes based upon media reports of high salaries within particular sections of the economy. It seems that many new graduates believe they have a right to a high salary in a graduate position with a large company with an assured route to senior management; this notion often takes some time to be dispelled. Indeed, many new graduates receive salaries well below those advertised by the large firm recruiters (DfEE, 1999). Universities may be responsible for fostering the illusion that a degree is a guarantee of high-level employment. A greater emphasis on small firms in case studies used in a variety of undergraduate studies could raise the profile of this potential career focus.

Several of the participants in the scheme acknowledged with hindsight that they could have done more to develop their employability skills, for example through taking up voluntary work and earlier career planning.

Traditionally, universities have held relatively little responsibility for supporting students after graduation. Graduate feedback has highlighted the demand for practical support, in which graduates are actually introduced to firms and supported through the early stages of employment. This is especially necessary if graduates are to take up employment in small firms that may not normally employ new graduates and which do not have the training and development programmes offered by larger employers.

Under-employment

Graduates are faced increasingly with under-employment – that is, having to accept positions that fail to fulfil their potential – because they cannot offer relevant skills or work experience. Often, financial pressures force graduates to take manual or shop work rather than remaining unemployed. This presents the dual dilemma of not having time to seek 'graduate level' work whilst becoming typecast as having only low-level skills and experience. Many of the new graduates on the scheme who are under-employed are taking up a graduate level placement on an unpaid basis for one day per week as the means of gaining vital employment skills.

Employer expectations

Employers indicate that they need graduates to make a contribution immediately on starting work. This seems especially true of the smaller firms that do not have experience of employing new graduates. However, one of the attributes that employers consider useful when employing graduates is that they generally have the ability to learn fast.

Employers often want to employ their graduate from the scheme on a permanent basis after maintaining the apprenticeship placement for just five or six months. The project team has been pleasantly surprised at how rapidly employers will employ a graduate on a permanent basis in order to retain the individual. This is a successful outcome, as the employer has recognized the graduate potential and may employ others.

Employers have indicated that they value the monitoring and review support offered under the scheme, and this has been increased within budget limitations. Some employers prefer frequent – monthly – review meetings at the start of an apprenticeship placement. This is especially true of organizations that previously have been involved with training programmes offered by further education colleges and training companies involved in Training and Enterprise Council funded programmes since such regular monitoring is common in these initiatives.

NVQs

The attitude of the employer to NVQ accreditation has great influence. In the first phase of the scheme, there was an attempt to introduce participants and their employers to job-related NVQs; this was not a success and subsequently was abandoned in favour of a focus on key skills.

In order to ensure that graduates on the scheme have an opportunity to achieve accreditation for their work-based competence, a series of weekly skills workshops has been implemented. These evening sessions allow graduates to network with their peers and share placement and other experiences.

A key reason why many employers were not attracted to occupation-specific NVQs is that, in many cases, the graduate does not have a work environment able to support the generation of sufficient evidence to complete a full NVQ at an appropriate level. However, employers are generally very supportive of the key skills programme.

Lifelong learning

The scheme introduces graduates to work situations in which they must learn to adapt and be flexible in a very short space of time. Their ability to develop towards the level of competence required by the employer is discussed at monitoring and review meetings. This process gives the graduate feedback on their work performance. Graduates are encouraged to set objectives for their continuing professional development in order to instil the ethos of lifelong learning. The process of continuation of learning in the workplace may also offer a good example to the employer to take up training for other staff in the organization. The scheme offers an opportunity to encourage a learning culture, which has been suggested as necessary for the viability and competitiveness of small organizations (NAGCELL, 1999).

A transferable model

The scheme has evolved significantly since its inception in 1996 and is now a mature element of the university's provision. However, it has been developed as a transferable model, and thus has the potential to be taken up by other institutions. The scheme has already attracted many students who have studied at other universities. Potential exists for a network of institutions offering a service equivalent to the Luton Graduate Apprenticeship Scheme and the DfEE has commissioned the university to undertake a national programme of dissemination.

Throughout the operation of the scheme the project team has been impressed with the level of graduate motivation and enthusiasm. The request for a continued social and professional link with the university is currently being explored with the Students Union and the Careers Service. Such a development gives impetus to the creation of alumni programmes able to mix social and professional development.

REFERENCES

Association of Graduate Recruiters (AGR) (1995) *Skills for Graduates in the 21st Century*, AGR, Cambridge

Association of Graduate Recruiters (AGR) (1999) *Graduates Working Out*, AGR/Careers Service Unit, Cambridge

Bailey, M, Fallows, S and Weller, G (1999) A structured methodology for use in undergraduate work related learning programmes, in *Proceedings of the 1st International Conference on Researching Work and Learning*, eds K Forrester *et al*, University of Leeds, pp 471–485

Connor, B *et al* (1997) *What do graduates do next?*, The Institute for Employment Studies, Grantham Book Services Ltd, University of Sussex

Department for Education and Employment (DfEE) (1996) *Evaluating Developments in Higher Education*, Department for Education and Employment, Higher Education and Employment Division, Sheffield

Department for Education and Employment (DfEE) (1998a) *The Learning Age: a renaissance for a new Britain*, Command Paper Cm 3790, The Stationery Office, London

Department for Education and Employment (DfEE) (1998b) *Evaluating Development Projects: A guide for contractors,* Department for Education and Employment, Higher Education: Quality and Employability Division, Sheffield

Department for Education and Employment (DfEE) (1999) *Skills and Enterprise Executive,* Issue 2/99, Department for Education and Employment, Skills and Enterprise Network, Sheffield

EDEXEL (2000) Details of the Capability Award are available from: EDEXEL Foundation, Central House, Upper Woburn Place, London WC1H 0HH

Elias, P *et al* (1999) *Moving On – Graduate Careers Three Years After Graduation*, DfEE/Higher Education Careers Service Unit/Association of Graduate Careers Advisory Services/Institute for Employment Research, University of Warwick

Fallows, S (1998) Evaluation of higher education developments, *Local Economy Quarterly*, **5** (4), pp 22–34

Harvey, L, Moon, S and Geall, V (1997) *Graduates Work: Organisational change and students' attributes*, Centre for Research into Quality, University of Central England, Birmingham

Hawkins, P and Winter, J (1997) *Mastering Change: Learning the lessons of the enterprise in higher education initiative*, DfEE, Higher Education and Employment Division, Sheffield

National Advisory Group for Continuing Education and Lifelong Learning (NAGCELL) (Fryer Committee) (1999) *Creating Learning Cultures, Next Steps in Achieving the Learning Age*, The Stationery Office, London

Purcell, K and Pitcher, J (1996) *Great Expectations: The new diversity of graduate skills and aspirations*, Higher Education Careers Service Unit/Association of Graduate Careers Advisory Services/Institute for Employment Research, University of Warwick

University of Luton (1998) *Strategic Plan 1997–98, 2001–02*, University of Luton (paragraph 3.22)

Weller, G (1998a) *Bridging the Gap Between Higher Education and Employment: Report on the Graduate Apprenticeship Scheme*, University of Luton

Weller, G (1998b) *Report on the Graduate Higher Level Key Skills Programme*, University of Luton

12

Springboard: student-centred assessment for development

Milton D Hakel and Eleanor A W McCreery
Bowling Green State University
USA

SUMMARY

Springboard, at Bowling Green State University, is an innovative course that places first-year students in a series of videotaped problem-solving sessions. The goal for each Springboard student, with aid from a coach, is to build competency in a core set of learning, employment and life skills: communication, analysis, problem solving, judgement, leadership and self-assurance. These skills are the key to effective performance on campus and in the world beyond the campus. Emphasizing these skills along with the capacity to manage immediate feedback encourages students to go beyond *knowing* to being able to *do* what they know.

Springboard is unique because:

- It focuses on learning and employment competencies rather than information retention.
- It matches each student with a coach who provides feedback and support, acting as a mentor for the student during the first year.
- It uses computer and video technology to tailor individually and observe directly performance in student-to-student interactions and student-to-coach interactions.
- It maximizes 'the teachable moment' by attending to first-year students at the most impressionable stage of their higher education.

● It relies on immediate, thoughtful, and ongoing feedback by trained coaches to help students rapidly develop accurate awareness of how they perform and how they manage feedback.

In the context of a state university, Springboard is extraordinary in providing first-year students with direct development of a set of meta-academic skills that better prepare them to learn and to work in a rapidly changing world. Uncommon for state universities, Springboard immediately connects faculty members, university administrators, graduate students and volunteers as coaches with first-year students as individuals, creating a powerful learning experience for both students and coaches.

Springboard students report improved performance in traditional coursework, a stronger sense of identification with the university, and an easier transition to university life and work as a result of this experience.

An additional benefit emerging from Springboard is the development of feedback, coaching and mentoring skills by the coaches themselves. Their experiences are as meaningful as those of the first-year students. The ability to observe and to provide immediate feedback leading to improved performance is a skill that separates the great teacher from the capable one or the great manager from the merely good one. Many coaches report that their Springboard experience is helping them in their professional and personal lives.

Springboard has yielded some unexpected and surprising results that require investigation. For instance, there appear to be no differences in the value of the feedback experience across gender, ethnic or economic class lines. Many first-year Springboard students arrive at Bowling Green from relatively homogeneous communities. These students have little experience in interacting with people of differing ethnicity or economic class. By exposing these students to coaches of different gender, ethnicity or economic class, who provide them with feedback and are invested in their success, students' tolerance and 'world view' is expanded and enriched. The Springboard interaction not only develops a core set of skills but also is uniquely meaningful in the students experience and educational development.

BOWLING GREEN STATE UNIVERSITY

Bowling Green State University (BGSU) is a public, state university founded as a teacher-training institution in 1910. Its 1,338-acre campus with 113 buildings is located in Bowling Green, Ohio, 23 miles south of Toledo. More than 17,500 undergraduate students and 1,750 graduate students are enrolled in 165 undergraduate degree programmes and 13 masters degree programmes in more than 60 separate fields of learning. Two specialist degree programmes and 14 doctoral programmes are also offered.

Bowling Green is undergoing a renaissance of its core mission, aspiring to become the premier learning community in Ohio and one of the best in the nation. It is led by President Sidney Ribeau. Bowling Green's more than 750 full-time faculty pursue this mission through a commitment to first-rate teaching in addition to research and scholarship activities.

President Ribeau's vision for Bowling Green is summarized in the simple and elegant slogan: 'Students First'. Students First, as embodied in the Springboard programme, is built on the belief that Bowling Green must create an atmosphere of intellectual excitement. 'How do you get students so intellectually alive, so turned on,... that they will learn in spite of anything the institution does?' Dr. Ribeau asks. '[Our goal is to] activate human beings intellectually in such a way that they will be lifelong learners. That's what we're trying to do when we talk about creating a premier learning community.'

SPRINGBOARD'S ORIGINS

When one looks at the issues facing both the first-year student and the university, it is apparent that the first year is extraordinary as a 'connecting year' for both. Most BGSU students come with heightened sensitivity to input, insecurities, and fear of the work ahead due to the need for fitting into a new, challenging environment. What became clear is that colleges and universities have an opportunity to leverage this heightened sensitivity.

Springboard's inspiration comes from two proven models that leverage 'the teachable moment'. The first is found in the pioneering work of Alverno College in Milwaukee, Wisconsin (see Chapter 3 in this book, and also Mentkowski, 2000). The second model resides in the leadership development practices pioneered by the Center for Creative Leadership (CCL), Greensboro, North Carolina. Each year more than 25,000 people participate in the Center's programs at its campuses in Greensboro, Colorado Springs, San Diego, and Brussels, or at corporate sites around the world (Conger, 1992). CCL's staff has learned how to collect and present developmental feedback in ways that minimize defensiveness and promote growth, and Springboard's coach role finds its main inspiration in CCL's feedback specialists and process advisors.

ABOUT SPRINGBOARD

Defined broadly as a series of personal development seminars, Springboard's curriculum is designed to help students achieve constant progress on six core competencies based on immediate, directly observed feedback using video and computer technology. The six competencies are:

- communication: the ability to make clear oral presentations of facts and ideas, to express ideas clearly in writing and to do this appropriately for different audiences;

- analysis: the ability to identify how a situation compares with previously defined standards, goals or priorities, to identify the important elements of a problem situation, to seek out relevant information and to determine possible causes;

- problem solving: the ability to create potential solutions, and to plan, organize, and implement a solution that best fits the available resources and avoids 'roadblocks';

- judgement: the ability to reach logical conclusions and to make high-quality decisions based on available information;

- leadership: the ability to motivate and guide people to accomplish a task or goal;

- self-assurance: the ability to feel comfortable, safe and secure in new or unfamiliar situations, to show confidence and enthusiasm, to take risks, to try new things, and to learn from experiences.

Springboard is an elective one-credit course (one-thirtieth of a year's work) presently offered by the Department of Psychology. There are no lectures, assigned readings, or examinations. It consists of seven group meetings during the semester, each devoted to helping the 12 students in each section to improve in one or more of the core competencies, and five individual meetings with one's coach. Videotaped meetings are reviewed closely by the student and coach together to evaluate performance, reinforcing positives and discussing areas for improvement. At each meeting a problem-solving exercise is presented with which students grapple individually or in groups.

Problems are patterned after real-life situations that first-year students can expect to face in their academic and professional careers. The class activities call for common problem-solving skills – setting priorities, participating in group decision-making, and the like. For instance, students report that what they like least about Springboard is the dreaded 'In-basket' assignment. The In-basket exercise approximates what one might find in a fast-paced, demanding job: a series of notes, memos, and letters to the student require decisions about conflicting problems that must be resolved in the course of one meeting, without anyone's assistance to help sort through the decisions to be made. The problems posed are tailored to the particular student, based on biographical information they've entered into a database, and call for analysis under pressure, priority setting, judgement, skilful communication, and self-assurance. Each action and decision is later reviewed with one's coach. The result is an exercise that combines the core competencies in a real-life setting with the added benefit of the development of appreciation for constructive feedback.

In the present design for Springboard, three of the group sessions involve videotaping students' performances. The notion for first-year students that their interaction in this class will be taped is intimidating at first, but is proving to be an incredibly helpful way of learning. Usually students become so engaged in the problem-solving that they quickly forget about being taped. More importantly, the students see themselves growing and improving their performance over the course of one three-month semester. Directly observing one's performance combined with immediate and supportive feedback is powerful as a learning tool. A key to making this work is that students are not graded comparatively, but rather against a grade contract calling for attendance and participation.

There are seven 90-minute class sessions in Springboard, and five additional meetings with one's coach:

- Just the facts: introduction to course and electronic interview.
- Getting to know you: meet your coach (video).
- Feedback meeting: watch video with your coach.
- Essence of America: leaderless group discussion (video).
- Feedback meeting: watch video with your coach.
- Day in your senior year: in-basket exercise.
- Feedback meeting: review decisions with your coach.
- Speaking from your heart: extemporaneous talks (video).
- Feedback meeting: watch video with your coach.
- Reflections and directions: review Springboard activities.
- Development goals session: create development plan with your coach.
- Commencement: celebration of lively learning.

Coaches are self-selected volunteers, coming from the campus and the greater Bowling Green community. During their training coaches take part in several key Springboard activities (being videotaped while giving an extemporaneous talk, completing the in-basket) so that they see the exercises from the participant's viewpoint. They meet for a half-hour overview and strategy session before each group meeting. Coaches are encouraged to be friendly, energetic, non-judgemental, positive, insightful, and supportive good listeners.

Technology supports Springboard in several ways, most obviously through videotaped sessions that are reviewed with one's coach. Database technology stores information collected during the electronic interview, information that then is used in the 'Getting to know you' session (the first contact with one's coach), and then later in the 'Day in your senior year' session, the in-basket exercise. E-mail is used routinely for notices and scheduling and anonymous e-mail is collected for course and session evaluations.

SPRINGBOARD AS BEST PRACTICE IN EDUCATION

It has long been recognized that students learn more as teacher–student interaction increases (Chickering and Gamson, 1987). Studies consistently demonstrate that academic performance improves in direct relation to smaller class size. When lecturing, the most prevalent form of post-secondary teaching, has been analysed, findings show that students retain less than 20 per cent of what they hear in a lecture one week later, as compared with upwards of 70 per cent when students are individually tutored. It is the ongoing, individual reinforcement and feedback that tutors provide that generates this improvement in learning. Summarizing years of research on college teaching and student learning, Chickering and Gamson's (1987) 'Seven Principles for Good Practice in Undergraduate Education' indicates that best practice in teaching:

- encourages student–faculty contact;
- encourages cooperation among students;
- encourages active (versus passive) learning;
- gives prompt feedback;
- emphasizes time on task;
- communicates high expectations;
- respects diverse talents and ways of learning.

By design, Springboard implements each of these best learning practices. The key innovation is the assignment of a volunteer coach, as a proxy for the professor, to each student to maximize individual contact. With no lectures, Springboard provides active learning, making the most of individual and group problem-solving at each session with immediate feedback. And, given that each student is helped to improve by an individual coach, the student's unique talents and ways of confronting new problems fosters creativity and individuality. In sum, Springboard creates an atmosphere that enhances learning and emotional engagement.

SPRINGBOARD'S IMPACT

Springboard embodies best practices in promoting student learning, with qualitative and quantitative evidence showing its impact. Much was learnt through interviews and focus groups conducted by an independent consultant in autumn 1997. These observations are supplemented by a comparison of Springboard versus non-Springboard first-year students from the Bowling Green Undergraduate Experience Questionnaire, as well as continuation statistics.

Interviews and focus groups elicited comments from both students and coaches on the value of the Springboard experience. Common themes include:

- First-year students reported that Springboard's emphasis on interaction with their coaches and fellow students helped them adjust and 'connect' with others in their new environment.

- Students reported that Springboard helped them learn to develop and be consciously aware of core skills that help them become more comfortable in their other classes.

- Students reported that they learned to appreciate rather than fear feedback as a valuable component of improving core skills and academic performance.

- Students reported an increase in self-assurance and communication skills as a result of the directly-observed, videotaped format of Springboard.

- Students were unanimously enthusiastic about Springboard because of the active role they and their coaches played in completing the curriculum versus a passive role in lecture-based classes.

Students spoke about Springboard in the following ways:

> The best part of Springboard was knowing that I had my own teacher who actually knew me and who gave me confidence that I could solve the problems and perform well in front of others.
>
> At first, knowing that they were videotaping everything I said and did was really weird. But once I realized that we [the student and the coach] were going to discuss what I did constructively and [I would] not just be criticized, I forgot about the cameras and just did the best I could.
>
> I guess the best thing about Springboard was the way it helped me build self-assurance based on constructive feedback. At first I wasn't sure what this was about, and then I learned that my coach was someone who wouldn't let me fail. There is great comfort and encouragement in knowing that. In my other classes I sometimes feel like teachers are trying to

set me up to fail, but Springboard taught me that if I monitor my performance and seek out feedback, there's no way that'll happen.

Springboard makes adjusting to college a lot easier. You quickly get
close to other students and learn that we all have the same the worries
about being able to cut it [at a university] – you know, homesickness, that
sense that you aren't as smart as the other kids. Besides, it [insecurity
about college] was something I could talk with my coach who seemed to
really care and gave me self-assurance that I could do it.

Springboard was a great experience. I had no idea what college
would be like and Springboard made me feel instantly at home. I
learned so much about myself and my abilities and I became more comfortable in all my other classes. Now I have no fears about college.

Springboard helped me learn that I had skills that I did not know I
had and will serve me in whatever I choose as my major in a year or so.
To feel self-assured that I can analyse and solve a problem and then
communicate why I chose that solution helps me in whatever discipline I
select as my major.

All this one-on-one and group work helped the class develop its own
culture almost immediately. It was like walking into Springboard sus-
pended the normal classroom experience, at least for a few hours.

A significant result from the Bowling Green Undergraduate Experience
Questionnaire indicated that Springboard students felt they made the right
choice in attending Bowling Green by a wide margin over their peers. Overall, 36 per cent reported that they had made the right choice versus 22 per
cent in the non-Springboard sample. When asked why, students credited
their Springboard experience with helping them to integrate quickly and
more fully than their classmates. This ability to integrate into the learning
environment bodes well for retaining these students at Bowling Green for
the course of their higher education.

Further, the Undergraduate Experience Questionnaire shows that
first-year students who took Springboard in the initial pilot study scored well
in comparison with their peers in areas where interaction with faculty and
fellow students would lead to improved outcomes. The Springboard students were more likely than others, at rates 10 per cent higher or more, to:

● communicate with faculty members using e-mail;
● do additional readings on topics that were introduced or discussed in
  class;
● participate in study groups;
● try to explain the material they had learnt to another student or friend;

- make friends with students from major fields very different from their own;
- participate in student organizations.

In addition, Springboard participants continue their studies at a higher rate than students who do not enroll in Springboard: 78.3 per cent of all first-year students return to BGSU for a second year of study, and for those who participated in Springboard, this rate is 83 per cent.

CONCLUSION – IT'S LEARNING THAT COUNTS

What is needed is a paradigm shift to a learning-centered approach. Springboard represents an effort to create a programme that integrates many of the key ingredients of Alverno's, CCL's, and others' successes into the educational programme of a state university. It seeks to engage students in their own learning about themselves as learners, and through this to connect them with the world of ideas. It does this by working directly with the major instrumental concern of students – how can I become more successful? It re-focuses that concern onto underlying questions about several skills – how can I become a better communicator? Analyse situations accurately? Solve problems more easily? Make better judgements? Provide leadership? Show self-assurance?

The sustaining motivation for change in higher education needs to come from students, specifically from the results that students achieve, and from their excitement about learning. Programme assessment, now required for re-accreditation of colleges and universities in the United States, points us in the right direction, but as practised on most campuses, it seldom engages students' motivation. Developmental assessment reinforces learning by focusing on individual progress in the context provided by publicly stated criteria. Springboard taps directly into student motivation, and its success shows that developmental assessment can be implemented in large state-assisted universities. It works because students see assessment as being worth their while.

REFERENCES

Chickering, A W and Gamson, Z F (1987) Seven principles for good practice in undergraduate education, *AAHE Bulletin*, pp 3–7
Conger, J A (1992) *Learning to Lead: The art of transforming managers into leaders*, Jossey-Bass, San Francisco
Mentkowski, M and Associates (2000) *Learning that Lasts: Integrating learning, development, and performance in college and beyond*, Jossey-Bass, San Francisco

13

Use of case studies in the development of key skills

Dick Glover and Maggie Boyle
University of Leeds
UK

SUMMARY

The Context project has successfully integrated students' key skills development with academic content learning. Over the three years 1997–2000, the project team has carried out a number of specific development projects at the University of Leeds, and contributed staff support to other projects elsewhere. The project is described in this example. Some work has been carried out with partner organizations external to the universities involved. These partners have provided assistance such as access to information, staff time and funds for additional work.

INTRODUCTION

The Context project, established in 1997, set out to investigate the use of case studies in higher education that:

- cover academic content: otherwise staff will not use it and students will not see its relevance;
- develop students' personal skills: through working in teams, problem solving, making decisions, making presentations, handling uncertainty, writing reports;
- are set in a work-related context: so learning is made realistic and based on real-world situations;

● encourage reflection on the learning: so students can talk confidently about their abilities and experience and understand that employers value these attributes.

The key target outcome is the integration of student personal development with the academic curriculum. Context has a number of strong examples of how this can be done successfully.

The Partnership Trust funded the project from September 1997 to August 1999. It is a UK-wide project based at the University of Leeds and is in partnership with the Careers Research Advisory Centre (CRAC). Context increased its initial budget by 35 per cent by generating income from other sources through sponsored case study development, and through providing staff training and development in other universities.

Context has reported annually to interested parties[1] and has developed an online database of learning materials[2] whose effects at least approximate the four key aims. It has also attempted to provide a national focus for this approach to integration of skills development with academic learning.

In 2000, Context is still actively supporting learning materials development and staff involved in course design in universities where funding can be found to cover the costs involved.

DERIVATION OF THE PROJECT

The Partnership Trust[3] wished to implement a project that aimed to encourage the use of 'case-study-based learning' in UK universities. The University of Leeds, in combination with CRAC[4], bid competitively for the funding and was successful. The project was named Context: 'putting learning into context'.

Context sought to develop ways in which key elements of CRAC Insight into Management courses could be fitted into normal student learning processes. Considerable student motivation and high-quality learning about career choice typify Insight into Management courses. To introduce this type of learning successfully into the academic curriculum (as opposed to using the existing materials in purely skills- and career-focused modules), Context had to find ways to integrate academic learning successfully into case study design.

The term 'case study' is ambiguous. The Harvard Business School, among other universities, has long had a large series of 'case studies', which it both uses and sells. These are predominantly static, analytical, with a view taken in hindsight. CRAC Insight into Management case studies are typically active, participative and about current real events.

Students are briefed about a business, government or social problem and asked to make decisions about future actions. Sometimes this involves role-play. Such case studies are inviting and challenging and therefore highly motivational. Because student teams work on them (as opposed to individual students), learning is achieved on at least two levels: about the situation (content or curriculum learning) and about team working and other skills (process learning or skills development).

WHAT SKILLS?

There is a multiplicity of lists of skills that students might usefully acquire. Rather than produce another set of definitions, Context has focused on how to achieve specific skill growth. So, in any given situation, the key step is to define which skills the focus should be on, from the outset of a case design task.

Context has referred to these generically as intended learning outcomes. They encompass both content and skills. Many academics are proficient in writing academic learning outcomes; less so at writing skills-related outcomes. Context has found that it is essential to develop learning outcomes thoroughly before attempting to design a case study. Above all else, clarity of purpose is essential.

Context has also found that an existing case study can often be refocused onto different learning outcomes (in the skills part) by adjusting in small ways the task that students are asked to tackle.

The essential step is to decide which specific skills to aim to achieve. Almost always, Context cases involve teamwork, as the Context team has taken the view that students are unlikely ever to have too much practice in this! Cases have always focused on the development of skills such as problem solving, decision making and negotiation in addition to team working.

Forms of case output can provide direct focus onto a variety of communication skills. Written communication skills can be targeted by a group report, verbal through presentations, visual through the creation of posters. In each case, the Context team would prefer to limit the scope (length of report, time of presentation, size of poster) so that students are encouraged to encapsulate key messages, rather than be unspecific; to be focused in reporting rather than verbose.

The Context team used the Association of Graduate Recruiters' work on graduate skills (AGR, 1995), and noted the desire that recruiters had expressed for independence of thinking, action and interaction. Thus, it makes sense to only tell part of the real story in briefing papers and where possible to encourage students to research related materials (eg via the library, the Web or people contact) to complete their own briefing.

This in turn provides considerable variety of output, so that when students see the work that others have done, there is yet more learning potential for them. This suggests that open reporting is valuable, and that student work should in some way be published within the course or module group.

HOW TO USE CASES

The normal academic timetable appears to severely inhibit what can be done. A pattern of one-hour (or in reality 50-minute) sessions can seem to restrict opportunity for team-based work. In the case of the traditional student (full-time student and recent school-leaver) Context found that it is effective to challenge students to find their own meeting space and time, provided that a little care is taken in group formation to avoid putting together people who live in opposite directions away from the campus. These students' time management is often weak to begin with, but improves with practice, especially if deadlines are made inflexible. Work is done when people can arrange to meet, often at weekends and in evenings. Less work was done that involved part-time and mature students, about whom some of the above observations may be less typical.

Often, it is worthwhile setting a large team task at the beginning of a module or course, even when students have not yet been taught all that they will need to know. There is an improved focus on lectures as a consequence ('we know why we need to know about…'); teams learn to make sure that they are all represented even if they are not all present.

WHAT IS A GOOD CASE STUDY?

First and foremost, it should be based on a real situation. Students seem wary of contrived materials; it most certainly focuses their minds if they can perceive (and even better see) the reality on which a case is constructed.

Briefing materials should use the terminology of the real situation. Tasks should be 'real' in nature. In businesses and elsewhere, focus is generally on appropriate action, rather than on analysis of past events. Cases should put students into situations where they must make and commit themselves to decisions as well as analyse events. Case writers need to remember that often: 'right' solutions are many and varied, 'best' solutions may only be defined in hindsight, and action (taking decisions) is usually infinitely preferred to inaction (deferring).

Thus cases need to be written as openly as possible, allowing students to make choices. To this end, the Context team has found it sometimes necessary and useful to distort reality, so as to avoid having a single obvious solution to a problem, and this seems to be acceptable and workable.

INVOLVING OUTSIDERS

There is great merit in seeking to involve outsiders, especially those who have direct experience of the situation simulated through a case study. The opportunity for students to receive feedback from someone who has direct experience of the problem that they have worked on provides substantial benefits, but it is necessary to ensure that such feedback is balanced, not all critical, or superficially positive.

It is important to remember that the deployment of skill is often confidence related, that people who are skilful often use only those skills in which they are reasonably confident of success. Over-critical feedback damages self-confidence, and superficial feedback diminishes the value of the experience. Industry frequently focuses on skills, but the reality is that many managers are less skilful than they would like their recruits to be. This is not hypocritical: it is reasonable for business (and other) managers to seek to improve their organization's skill base, and if employers focus on skills when they are recruiting, educators must do so too, or leave their students at a disadvantage in the job market.

SECONDARY BENEFITS

There are many secondary benefits that the Context team has seen arise.

Multiple uses of case studies have occurred: cases have been used inside the organizations that they are about. Thus organizations that initially were asked to help provide data on which to base new cases have been found to use the cases for their own staff development purposes. Use in other departments and universities is much less common: the 'not invented here' syndrome may still be predominant, and if so, this is a serious block to rapid progress.

It is probable that working on student skills using case studies has indirect effects on academics. Their understanding of the real application of their own specialist knowledge may improve, their own interpersonal skills may improve, and their breadth of teaching skills is very likely to improve.
Work experience is much in demand now. This can provide students with excellent insights to organizational and work culture as well as to how their subject study is relevant to work. However, not all students can (or are likely to) access high quality work experience. Case studies, through providing access to simulations of work, can give students some of those learning outcomes.

SOME EXAMPLES OF CONTEXT CASE STUDIES

SusDale

This was developed for a new geography module, which focused on 'interpretation of environment', on how people see different things in an environment depending on their situation.

It was written in two versions. One lasts eight to ten weeks, as the backbone activity on a second-year undergraduate module, and the other lasts three to four hours as a stand-alone activity.

The partner organization was the Yorkshire Dales National Park Authority, which now uses the short version regularly with sixth form and FE college students, typically 16 to 19 years of age, to help them to understand the nature of a national park and the stresses that such a body creates within its community.

The long version, designed for higher education use, sets students into role groups and invites interaction between groups over an extended period, ultimately seeking agreement between communities as diverse as hill farmers, hill walkers, local business owners and the Park Authority. The short version is a role-play where individuals within a meeting take on the same roles.

As with all new case developments, the Context team spent some time with the students after it had been used, reviewing with them how it had worked and what they had learnt. The undergraduates listed all the following skills as having been developed as a direct result of participation:

> negotiation; role-playing; compromising; communication; presentation; controlling large meetings; evaluation; interpretation; team-work; debating; questioning; analysing; seeing the views of others; forward thinking; report writing; leadership; following a policy; creating a policy; empathizing; listening; argument (maybe not a skill!); persuading; probing; chairing; participating; increased self-awareness.

The students were then asked where these skills might find new applications in their lives:

> when playing sports; socializing; buying a car; at work; in other modules; in caring professions; in their own environment group; in teaching.

Seatons

The Seatons case is quite different. It runs for about three hours, and presents students with information about a chemical business that has some specific pollution risks. The company is a real business, although the data has been subtly changed so that commercially sensitive information is not revealed. The students are given a range of investment proposals, some cheap and quick, some expensive and with a longer implementation timetable. They are asked to develop a programme that is within the resource limits of the business (money and skills available), and that meets both business priorities and environmental priorities.

Outcomes are very varied, and considerable insight is achieved into practical environment management issues. The case has been used with undergraduate students, who said of the experience:

> It was a challenge and it forced you to be decisive. I like weighing up pros and cons of different situations so it was enjoyable.

> I found it interesting reading the different opinions and then analysing them. I also found it interesting to see how other people thought. It gave me an idea of what I perhaps hadn't thought about.

> The limited time made the exercise seem realistic – making key decisions under pressure.

> It was applied to something real and modern that has actually happened. This makes it seem more relevant.

> Overall the exercise was very useful in terms of examining the decision-making process and practising communication skills.

It has also been used with students studying Geography at Masters level:

> Stimulating and useful process to look at group dynamics and environmental issues. Particularly feedback from author and review of what Seatons actually did.

> Very worthwhile exercise, people do get involved which shows their interest and creates a good learning environment. Revelation concerning decision-making process.

> Very useful exercise that will hopefully be quoted in later job interviews.

> Good exercise altogether. Valuable practical experience in real-life problems. Many valid points learnt.

> Led to interesting and stimulating discussions. A useful interactive exercise.

> The use of a hands-on approach actually solving a problem within a group and within a time frame, and also comparing results with other groups. How different groups can create such different results.

On a number of occasions it has also been used as a staff-development exercise on Context workshops for staff wishing to learn more about how cases might be used. The Context team found the strongest impact came when students were doing the case study alongside the staff, and recall amazement at the dynamic and motivated students on the other side of the room!

A series of cases on flood warning and defence issues

One academic at the University of Leeds School of Geography sought materials with which to redesign an undergraduate module on Hydrology. At that time, the Environment Agency, which covers England and Wales, saw benefit in supporting the development of such materials: flooding was and probably still is a major issue in England and Wales. Cases were created that covered issues such as developing a national flood-warning strategy, selecting a flood-defence scheme, forecasting river flows and planning river-flow monitoring systems.

The Environment Agency provided the funds necessary to make these cases possible. All four cases have been used, and it is expected that the Environment Agency will make them widely available towards the end of 2000. In the meantime, they are available on request from Context.

Pudsey

Context also developed a case study specifically for use with academic staff. This is designed to help them to see under what circumstances the use of case studies may be relevant. The University of Pudsey[5] is an imaginary university; the participants are cast in the role of junior department members in a department with some learning and teaching issues. The case enables staff to rehearse the arguments for and against a variety of teaching and learning strategies, and it is thus extremely effective training material.

The most common response to this case – usually within ten minutes – is 'Did you base this on my department?', which is probably a genuine reflection on the use of realistic materials.

GETTING COPIES OF CONTEXT CASES

All except Pudsey are available for download. Check the Context Web site[6] for Seatons, and use the contacts listed there for information about the other cases. Pudsey is special: the Context team sees this as one of a series of staff-development activities, and believes that the provision of staff training and support is a continuing activity for Context into the future. The Context team will be happy to talk to readers about providing development project support and staff training, which, whilst based on using and creating case studies, can be tailored to meet specific needs.

WHAT OTHER SUBJECTS HAVE BEEN INVOLVED?

At the University of Leeds in the Context years: Geography, Philosophy, Civil Engineering, Computer Studies, Mechanical Engineering and Fuel and Energy. Before Context (and thus through the Enterprise project at The University of Leeds): Maths, German, The Environment Centre, Biochemistry, Classics and Law.

At the universities of Northumbria and Newcastle (the Cases to Advance Student Employability or CASE project): Geography, Politics, German, Fine Arts and Social Policy.

At the University of Newcastle (the Teamwork for Education and Employment Network in Arts or TEENA project): Museum Studies, Archaeology, Modern Languages and Music.

ENDNOTES

1. 'Context' Annual Report Summaries, available from Maggie Boyle.
2. www.context.tlsu.leeds.ac.uk
3. The Partnership Trust was formed as an offshoot of the Council for Industry and Higher Education in about 1989, primarily to raise funds from industrial sponsorship for the *Innovation in Teaching Awards Scheme* until the late 1990s. The Awards Scheme provided cash prizes for excellence in teaching in higher education in a range of categories. The Partnership Trust formally ceased to exist in March 2000.
4. The *Careers Research Advisory Centre* based in Cambridge. See www.crac.org.uk for full details of CRAC's work.
5. Pudsey is a small town near Leeds; Pudsey Bear is the name used as a logo for the BBC's *Children in Need* Charity. There is no connection with this charity. There is also no University at Pudsey!
6. www.context.tlsu.leeds.ac.uk

REFERENCE

Association of Graduate Recruiters (AGR) (1995) *Skills for Graduates in the 21st Century*, AGR, Cambridge

14

Using the national key skills framework within a higher education context

Sue Bloy and Jean Williams
De Montfort University
UK

SUMMARY

Since the early 1990s, De Montfort University has been developing a cross-institutional approach to key skills.

This chapter provides an introduction to De Montfort University, a synopsis of key skills developments at the university, and an overview of the national key skills framework.

Three aspects are then used to illustrate how the university's key skills policy is working in practice:

- Curriculum review: making the 'subject' the central focus of key skills development within undergraduate study.
- Students' self-assessment of their own key skills on entry to the university: providing a picture of students' learning support needs at the point of transition to higher education.
- Individual key skills development: some concluding observations on key skills as part of the broader culture of an individual's learning experience.

INTRODUCTION TO DE MONTFORT UNIVERSITY

De Montfort University has evolved from a diverse range of specialist institutions. The university's long history of learning, teaching and research is

151

founded in the technical and trade education of the late 19th century. The name itself is associated with Simon De Montfort, Earl of Leicester, a distinguished figure in English history and widely credited with establishing the first parliament in 1265.

The university is one of Britain's largest higher education institutions, with around 30,000 students based at four UK centres: Bedford, Leicester, Lincoln and Milton Keynes. Programmes of study range from further education to PhD level in agriculture, the arts, business, computing, design, education, engineering, health, humanities, sport and the sciences. The university also offers programmes in South Africa, Europe and the Far East.

The university maintains strong links with industry and places great emphasis on equipping students with the skills, confidence and creativity that today's workplace demands.

A SYNOPSIS OF KEY SKILLS DEVELOPMENTS AT THE UNIVERSITY

The university was one of over 60 institutions to receive funding (1990–1995) within the Enterprise in Higher Education (EHE) scheme of the Employment Department (latterly the Department for Education and Employment). EHE had as its primary aim the preparation of graduates for the world of work, linking developments in higher education with the needs of employers and has been viewed as one of the largest catalysts for change in higher education:

> Successive national evaluations of EHE have demonstrated that the initiative was a catalyst for change... Significant parts of the HE curriculum have become more relevant to employment and employer needs. As a result, learners are becoming better prepared for working life by developing lifelong learning and other key skills.
>
> (Hawkins and Winter, 1997)

De Montfort's approach to EHE placed the emphasis on preparing students with the skills needed in learning, working and life and a major outcome was the development of an institution-wide model for Personal Transferable Skills (De Montfort University, 1995). The model drew on the university's wide-ranging undergraduate provision, within which many programmes lead to professional qualifications and exemptions. Staff and students across the university contributed to the model through surveys and focused interviews and account was taken of national key skills developments.

The Personal Transferable Skills model comprised the four skill areas of communication, groupwork, personal effectiveness and problem solving. A fundamental aspect of the model was to ensure that programmes of study addressed the skills explicitly and an audit of the personal transferable skills within programmes of study was undertaken. A Certificate of Achievement in Personal Transferable Skills was offered to students who obtained evidence of skills achievement from their undergraduate study, authenticated by tutors. A move was made therefore to elicit skills outcomes from modules and to provide a value-added qualification for students.

In the light of national developments in the late 1990s, in particular the Dearing Inquiry into Higher Education (NCIHE, 1997), the university's model was extended to include numeracy and information technology. Students were again offered the opportunity to gather evidence of their skills achievement in an assessed portfolio, for which they would receive additional certification. The emphasis at this point was on students' reflection on their achievement in academic, extra-curricular and work-based activity, as well as on tutor-assessed evidence.

While students were initially keen to be involved in both of the above schemes, most found that the priorities of study, part-time employment and personal and social pressures prevailed. As a consequence, only a small number of enthusiastic and committed students claimed certification. Evaluation of these earlier approaches has led to the embedding of skills outcomes within modules as an holistic part of the student experience rather than using a value-added model. More specifically, the emphasis is now on providing students and staff with a framework of learning support and guidance in respect of academic and personal achievement.

Further funding from the Department for Education and Employment (DfEE) provided an additional catalyst for establishing and implementing the university's approach to key skills, through a successful bid to the 1997 Development Fund (DfEE, 1997). A key outcome of the university's project, The Diagnosis, Guidance and Support and Recording Achievement of Key Skills in Higher Education, has been Academic Board endorsement of the university's key skills policy:

> The national standards for key skills are to be adopted across the full range of the university's awards as benchmark outcome statements. All students will be entitled to equal access to guidance and support for the development of a profile of key skills.

This synopsis has shown that the DfEE has played a significant role in supporting developments at the university. However, mention should also be made of the importance of collaboration and networking between institutions in the implementation of approaches to key skills in higher education. Through EHE, the DfEE brought staff together from different institutions to learn from each other's experience and continued this by establishing around 34 discipline networks. One of these, the Ability Based Curriculum (ABC) Network, of which De Montfort University was a founder member, comprised a group of individuals from nine UK institutions and Alverno College (USA), who shared a common interest in key abilities (skills). In 1994, six of the institutions had participated in a three-day conference in York (Employment Department, 1995), at which the foundations for the creation of the ABC Network were laid. A comparative overview of key skills developments in the network member institutions (Otter, 1997) provides a useful snapshot of approaches to key skills.

AN OVERVIEW OF THE NATIONAL KEY SKILLS FRAMEWORK

Before considering how adoption of the university's policy is working in practice, it is necessary to understand the context of the national key skills framework, and in particular, what is meant by the concept of level.

The national key skills framework is defined by three regulatory bodies: the Qualifications and Curriculum Authority (QCA) for England, the Council for Curriculum Examination and Assessment (CCEA) for Northern Ireland and the Qualifications, Curriculum and Assessment Authority for Wales (ACCAC). The framework comprises six key skill areas:

- application of number;
- communication;
- improving own learning and performance;
- information technology;
- problem solving;
- working with others.

Key skills are defined in learning outcomes at national Levels 1 to 5. Table 14.1, taken from the QCA guidance on Levels 4 and 5 (QCA, 2000a) demonstrates the main differences between the key skills levels. As an individual moves up the levels, he or she is expected to take more responsibility for decisions on how to apply these skills to different tasks, problems and situations. In moving up the levels, the abilities required at the lower levels are subsumed.

Table 14.1   Qualifications and Curriculum Authority – skills descriptors

LEVELS 1–3
Levels 1 and 2 are mainly to help you develop the basic skills that underpin key skills and to increase your confidence in applying your skills to largely routine situations. **Level 3** marks a shift from being able to deal with straightforward tasks to being able to respond to the demands of more complex activities. The key skills units at Level 3 require more explicit reasoning ability and increased personal responsibility for making decisions about your own learning and how tasks are organized.
LEVEL 4
This level requires you to have substantial autonomy and responsibility for managing activities and identifying how the key skills relate to your situation. Each of the key skills units requires you to: • develop a strategy for using the relevant key skill over an extended period of time, and plan how you will do this; • monitor progress, critically reflect on your performance in using the relevant skill, and adapt your strategy, as necessary, to achieve the quality of outcomes required; • evaluate your overall strategy and present the outcomes from your work, including ways of further improving your skills.
LEVEL 5
Personal Skills Development This level requires you to demonstrate an integrated approach to applying skills in communication, working with others and problem solving. The aim is to improve your own learning and performance in the context of managing dynamically complex work. The unit requires you to: • explore the demands of your work, including your own skills-development needs, and formulate viable proposals for meeting these demands; • plan how to manage your work, meet your own skills-development needs, and gain the necessary commitment from others; • manage your work, adapting your strategy as necessary to resolve problems and meet new demands, and formally review your use of skills; • evaluate your overall performance and present the outcomes, including ways of enhancing your skills in the future.

It is the view of the authors that one might expect students to be entering higher education with Levels 2–3 and during the first year of undergraduate study be applying Level 3 in the key skills identified as essential for their chosen subject. Level 4 is that which students should be aiming to achieve in the range of key skills identified as essential by a discipline on completion of an undergraduate programme.

Level 5 is aimed at an individual's continuing professional development and in the short term it is unlikely to be used widely in the context of higher education, except perhaps in certain Masters level work-based studies. However, as postgraduate education becomes subject to the same pressures as undergraduate education, with for example the need to complete qualifications within a tight time frame, it is feasible that postgraduate students will more generally need to apply skills at Level 5. Recognition of achievement at Level 5 may, therefore, become a feature of 'added value' for postgraduate students.

CURRICULUM REVIEW

While the university's key skills policy will eventually be applied across the full range of provision, from further to higher and postgraduate study, implementation is commencing in undergraduate programmes of study. At undergraduate level, the basic unit of learning is the module, with clusters of modules being brought together in diets, usually in a distinct academic subject. Diets are themselves managed under the authority of subjects, through Subject Authority Boards, which are standing committees of the Academic Board.

As a first phase, subjects are identifying the essential and desirable key skills, measured against the national specifications, for students in Part 1 (year 1) and on graduation. This is providing a framework against which modules can make explicit which key skills, by level, are learnt, practised and/or formally assessed. By providing clarity for students regarding the key skills that they will be expected to develop and apply within their study, and in particular, where these will be assessed as learning outcomes, the importance of the skills as a valued aspect of the student experience is being emphasized. The embedding of key skills in the curriculum is seen as the best way of ensuring that students acquire and enhance their skills profile.

Use of the national framework will assist in promoting the concept of continuous curriculum development and partnership with the compulsory and post-16 sectors. With the introduction of the Curriculum 2000 qualifications framework (QCA, 2000b) in schools and colleges, students will be entering higher education with recognized levels of key skills alongside advanced-level qualifications. They will expect to have their current key skills achievement acknowledged and the admissions tariff that is being introduced by the Universities and Colleges Admissions Service (UCAS) in 2000 will award points for key skills achievement (UCAS, 2000).

In this climate of change, adoption of the national framework as benchmarks within the university's own provision will assist in ensuring consistency and comparability across subjects and will provide clarity for students and staff of the university and for potential applicants, parents, employers and external agencies. Furthermore, use of the standards within the undergraduate curriculum will provide opportunities for students to further enhance their key skills at the higher levels.

STUDENTS' ASSESSMENT OF THEIR KEY SKILLS ON ENTERING THE UNIVERSITY

As already noted, developments have been focused initially upon undergraduate programmes. It was felt important to underpin this with an assessment of the level of the key skills of full-time undergraduate students entering Part 1 in September 1999. Analysis of the self-assessment exercise undertaken by students, and their identification of learning development needs, is providing the university with an evidence base of students at the point of transition to higher education both on an institution-wide basis and more specifically within subject areas.

Methodology

There have been few studies (Powell, Conway and Ross, 1990; Macdonald-Ross and Scott, 1997) looking specifically at students' objectively assessed level of skills competence. A small-scale study undertaken in 1997 (Murphy *et al*, 1997) did objectively assess the key skills against the national standards at Level 3 of a sample of 200 students. Students drawn from ten universities also completed their own self-assessment in these skills which was compared with that of their previous school or college tutors. Among other findings, the latter study revealed that students were not entering higher education with the levels of skills that had previously been assumed. This indicated that there was perhaps a need to look at a wider range of levels, hence the decision taken in the De Montfort survey, to apply Levels 1 to 3 in communication and Levels 1 to 4 in application of number.

It should be noted that the exercise undertaken at De Montfort was intended to be a measure of students' own level of confidence and a means of raising awareness of the expectations that are likely to be placed on them in undergraduate study. In order to ensure substantial coverage of the undergraduate intake, an assessment instrument was devised that could be delivered to large numbers of students from a varied subject base and background in an equitable manner (De Montfort University, 1999). Self-assessment exercises based upon methodology already used within existing learning and support provision at the university were deployed to engage a large sample of students across the full range of the university's undergraduate provision.

The assessment concentrated on the three skills of communication, application of number and information technology (IT), with the wider key skill of improving own learning and performance underpinning the whole exercise. Activities completed by students were related to their perceptions of higher education and to the university's expectations of the skills levels of undergraduates. The activities were designed to challenge students and raise their understanding of the need to take responsibility for their own learning and development. Communication (oral, written and reading) at Levels 1 to 3 and application of number at Levels 1 to 4 were covered using a range of exercises that enabled students to make a judgement of their own confidence in the skills. IT was addressed by a questionnaire which sought students' experience of and confidence in a range of practical applications of information and communications technology (ICT).

The results

While the opportunity to participate in the self-assessment exercise was included in induction programmes, participation was on a purely voluntary basis. However, 3,013 students, over half of the full-time undergraduate intake, completed the exercise, covering the full range of subject provision. This included students from all six faculties of the university and collaborative provision in a number of the university's associate colleges. Analysis by age and gender, which is only available for 1,502 (under 50 per cent) of the students, closely reflects the profile for full-time undergraduate students as compared with the undergraduate profile for the 1998/99 intake, as shown in Table 14.2.

Table 14.2 Comparison of profile of students completing self-assessment with undergraduate profile for 1998/99 new entrants

1998/99 Undergraduate profile for new entrants	1999/2000 Self-assessment survey profile
Age	*Age*
78% under 21	75% under 21
11% 21 to 25	11% 21 to 25
11% over 25	14% over 25
Gender	*Gender*
52% female	59% female
48% male	41% male

Figure 14.1 shows the global results for oral and written communication and reading. Students assessing themselves at Level 3 in communication perceive that they are well prepared for, or at least feel confident in, meeting the challenges that lie ahead. Those students who assessed themselves at Level 2 should find that the learning opportunities presented to them during the first year of undergraduate study will enable them make the transition to the demands of higher education. However, those students who assessed themselves at Level 1 are likely to need directed support provision in order to make the most of the higher education experience. An interesting outcome was that all faculties demonstrated a very similar pattern in all three aspects of communication, thus perhaps dispelling some assumptions regarding proficiency in certain subject areas over other others.

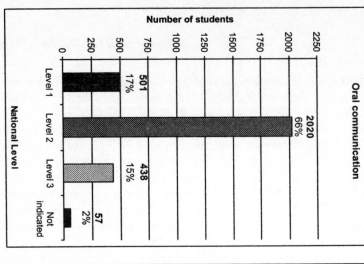

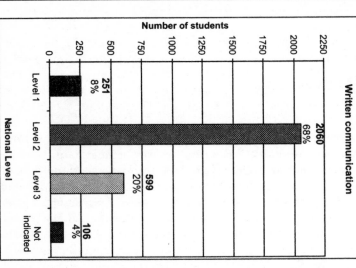

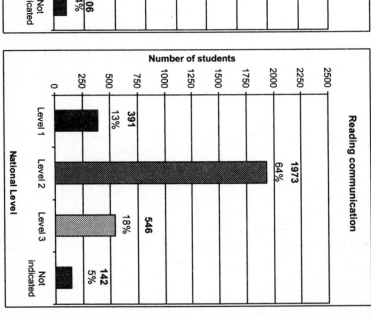

Figure 14.1 Global results of self-assessment levels for communication (oral, written and reading) including associate colleges (Tresham, North Oxfordshire and Bedford).

The results for application of number were more widely spread, reflecting the subject area being studied (11 per cent at Level 1, 30 per cent at Level 2, 37 per cent at Level 3, 16 per cent at Level 4). The results of the IT questionnaire reveal that students in general are entering higher education with a relatively high level of confidence in ICT, with 38 per cent of students declaring that they had some ICT experience and 39 per cent that they had considerable experience. However, it should be noted that 14 per cent of students indicated that they had little or no previous experience and that of these, analysis by age has shown that a higher proportion were mature students. This is itself a clear indication of the need to provide basic ICT training and support for some students entering higher education.

As has already been stated, the self-assessment was of students' confidence and was undertaken within the first week at university. Students were instructed to be ruthlessly honest with themselves and it is possible that they underestimated their actual level of skill, particularly in aspects of communication. The results may indeed reflect students' concerns about meeting the challenge of higher education, and could therefore be an indication that higher education should be much clearer about the expectations that will be placed upon students. In all areas, a small proportion of students did not indicate their self-assessed level, but this is not felt to detract significantly from the overall picture.

An evaluation of the exercise, including questionnaire surveys of students and staff and focus group discussions with students, is informing revisions to the key skills induction programme for the next academic year. The majority of students who participated in 1999/2000 said that they had not previously undertaken such an activity and valued the opportunity to reflect on their own key skills. Further developments, including the use of a range of objective assessments alongside the self-assessment exercise, are being trialled in the first instance with small samples taken from students who entered the university in the spring term 2000.

As far as can be ascertained, no other survey has been conducted on the scale of that undertaken at De Montfort University. Notwithstanding the possible margin of error due to the self-assessment nature of the exercise, it has provided the university with a snapshot of the key skills that students bring with them and of the development opportunities that need to be provided for students entering higher education. While much of the support that students were seeking is already provided both within the curriculum and through a range of support services, the survey has informed a review of learning support provision across the university. The review has identified the need to clarify that support which should be provided as a central resource and that which is better served at the point of curriculum delivery.

INDIVIDUAL STUDENT SKILLS DEVELOPMENT

In conclusion, by exploring one UK university's approach to key skills, this chapter has attempted to demonstrate that such developments need to be viewed within the context of the subject, the institutional culture and the national educational agenda. However, in addition, the role of the individual student must be seen as paramount. The student experience in higher education can be represented as part of a cycle, commencing pre-entry, through induction, engagement in the curriculum and extra-curricular activity, to graduation and on into employment and continuing professional and personal development.

While this chapter addresses specifically key skills in the context of higher education, it is important to recognize that in the development of student entitlement and provision, the cycle can also be applied to learning before and beyond higher education. Throughout an individual's life, there are issues relating to choice and the consequential decisions that have to be made regarding progression to the next stages. In choosing to participate in higher education, an individual student has elected to engage with a system that requires them to develop both knowledge and skills. As part of a supportive learning environment students can be encouraged to diagnose their confidence and competence in applying skills at each level. Students should not be expected to achieve all skills at the same level but be encouraged to be proactive in improving those skills that may enhance their academic and extracurricular profile. By suggesting subject-specific skills development and a broader range of learning support activities, one aim of higher education is to encourage students to develop personal autonomy in order that they can respond to the immediate learning experience and any subsequent new learning environments in a structured manner. In this way key skills become part of a broader culture of learning, rather than a tool for remedying perceived variations in ability. Thus pre-graduation experiences can be seen to form the basis of a student's graduate identity, to be further maintained and developed.

ENDNOTE

1. Figures supplied by Planning Support, De Montfort University, taken from the University's returns for HESES (Higher Education Student Entry Statistics) and HESA (Higher Education Statistics Agency).

REFERENCES

De Montfort University (1995) *Enterprise Learning Initiative, Five Year Review, 1991–1995*, De Montfort University, Leicester

De Montfort University (1999) *Improving Your Learning: Introductory workbook to key skills in higher education – self-assessment and action planning for the development of key skills*, De Montfort University, Leicester

Department for Education and Employment (DfEE) (1997) *Higher Education and Employment Development Programme Prospectus*, DfEE, Sheffield

Employment Department (1995), *Institutional Change Towards an Ability-based Curriculum in Higher Education*, Report of a three-day conference held in York, 3–6 July 1994, Employment Department, Sheffield

Hawkins, P and Winter, J (1997) *Mastering Change: Learning the lessons of the Enterprise in Higher Education Initiative*, DfEE, Sheffield

Macdonald-Ross, M and Scott, B (1997) A postal survey of OU students' reading skills, *Open Learning*, **12** (2), pp 29–40

Murphy, R *et al* (1997) *The Key Skills of Students Entering Higher Education*, University of Nottingham School of Education

National Committee of Inquiry into Higher Education (NCIHE) (1997) *Higher Education in the Learning Society*, HMSO, Norwich

Otter, S (1997) *The Ability-based Curriculum – Some snapshots of progress in key skills in higher education*, www.brookes.ac.uk/services/ocsd/abschome

Powell, R, Conway, C and Ross, L (1990) Effects of student predisposing characteristics on student success, *Journal of Distance Education*, **1**, pp 5–19

Qualifications and Curriculum Authority (QCA) (2000a), *Guidance on the Higher Level Key Skills Units: Levels 4–5*, www.qca.org.uk/keyskills/

Qualifications and Curriculum Authority (QCA) (2000b), *Curriculum Guidance for 2000*, www.qca.org.curric2000/

Universities and Colleges Admissions Service for the UK (2000), *The UCAS Tariff – A new points score for entry into higher education*, www.ucas.ac.uk/new/press/tariff

15

Helping academic staff to integrate professional skills

Barbara de la Harpe and Alex Radloff
Curtin University of Technology
Australia

SUMMARY

Employers worldwide want graduates who have work and life skills and are especially looking for graduates who have well-developed communication, team-work and problem-solving skills. Students are most likely to develop them when the skills are integrated into regular course work and are taught by the subject teacher. Teaching both subject content and skills challenges academic staff to reflect on and, where necessary, to make changes to what and how they teach and assess.

The Business School at a large Australian technological university has, since 1998, been implementing a project aimed at integrating the skills that the employers of their graduates value into the undergraduate curriculum. A major part of the project has involved supporting staff in making the necessary changes to their curricula and to reconceptualize their roles as teachers.

The support has aimed to help and encourage staff to:

- reflect on their teaching practice and on student learning and skill development;
- introduce innovative ways to develop skills;
- monitor the teaching and learning outcomes as a result of the changes they have made;
- document and disseminate their experiences.

Support has included working with staff one-on-one, having group meetings and seminars, developing teaching and learning resources, and providing advice on researching teaching practice. Experience so far shows that support that is based on principles of good practice is effective and well received by the staff who choose to use it. However, the challenge is to encourage more staff to engage in such activities. Staff can meet the challenge of their changing roles when there is a focus on learner-centred conceptions of teaching, effective leadership, appropriate incentives, and adequate time for change.

INTRODUCTION

The chapter begins with a description of the institutional context and an outline of the project. The support provided to staff to help them integrate skills into their subjects is then described. This is followed by reflections on what aspects of staff support worked. The chapter concludes with a brief overview of the key issues that need to be addressed in order to encourage staff to respond to the need for change and to engage in professional development.

The institutional context

Curtin University of Technology – one of four public universities in Perth, Western Australia – is a large, multi-campus university with approximately 25,000 students from diverse cultural and language backgrounds enrolled in a wide range of courses. It has four teaching divisions, of which the Business School is one. The Business School consists of seven schools (departments): Accounting, Business Law, Economics and Finance, Information Systems, Management, Marketing, and the Graduate School of Business.

The Business School has just over 5,500 undergraduate students enrolled on the main campus, an attractively landscaped low-rise suburban site some 10 kilometres from the centre of Perth. Approximately 40 per cent of the Business School students are international, with most coming from the South-East Asian region. The majority of first-year students are school leavers aged around 17 or 18 years.

Undergraduate students are enrolled in a three-year Bachelor of Commerce degree with a single or double major chosen from 23 areas offered by the first six schools listed above. In the first year, students must complete six common core units, namely Accounting 100, Legal Framework 100, Economics 100, Information Systems 100, Management 100 and Marketing 100.

There are approximately 200 full-time academic staff and numerous part-time or sessional staff involved in teaching in the undergraduate programme.

THE PROFESSIONAL SKILLS PROJECT

At the beginning of 1998, the acting executive dean of the Business School initiated the Curtin Business School professional skills project. The project responded to feedback from employers as well as from graduates which underlined the need for business schools to produce graduates with high levels of the skills needed for success in the world of work and for life. The project was selected as one of the case studies in the Australian Technology Network Project on Graduate Capabilities (ATN, 1999).

The project began with the setting up of a task force comprising representatives from each of the six Business School subject areas, employers, students, the Centre for Educational Advancement (CEA), and the library. It met regularly for eight months and, based on input from members, the research literature and employer surveys and following extended debate and discussion, identified a set of professional skills relevant to business graduates:

- communication (divided into three components: writing, presenting, and speaking out);
- computer literacy;
- information literacy;
- team working;
- decision making.

In coming to a consensus on which skills to focus on, the task force used a bottom-up approach, encouraged ownership and collegiality, and recognized disciplinary differences in skill selection and development (CBS Professional Skills Task Force, 1999).

Integration of skills into units began in first semester 1999 with first-year units, and will over time include units in second and third years of the programme. Unit coordinators in each of the schools were asked to select from the list the skills they considered most appropriate to their subject and to integrate them into their subject through changes to curriculum materials, teaching and learning activities and assessment tasks. They were given time release to work on their units.

A unit outline template was developed collaboratively by a sub-group of the task force and the first-year coordinators to provide a framework for the curriculum changes and to standardize the information provided to students. The template included headings such as a welcome, syllabus outline, learning objectives for content and skill, teaching mode and a semester calendar. The template also included compulsory statements of school and university policy such as those on plagiarism and copyright as well as important information and dates. The template was available electronically and staff were encouraged to use it.

When integrating skills, staff were asked, in line with Biggs (1996), to ensure that the learning objectives, teaching and learning activities and assessment tasks were aligned to include:

- learning objectives for each skill as well as learning objectives for the content;
- a programme for the semester showing where each skill would be taught and assessed;
- marking guides showing assessment criteria and allocation of marks for both the skill and content components of the task;
- an icon for each skill (see Table 15.1) placed next to the learning objective, teaching and learning activities, and assessment tasks to highlight the alignment between them.

Staff were helped and encouraged to make the necessary changes to their units, monitor the impact of the changes they made, and document and disseminate their experiences. This emphasis on curriculum development has been shown to be a powerful way to encourage staff to engage in professional development to improve teaching and learning (Zuber-Skerritt, 1992).

Table 15.1   Icons for each of the professional skills as used in unit outline template

Icon	Professional skill
✍	Writing
☺	Speaking out
👥	Presenting
💾	Computer literacy
📖	Information literacy
💡	Decision making
🤝	Teamwork

PROVIDING STAFF SUPPORT

From the beginning of the project it was recognized that staff would need support to reconceptualize their roles and what and how they teach. Specifically, it was important that staff accepted that, in order to help their students develop skills, their role had to change from mainly content experts to teachers of content and skills. Traditionally, academic staff have considered themselves as mainly content experts rather than as teachers, since, as Sutherland (1996: 91) points out,

> [they] have spent their professional lives developing skill and confidence in their abilities as chemists, sociologists, rhetoricians, and art historians. Their training and focus has been on content, and few have been supervised or mentored in teaching and evaluating students.

However, in order to help students to develop not only subject knowledge but also skills for work, learning and life, staff need '... to think of themselves as teachers as well as specialists in their discipline area... The message is that an academic needs to be a discipline expert and a teacher' (Kember, 1998: 23).

Therefore, to help staff to address these changed expectations about their role, they were offered support aimed at helping them to integrate skills into their units. Funds were provided for staff time release, development of teaching and learning resources, catering for seminars, administrative support, and for a member of staff from one of the schools with a reputation as a good teacher (a subject specialist) and an educational consultant (the first author) to work half time on the project.

The support activities offered and coordinated by the educational consultant included working with staff individually, providing seminars on teaching and assessing each skill, contributing to discipline-based meetings, and developing and collating teaching and learning materials. Further, it was also recognized that the success of the project depended on leadership from senior staff. Thus, every effort was made to include these staff as both champions of the project and as participants in staff support activities.

In line with good practice in staff development, the support offered:

- was ongoing;
- included a range of activities;
- focused on curriculum change;
- encouraged staff to reflect on their teaching practices;
- included teaching and learning resources and practical advice;
- recognized and tried to address the different needs and concerns of staff;

● encouraged collegiality within and across schools.

Each of the support activities is briefly described below.

Individual support

Staff could meet with either the educational consultant or the subject specialist to:

● decide which skills were most appropriate to integrate into their subject;
● discuss how to teach and assess these;
● develop teaching and learning materials such as overhead transparencies, handouts and assessment guides;
● get advice on how to get feedback from their students about skills integration and development;
● get help in documenting and disseminating outcomes;
● clarify the project aims, and their role and responsibilities;
● discuss their concerns about skills integration.

Seminar series

Seven two-hour lunchtime seminars were offered across the 15-week semester in collaboration with staff from the CEA and the library. Each seminar focused on one of the professional skills, was based on a constructivist approach to learning, was learner-centred and collaborative, and provided a safe environment where participants could feel free to share their experiences, feelings and concerns, and to address their conceptions of teaching and learning. Seminars also included ideas and strategies for teaching and assessing the skill. The seminar series was widely advertised and Heads of School were personally invited to attend and asked to encourage their staff to participate.

School meetings

Heads of School were asked to hold meetings to discuss the project. Meetings were deliberately held in schools in recognition of the importance of the disciplinary context and to encourage ownership of the project. The meetings gave staff a chance to discuss the philosophical and educational basis for the project, ask questions, raise concerns, and find out about the support available to help them integrate skills into their subject.

Teaching and learning resources

For each of the skills, teaching and learning resources were collated into a resource file. Resources included handouts, worksheets, checklists, proformas and assessment guides which staff could use or adapt, as well as material about skills and their development. The resource file was made available to staff through the educational consultant or the project director.

Staff views about the support provided was gathered using formal and informal sources of feedback.

WHAT WORKED?

All staff who participated in any of the activities described above commented positively about the support that they received. The 24 staff who met with the educational consultant or the discipline specialist one-on-one said they found the approach helpful in selecting skills and making the necessary changes to their unit. Seven staff chose to document and disseminate their experiences of integrating skills. Staff who did so are continuing to refine the changes they made to their units in line with the project aims.

The feedback from the 38 staff who attended one or more of the seven seminars was positive. Participants most often mentioned as benefits of attending: meeting colleagues; talking and comparing experiences with colleagues outside their school; enhancing teaching ideas; learning new techniques; crystallizing ideas; and reflecting on teaching practice and thinking about what students think and need. They also liked the format and style of the sessions, highlighting the 'friendly but thought-provoking atmosphere', 'open discussion on the ways students' skills can be developed', 'group discussions', 'sharing problems and strategies', and the 'enthusiasm of the presenters'.

Staff in the four schools that held meetings found them particularly useful for clarifying the aims of the project. They also used the meetings to air their concerns and resistance – philosophical and practical – to integrating skills, making comments such as 'I shouldn't have to teach this – it should be taught in a specific skills unit', 'if we had well-prepared students in the first place, there would be no need to teach these skills' and 'I don't know how to teach this. I'm an expert in… and can't be expected to teach anything else'.

Staff who accessed the resource file most often selected assessment checklists and proformas which they could use for giving feedback to students on their assignments. Staff feedback showed that what they found to be most useful were ready-made, subject-specific materials rather than ones that they had to adapt.

In addition to the staff support activities provided, a number of other activities associated with the implementation of the project proved to be useful in helping staff recognize the importance of making changes to their teaching to support student skills development. Staff who were nominated to be on the task force became very committed to the project and acted as champions for change. Unit coordinators and Heads of School who were interviewed as part of the evaluation of the project appear to have benefited from the opportunity to talk about and reflect on the aims and philosophy of the project. A staff member who visited an overseas university that was involved in a similar project returned full of enthusiasm for the project. Finally, most of the 14 staff who were approached to help gather student feedback about skills development through administering questionnaires in their classes appear to have become more aware of the project.

Overall, staff who participated in one or more staff-support activities found them helpful. These staff formed a core of interested and enthusiastic teachers who were prepared to invest time and effort into integrating skills into their units. The challenge is how to get the majority of staff who do not appear to see the need to engage in professional development to participate in activities focused on teaching in general, and skills development in particular, a dilemma reported by others introducing new teaching ideas (Price and Rust, 1999).

Experience in providing staff support for the project has highlighted a number of key issues that must be addressed if staff are to meet the challenge of their changing roles.

KEY ISSUES

Staff conceptions of teaching and learning and their attitudes and beliefs about their role and responsibilities are at the heart of effective change. Staff need to become aware of their current conceptions and, where necessary, need assistance to change them to reflect a more learner-centred and process-oriented approach which is essential for skills development. Staff concerns about academic freedom and feelings of pride and insecurity must also be faced and addressed. Moreover, staff need to be realistic about their current skills and be prepared to commit to ongoing development. Professional development to help staff with this process is most effective when it acknowledges and builds on their existing expertise. It must be accepted, however, that not all staff will be able or willing to develop the necessary self-awareness and motivation needed to begin the change process.

Institutional issues can help or hinder the willingness of staff to start down the path of change. To help this process, staff in leadership positions must first themselves be committed to skills development and understand the need for change. They must also publicly support professional development activities, encourage staff to take responsibility for ongoing professional development, convince staff that part of their role is to ensure that graduates develop necessary skills, overcome staff resistance to change, and manage those staff who are unwilling to change.

What the organization asks staff to do and what it rewards must be carefully aligned. Thus, staff who put effort into their teaching and participate in development activities should be recognized and rewarded for their efforts. Where there are competing demands, staff will invariably put time and effort into what they perceive gets the most reward.

A realistic timetable for change needs to be set since time is needed to shift conceptions, attitudes and approaches to teaching and learning. Staff need time to debate and discuss skills development, to reflect on the implications for their subject, to experiment with new ways of teaching and to evaluate outcomes.

As part of performance management at all levels, expectations and consequences – both positive and negative – for achieving goals are needed. Only then are staff likely to take seriously the need for professional development and use the support provided to help them integrate skills into their units, and develop as reflective practitioners.

CONCLUSION

As Zuber-Skerritt (1992: 77) says,

> [an] institutional policy, backed up by the power of persuasion and enforcement from the top and a supportive environment at the bottom of the hierarchy with the assistance and guidance of professional consultants, seems to be a necessary condition for continuous development to be undertaken by *all* academic staff.

Thus, helping staff to reconceptualize their roles to include a focus on skills requires commitment and motivation on the part of staff, strong leadership, and a range of staff-support activities. Making the shift will lead to greater student satisfaction and professional rewards for staff, and ensure that graduates have the skills needed for work and for life.

REFERENCES

Australian Technology Network (ATN) (1999) *Australian Technology Network Project on Graduate Capabilities*, URL: www.cea.curtin.edu.au/ATN/index.html

Biggs, J B (1996) Enhancing teaching through constructive alignment, *Higher Education*, **32**, pp 347–64

CBS Professional Skills Task Force (1999) *Integrated Professional Skills Project: Report of the Phase One task force*, Curtin Business School, Curtin University of Technology, Perth

Kember, D (1998) Teaching beliefs and their impact on students' approach to learning', in *Teaching and Learning in Higher Education*, eds B Dart and G Boulton-Lewis, ACER Press, Camberwell, Victoria

Price, M and Rust, C (1999) The experience of introducing a common criteria assessment grid across an academic department, *Quality in Higher Education*, **5**, pp 133–44

Sutherland, T E (1996) Emerging issues in the discussion of active learning, in *Using Active Learning in College Classes: A range of options for faculty*, eds T E Sutherland and C C Bonwell, Jossey-Bass, San Francisco

Zuber-Skerritt, O (1992) *Professional Development in Higher Education: A theoretical framework for action research*, Kogan Page, London

16

Lessons learnt: a case study in the assessment of learning outcomes

Donna Wood McCarty
Clayton College & State University
USA

SUMMARY

Since the mid-1980s, the faculty and administration of Clayton College & State University have been working to develop an effective system of student learning outcomes and assessment. Initially, the faculty and administration developed an elaborate system that proved to be too difficult to sustain effectively over time. The programme was carefully evaluated in the mid-1990s and has been redesigned extensively, based upon the lessons learnt from the initial attempt.

INSTITUTIONAL OVERVIEW

Clayton College & State University is a commuter campus of approximately 4,500 students in a southern suburb of Atlanta, Georgia. The institution was established in 1969 as a community or 'junior' college. Since that time, Clayton State has become a senior college awarding a variety of baccalaureate degrees.

OVERVIEW OF PURPOSES OF ASSESSMENT

The faculty and administration of Clayton College & State University have always made a strong commitment to provide educational programming of the highest quality. In the United States as well as in many other nations, the public perception that educators (particularly in the public sector) must be accountable for demonstrating that they are preparing students adequately to take their places in society has driven many educational reforms. In a foreword to a series of essays, *Assessment in American Higher Education*, Secretary of Education William J. Bennett commented (1985: i–iii):

> I am encouraged by signs that our colleges and universities are now recognizing the need to improve the quality of undergraduate education... From the perspective of society at large, the worrisome inadequacies are inadequacies not so much of processes as of *outcome* and *performance*. At the undergraduate level, we might – at the risk of oversimplifying – state the fundamental problem thus: We are uncertain what we think our students should learn, how best to teach it to them, and how to be sure when they have learned it.

Clayton State has responded to these demands by emphasizing the use of assessment as a tool not only for the evaluation of quality, but also for enhancing student learning and performance. The view is that both purposes for assessment (the evaluation of quality and the enhancement of learning) are essential for creating and maintaining quality educational programmes to meet the needs of the student, the community, and the nation.

OVERVIEW OF ORIGINAL PROGRAMME OF OUTCOMES ASSESSMENT

During the early to mid-1980s, when the student learning outcomes/assessment movement was gaining momentum in the United States, Clayton was a community college (Clayton Junior College) with programme offerings only at the associate degree level. The institution's president, Dr Harry S Downs, developed the strong belief that defining and assessing outcomes had the power to transform the teaching/learning process. The subsequent efforts of the Clayton faculty followed the principle that colleges and universities should design their curricula around the competencies, skills, or abilities that students were intended to develop. In particular, the assessment work of the faculty at Alverno College, in Milwaukee, Wisconsin had a powerful effect on the design of the programme of outcomes assessment at Clayton (Alverno Productions, 1976; Loacker *et al*, 1984). The Alverno view of assessment as 'a multidimensional process of judging the individual in action' (Loacker, Cromwell and O'Brien, 1985) was central to the Clayton approach, which was designed to be 'outcome-focused, assessment-based, learner-centered' (Clayton State College Outcome Handbook, 1988, 1993).

The President engaged the faculty in the process of debating the essential abilities that graduates of the institution's programmes should have – a process that went on for several years and became rather heated at times. After a great deal of discussion and effort, the faculty determined that there were two 'skill' outcomes and six 'perspective' outcomes that were essential to the higher education experience they sought to provide for their students.

The skill outcomes were communication and critical thinking. The perspective outcomes were aesthetic, contemporary, historical, mathematical, scientific, and value.

Once these outcomes were agreed upon and established, the faculty set about the task of developing detailed sets of generic criteria for assessing the quality of student work in these skills and perspectives across the entire curriculum. While many educators of the time equated assessment with testing, some of the leaders in the assessment movement urged educators to move beyond the description and testing of skills and abilities to the creation of performance standards, and the Clayton faculty worked diligently to develop criteria for performance assessment. These faculty efforts culminated in a handbook detailing each of the skills and perspectives and their respective performance criteria (Clayton State College Outcome Handbook, 1988, 1993)[1].

One of the hallmarks of the Clayton programme was the emphasis on the judgement of student performance, which was consistent with the approach advocated by Adelman (1985). Adelman noted that even competency-based programmes tend to 'provide guidelines for *what* students are expected to do, not how well they are expected to perform... the exceptions, though, are worth noting, eg in an institutional programme – Clayton Junior College's communication assessments' (1985: 78).

At Clayton, a curriculum map was developed in which the particular outcomes to be taught in each course were designated. The intent was for the student learning outcomes to drive the curriculum in that the sequence of instruction in these outcomes was to be decided and then the courses were to be redesigned around them. This method contrasted with the more typical approach of the fitting of outcomes into the current set of courses. 'Outcome Councils' of interdisciplinary faculty were appointed and charged with the task of overseeing their respective outcomes and designing training for faculty in using the criteria effectively and consistently for assessing student work. Since the criteria were developed using eight-point scales, faculty had to learn to assign a score of 1–8 on each criterion in the set for a given outcome, and the need for reliability between the raters for particular courses was a concern of the faculty.

Another important aspect of this programme was the mechanism for reporting, collecting and using student performance scores. Since the purposes for assessment at the college were both to monitor and promote individual student learning and performance and to evaluate institutional effectiveness, the data produced by this programme must be used to meet these objectives. To enhance student learning, the faculty were mandated to provide systematic feedback to each student on his or her performance on the outcomes assessed in each course. Students who did not attain the necessary performance levels in certain outcomes (such as written communication) were required to remediate to improve their skills. To evaluate institutional effectiveness, the administration, in conjunction with the Outcome Councils, determined that each faculty member would be provided with 'assessment rolls' at the end of each grading period; each student's scores in all relevant outcomes would be reported on these rolls. These data were then submitted and entered into a computer for the purpose of analysis, reporting, etc.

These practices continued for several years as faculty and administrators grappled with the burdens that these procedures placed upon them. In some classes, faculty found themselves having to report multiple scores for each student in a variety of outcomes. Many of the faculty became overwhelmed with the number of outcomes and the multiplicity of reports to be prepared, eventually becoming convinced that these data were never going to be used effectively. The perception was growing that the programme required a huge amount of effort and resulted in relatively little benefit to students. Meanwhile, the amount of unused data increased steadily, prompting some faculty to use the term 'black hole in space' to describe the location of the assessment scores.

These experiences underscore the observation that it can be extremely challenging and labour intensive to maintain a system of consistent, accurate ratings of student performance, particularly for a large number of outcomes. When many different faculty (especially part-time or adjunct faculty who may not be able to participate regularly in faculty development opportunities) are rating students, the difficulties become even greater.

LESSONS LEARNT

In the early 1990s and culminating in May of 1993, the institution went through a self-study with the Southern Association of Colleges and Schools, one of the regional accrediting bodies in the United States. The process involved an in-depth examination of the practices of the institution, including the programme of student learning outcomes assessment. While many positive aspects of the Clayton programme were noted, this examination revealed a number of problems with the current system. Following the self-study, a faculty group (the Assessment and Effectiveness Working Group) was established to study the current programme thoroughly and to recommend strategies for redesigning it to function more effectively. The overriding objective of the working group was to place a strong emphasis on student learning and to help ensure that the assessment programme truly enhanced the teaching/learning process. The members of the group were to advise the Vice President for Academic Affairs, the chief academic officer, as to measures to be taken to improve the programme.

After thorough study, the Group set forth the following observations:

- The data collected were largely unusable for the stated purposes of assessment, primarily because an effective research design and adequate faculty development support had not been provided, particularly for part-time faculty members.
- While some individuals and groups of faculty used the student assessment programme effectively to enhance student learning and to gain valuable insights into teaching effectiveness, the purposes of student assessment were not being fulfilled consistently by all faculty, particularly those who were part-time. While a great deal of work had been done with the writing mode of communication, critical thinking, and some of the six perspectives, an examination of the data provided clear evidence that all of the outcomes were not being taught and assessed effectively.
- Given the size and complexity of the programme, all aspects could not be reworked to function effectively at one time. Decisions regarding programme priorities must be made.
- Teaching and assessing all eight general education outcomes across the curriculum had proved to be an overwhelming, unmanageable task. A careful re-examination of the set of outcomes for the purpose of prioritizing and streamlining the programme was needed.

Based upon this analysis of the existing programme, a set of basic principles was unanimously agreed upon and set forth by the members of the Assessment and Effectiveness Working Group (Clayton State College, 1994):

- Principle 1. Each of the purposes for assessment included in the college's mission statement is important and should be supported by an effective, carefully planned and implemented programme which functions within the context of an overall research design.
- Principle 2. Only meaningful, useful data should be collected.
- Principle 3. The programme must have strong faculty and student support and involvement, and must be manageable and user-friendly.
- Principle 4. The programme must be integral to and supportive of the teaching/learning process.
- Principle 5. Care must be taken to ensure the coherence and effectiveness of the student assessment programme (eg that the programme is clearly linked to institutional mission, that it fulfills the stated purposes of assessment, that it fulfils these principles, etc).

- Principle 6. The mechanisms for assessing and collecting data on student performance on the learning outcomes should be redesigned carefully to support rather than hinder the major purpose of such a programme: enhancement of student learning.

PROGRAMME REDESIGN

Following the analysis of the current programme and the establishment of the above set of principles, the faculty set about the task of redesigning the general education outcomes programme. The first step was taken in spring 1995 when faculty in the various departments were asked to examine the current list of outcomes for which they were currently responsible and to submit answers to questions such as the following:

- Which of these outcomes can be naturally integrated into the courses taught in the department/school?
- Which of these outcomes do not fit naturally and are difficult for faculty to implement?
- Which outcomes should be eliminated from the current set of general education outcomes?
- Are there any other outcomes that should be added to the set?

When the reports from the departments were evaluated, a clear theme was found throughout: communication and critical thinking should be emphasized and assessed across the entire curriculum, at both the general education and major levels. It was also clear from these reports that the faculty did not view most of the current outcome descriptions and assessment approaches as fully workable for themselves or their students.

The analysis of the departmental reports revealed that the attempt to produce and use sets of generic criteria for all disciplines and majors had not worked as well as had been hoped, especially for critical thinking. The result of this attempt had been the creation of rather rigid sets of criteria for assessing student performance that often did not satisfy any group completely.

Another important finding was that transfer of learning from one situation to another was an important issue that was not addressed sufficiently by the previous programme. Students tended to learn one specific way (ie the sets of criteria) to think critically and communicate and did not always realize that each of the disciplines and professions has its own unique set of expectations and methods to bring to the thinking and communication processes. Everyone agreed that students must learn to think and communicate flexibly and adaptively under varying conditions.

Perhaps the most important finding that emerged from the analysis of these departmental reports was that the faculty were seeking a common goal. They reported that they sought to enhance each student's ability to think critically within various domains, disciplines or content areas, and to communicate the product of that critical thought to a particular audience (ie through writing or speaking). Everyone agreed that the programme of outcomes assessment should foster flexible critical thought and responsive communication abilities.

The emerging model resulted in a streamlining of the outcomes assessed for communication and critical thinking; the perspectives were re-conceptualized as variants of critical thinking (for example, critical thinking in the sciences and critical thinking in the health professions). The new model was intended to promote flexibility and transfer of learning from one context to another just as successful people do in their careers and in their lives. Despite the seemingly vast differences between them, the practitioners of the various disciplines and professions are all engaged in using the methods of their fields to solve problems and develop reflective judgements, and to communicate their thinking to others. As preparation for life, students should be developing the same skills.

The goal was for the faculty to create specialized sets of criteria adapted from the generic components for the two outcomes. In critical thinking and communication there would be a liberal arts context at the core curriculum (the freshman and sophomore years of college) level and a professional context at the baccalaureate level (the junior and senior years of college). The liberal arts context would include critical thinking in the humanities, the sciences, mathematics, and the social sciences. The professional context would include critical thinking in business, the health professions, music, technology, and other areas appropriate to baccalaureate programmes at CCSU.

The new programme of outcomes assessment, then, involves isolating the key components of communication and critical thinking that cut across all disciplines and then carefully tailoring each of these components to reflect the particular methodology, terminology, etc of each discipline.

In addition to redesigning the general education outcomes programme, the faculty in the baccalaureate programmes were to re-examine the outcomes for each of the majors. Again, the intent is to create a programme of student learning outcomes that fulfils the principles described earlier in this paper as well as the purposes set for CCSU's academic assessment programme.

CONCLUSION

A change in presidents and priorities occurred near the beginning of the assessment redesign process, resulting in a major initiative to infuse technology into instruction. The Information Technology Project (ITP) has been the major institutional initiative for the past five years and has been a resource-intensive effort. The ITP programme currently includes common laptop computers and software for all faculty and students, unlimited Internet access, support and training, and the ability to dial in to the campus network from home. The effort to redesign the academic assessment programme temporarily became a lower priority item on the institutional agenda than the integration of technology into instruction, but the redesign effort is currently regaining momentum. It is hoped that the programme described above can be implemented fully and that its impact on student learning and institutional effectiveness can be assessed within the next few years.

ENDNOTE

1. The outcome statement and criteria for the current communication outcome can be viewed at the Clayton College and State University Humanities Department Web site: www.a-s.clayton.edu/humanities/ criteria/ default.html

REFERENCES

Adelman, C (1985) To imagine an adverb: concluding notes to adversaries and enthusiasts, in *Assessment in American Higher Education*, pp 73–82, Office of Educational Research and Improvement, US Department of Education and the American Association of Higher Education, Washington, DC

Alverno Productions (1976) Preface, in *Liberal Learning at Alverno College*, pp 2–5, Alverno Productions, Milwaukee, Wisconsin

Bennett, W (1985) Foreword, in *Assessment in American Higher Education*, pp i–iii, Office of Educational Research and Improvement, US Department of Education and the American Association of Higher Education, Washington, DC

Clayton State College (1988, 1993) *Outcome Handbook (Internal Report)*, Clayton State College, Atlanta

Clayton State College (1994) *Assessment and Effectiveness Working Group: Preliminary report and recommendations concerning the assessment of general education outcomes (Internal Report)*, Clayton State College, Atlanta

Loacker, G, Cromwell, L, O'Brien, K (1985) Assessment in higher education: to serve the learner, in *Assessment in American Higher Education*, pp 47–61, Office of Educational Research and Improvement, US Department of Education and the American Association of Higher Education, Washington, DC

Loacker, G *et al* (1984) Introduction and prologue, in *Analysis and Communication at Alverno: An approach to critical thinking*, pp i–v, Alverno College, Milwaukee, Wisconsin

17

It's a long hard road!

Alan Jenkins
Oxford Brookes University
UK

SUMMARY

The approach of this chapter is in part autobiographical, of part of my academic career in one UK institution. However, the issues it discusses are germane to others who have embarked on or are considering the long hard road of developing an institutional policy, culture and practices for developing students' key skills. In reading this account, readers need to know that it is presented from three time periods of my career:

- from 1975 to 1990 as geography teacher, developing with colleagues an innovative curriculum which now would be seen as developing key skills;
- from 1990 to 1995 as a central policy maker, developing at Oxford Brookes institutional requirements on key skills and also working with other UK institutions who were developing similar policies;
- from 1996 to 2000 as in part bemused onlooker, but also as an educational developer working across the institution.

While this account will draw out of this experience that which is of general relevance, it does ask readers to support the processes of transferring its messages to their context, for part of the argument is that effective policies for key skills have to recognize the particularities of time, disciplinary and institutional contexts.

THE INSTITUTIONAL CONTEXT

Oxford Brookes University is the former Oxford Polytechnic, one of the many non-elite higher education institutions developed in the 1970s as the United Kingdom moved towards a mass higher education system. It was somewhat distinctive in being in Oxford, and therefore attracting, to a largely residential campus, mainly 18–24 year old students, many from economically advantaged backgrounds. It was also then distinctive for being one of the few modular or credit-based institutions, with a degree structure very similar to those in North America and elsewhere. Then most UK institutions had linear-style degrees, with assessments largely by unseen exams at the end of the degree.

By contrast, students on Oxford Polytechnic's institution-wide modular course generally took two fields or subjects, though they also had the choice of doing modules from across the course (Watson *et al*, 1989). Most modules were one term or ten weeks in length, in a three-term academic year. Students' choice of what modules to take were in part determined locally, by the way subject groups or fields determined their course structure, but the modular rules and the institutional culture emphasized choice. Students were supported to make informed choices through a personal tutor system.

Thus when I joined the institution in 1975 to teach geography I had about five personal tutees, most of whom I saw regularly to discuss their programme and progress. As they approached graduation and in the early years of employment they would generally ask me to write them references. This I could do with a good knowledge of them through the personal tutor role and I had usually taught them geography in class sizes that in year-two and year-three options were generally 10–20 students. My references were informed statements.

However, what really affected student employability was their social background, their having a degree (even if it was in a non-vocational subject like geography) and that they were entering a buoyant labour market. Yet at the time (late 1970s) the issue of key skills was not part of the culture, policies or even practices of the institution. If it was part of the national agenda I doubt that any of the academic staff were aware of or concerned about such issues, nor seemingly were the students.

Yet aspects of the institutional culture, etc enabled these issues to come onto the agenda of staff and students. Within broad institution-wide rules, subject groups or fields had considerable choice over what and how to teach and assess. Also, knowledge of what was happening in one subject group could move across the institution through its then lack of any strong departmental structure, and through the various course committees that brought staff together to discuss common (modular course) concerns. The creation of an Educational Methods Unit in 1979–80, headed by Graham Gibbs, was a major stimulant to pedagogic innovation and an institutional culture that valued innovative curricula. In addition, a strong Student Services unit also ensured that student concerns were central to institutional discussions.

GEOGRAPHERS AND KEY SKILLS

Within the geography unit in which I taught we seized the autonomy we had, in particular over issues of assessment and teaching methods, to radically change how students learn. We largely dispensed with conventional lectures and unseen exams, and through trial and quite a bit of error, developed a curriculum where students worked in groups, carried out projects, self- and peer assessed their work, and the overt 'geography' curriculum centred on current environmental issues (Jenkins and Pepper, 1988). Such curricula are now more commonplace and often seen as developing key skills of team-work, etc. Our motives were initially entirely pedagogic, to enable students to learn (geography) more effectively. As staff we enjoyed experimenting with teaching that way, and our students largely enjoyed the experience and learned effectively.

The students also had to 'waste' much time as we learned these new teaching skills. For example, we all sat through some very ineffective student presentations, as students were initially given no guidance or training in how to present. Like us they learned the hard way. We had also not thought through how to organize an overall skills-based curriculum. One student comment encapsulates part of what we had to learn. He pointed out that that term he had had 28 meetings outside class for geography courses that required him to work in groups. As a mature student who was very conscious of the employability skills he was developing through the geography field, for reasons of his own time management, he was pleased that his other subject field had no such key skills emphasis.

Yet by then – the early 1980s – as staff we were well aware of the arguments for skills. They were part of the national and institutional discussions. We were also well aware that our own relatively privileged students were entering a much harsher employment market, and that to an extent we had a responsibility to support students in making that transition.

WHAT OF THIS IS TRANSFERABLE?

Looking back at that time and institutional context, and from what I now know (largely through that experience) regarding institutional and departmental issues on key or transferable skills, the following observations are of general relevance:

- Strong subject autonomy enabling staff to experiment and develop practices they think appropriate to their context can give ownership and vitality to how skills are integrated to disciplinary concerns.

- Whilst there are tensions between (staffs') disciplinary concerns, such that they can support many elements of the skills agenda, the form in which they do so will reflect disciplinary mores, etc. In an issues-based course such as the one I taught, very student-centred and skills-based practices could be readily developed. Other disciplines would have to decide what was appropriate to their context.

- Students and staff now don't need to reinvent the wheels we did. Much of what we learnt over some years, say about how to organize groupwork effectively, can be readily taught to staff and students. Courses on teaching methods, handbooks on teaching skills (eg Gibbs *et al*, 1994), and other staff development activities can play an important role in accelerating that individual, departmental and institutional learning.

- Modular courses that enable cross-institution knowledge of subject groups' practices can assist this process of diffusion of good practice.

- Modular courses also present challenges to ensuring that all students have opportunities to develop key skills (and such credit or unitized courses are the norm in North America, Australasia and now the United Kingdom). As an inspection by Her Majesty's Inspectors in 1990 of the Oxford Modular Course reported (Department of Education and Science, 1991: 8): 'the modular structure makes it difficult, but not impossible, to ensure the systematic development of interpersonal and communications skills.' The inspectors noted that in some subjects such skills were clearly identified and developed, and in others this was not apparent. One of their central recommendations to the institution was to develop an institution-wide framework to ensure the 'systematic development of subject-specific interpersonal and communication skills within each field' (Department of Education and Science, 1991: 11).

- The continued budget cuts and efficiency gains higher education institutions have faced worldwide in the 1980s and 1990s have accentuated these problems. For modular courses to be effective in supporting students in developing and reflecting on their learning of key skills, informed choice and effective support is required. As is common with many other UK institutions, Oxford Brookes attempted to do that in part through the personal tutor system. The inspectors observed that 'personal tutors can have up to 24 students at a given time and receive no timetable relief to carry out their responsibilities'. However, inspectors did not mention that these pressures largely stemmed from the Thatcher administration's (and previous Labour governments') continually cutting the 'unit of resource', while pushing and even requiring institutions to develop transferable skills for a changing and increasingly difficult labour market for graduates.

These last general observations on modularity, student guidance and support, and a 'right wing' and interventionist government agenda become central to the next phase of this story, the development of an institution-wide policy on skills, and the lessons that you may transfer from this case study to your context.

INSTITUTION-WIDE FOCUS ON KEY/TRANSFERABLE SKILLS

The Thatcher Government's determination to bring a stronger skills and employability focus to university curricula was driven through by the Enterprise in Higher Education (EHE) Initiative. This involved institutions bidding to the then Department of Employment for funding to deliver activities or outcomes that would enhance their institution's standing for being 'enterprising'. Oxford Brookes was successful in a bid that somewhat unusually went for a whole-institution approach to developing skills. (Most others focused on more specific initiatives, eg for particular departments.)

The Oxford Brookes commitment was both all-encompassing and imprecise. It stated that the institution would ensure that 'all students graduate with a profile of their enterprise skills and qualities' and 'all courses will be reviewed in terms of their delivery of enterprise skills'. It gained one million pounds to spend over five years to develop those general commitments into effective policy.

Before setting out how we did that, and then the lessons for elsewhere, I will accelerate this history to the present and then move back in time.

INSTITUTIONAL POLICY SUMMARIZED

Oxford Brookes has in place (April 2000) a university-wide policy that includes a number of requirements regarding transferable skills. There is a list of transferable skills that all subject groups at undergraduate level (eg history, occupational therapy) are required to help students develop. All such subject groups have to produce a skills map that specifies where particular skills are taught, practised and assessed. All subject groups must also give graduating students (and are encouraged to give incoming students) a graduate profile that specifies in a language clear to employers, the knowledge and skills (including key or transferable skills) developed through the discipline. (Examples of these skills maps and course profiles are on the Web at www.brookes.ac.uk/services/ocsd/obukeyd.html) Personal tutors and other support staff are encouraged to support students in developing a programme that supports their skills development and helps them present on graduation to potential employers a personal profile of their skills and qualities. (See below for further explication.)

DEVELOPING POLICY

To develop this policy, the institution hired an Enterprise Director, Lawrie Walker, who had extensive experience of developing such policies at high-school level. I moved out of the geography department to work half in the Educational Methods Unit, and half as Profiling Coordinator in the Enterprise Unit, to support Walker in developing policies to deliver our institutional commitment to the Department of Employment.

Readers will not be surprised that this institutional commitment was not widely known by staff before the contract was signed by senior management. On hearing about it, many staff were uncertain what were 'transferable' or 'enterprise' skills, and profiling was even more of a mystery. Indeed, my application for the profiling coordinator post opened with a statement that if they wanted someone who knew about profiling they should hire someone else. (I did know there was no candidate other than Lawrie Walker, so this was not necessarily a foolhardy statement.)

As staff, including school and department heads, started to realize what were the implications of our contract, there was a mixture of excitement and commitment, and anger and concern. The commitment came from two broad groups of staff. Those courses with a strong employability focus welcomed it both for its promise of resources to further develop their curricula, and for its legitimizing their valuing an employability focus; a vocational focus had been questioned by many in the institution as being inappropriate to higher education. Meanwhile, as Elton has argued (1999), the Enterprise Programme also legitimized and gave resources to groups in any institution with a strong focus on teaching. Such groups welcomed this opportunity to get hold of resources (money) that enabled them to push their agenda, even if it meant dressing it up in the language of 'skills' (Pope, 1994).

However, to other staff this skills focus was an attack on much of what they valued. They saw it as an assault on valuing knowledge and learning for its own sake. They feared and perceived it as an attack on the value of disciplines and of research, and of turning the institution (which in 1992 became a university) into a low-level vocational institution.

Even those with a commitment to the aims we were formulating were concerned (terrified is perhaps a more accurate word to describe their views) about the implications for their own workload. Did it not require a total rethinking of the curriculum? And as we started to understand that profiling was likely to involve personal tutors supporting students in developing their skills, this seemed to go against any sane view of what could be delivered. Some readers will recall the HMI statement of some tutors in 1990 having 24 personal tutees. Subsequently student–staff ratios and class sizes continued to degrade and the Thatcherite mantra of 'efficiency and effectiveness' told all of us that further cuts and demands to do more with less formed our present and our future. In that context personal tutors, virtually all academic staff, were generally adamant that this commitment to personal profiling could not be delivered.

I presume that you will recognize all these reactions and recall similar concern in your institution in designing and delivering policies that are both achievable and worthwhile.

DELIVERING POLICY

We started with a series of open meetings and discussion papers that sought to raise awareness of the role of transferable skills in curriculum design, and to report on other institutions that had already embarked along this road. In key committees and in closed meeting we also tried to grapple with what could be delivered and how. We were well supported by advisers from the Department of Employment, with whom we could honestly share our difficulties and hear their views of how we might proceed.

We circulated various lists of skills that external bodies such as the Confederation of British Industry had seen as the key or transferable skills valued by employers, implicitly and explicitly asking staff: could you deliver these? There was much discussion of whether skills should be taught and assessed as separate from the conventional disciplinary curriculum. We also encouraged the commitment of schools and departments by funding a range of local innovations that supported the overall aims of the programme. This was in part bribery, but it was also more or less effective cultural and curriculum change, whose lessons we sought to diffuse across the institution.

By year three/four of the programme we had arrived at a variety of policies that met the contract and which are summarized above and detailed later. This was achieved through an agreed list of key skills that were to be developed in all programmes, and university-wide requirements for course-based profiling and module design.

A UNIVERSITY-WIDE LIST OF SKILLS

The final list of skills that were decided upon did not come directly from the national and international lists or definitions of key skills. After these lists had been circulated, discussed and disputed, we changed tack. A small group of senior staff examined the current descriptions of courses that existed and asked: was there implicitly a list of skills that all or most courses and staff could sign up to? These were then circulated to the schools, and their reactions modified the initial list we had drawn up. Perhaps not surprisingly the final agreed list looked rather similar to the national lists we had circulated some 12 months before!

Those of us formulating central policy started saying, in effect 'We don't want you to do anything extra; indeed, we know you don't have the time. We just want you to make explicit to students and other staff what you're already doing.' Yes, this was somewhat Machiavellian in that there would be *some* extra work involved in making things explicit, but it was deliverable. Also no doubt some staff, and some heads, signed up to these policies as they feared something worse might replace them, particularly as the then Pro Vice Chancellor was a major backer of the Enterprise Programme and was also proposing even bigger curriculum changes (Roper, 1994). Certainly, some agreed to our modest changes with the idea of limiting the damage or further change to that level.

In 1993–94 all undergraduate courses were required to deliver the following university list of skills:

- self-management: a general ability to manage one's own learning environment;
- learning skills: a general ability to learn effectively and be aware of one's own learning abilities;
- communication: a general ability to express ideas and opinions, with confidence and clarity, to a variety of audiences for a variety of purposes;
- teamwork: a general ability to work productively in different kinds of team (formal, informal, project based, committee based, etc);
- problem solving: a general ability to identify the main features of a given problem and to develop strategies for its resolution.

There was and is no requirement that such skills be either separately taught or integrated into courses: that was and is for subject groups to decide. However, the most usual approach is for skills to be integrated with disciplinary concerns; the way these generic key skills are developed will typically reflect disciplinary mores.

ASSESSMENT AND ACCREDITATION OF SKILLS

There was, and still is, no university-wide requirement that skills be specified at a range of levels, and nor is there any requirement or expectation that skills be separately assessed. This reflected the fact that many staff and many student representatives were unsure of either the wisdom of or the available skill in making such assessments. Certain subject groups do now give more explicit and concerted attention to assessing skills, but that is their decision. It was the assumption and hope of those of us who decided on this cautious policy that the university would wish to tighten assessment and recording skills at some later time. It has not done so through any explicit further policy initiative, but the effective policy, practice and institutional culture have further embedded these practices through both internal and external quality-assurance procedures. Externally the commitment of both the Teaching Quality Assessment (TQA) procedures and the current Quality Assurance Agency's (QAA) requirements and values regarding key skills ensure that, at least on paper, courses do deliver these skills.

Here (as also with course-based profiling: see below), the institution-wide modular course was an effective ally to delivering effective institutional policies. Not only does the modular course bring staff together, it also has a set of university-wide rules which can quickly spread policy and shape practice across the institution. By year three of the three-year EHE contract the central Modular Course Committee agreed a set of small but significant changes. As courses came up to revalidation in their five-year rolling cycle, they had to set out all programmes and modules in a common format. This included:

- describing all modules in the language of learning outcomes;
- for each programme or subject, eg art history, setting out a course profile (see below) that includes the key transferable and disciplinary skills that students should have developed through that course;
- for each programme or subject, setting out a skills map or matrix showing students where the university's list of transferable skills are taught, practised and assessed in that course. They may also – and many do – specify where the disciplinary skills are developed.

TWO STEPS FORWARD: EXTERNAL ACCOUNTABILITY AND IT SKILLS

By 1996 the external DfEE money was gone, the contract was accomplished and Lawrie Walker, the EHE director at Oxford Brookes, was to move on to Thames Valley University. For myself, now working full time in the institution's learning methods unit, I had tired of focusing on skills, and anyway knew that for the policy to be further embedded it had to be taken forward by others. To an extent that has happened. In particular, the steady endorsement by the external TQA/QAA processes of those courses that have integrated skills has been a powerful and recurring message to all course teams to ensure that skills are delivered. Particularly important has been the recognition that assessors would verify through discussions with students and through the way students were assessed that the fine words on the importance of skills was matched by the ways the course was taught and assessed.

A further significant step forward was in 1999 when the university added a sixth required skill: a general ability to use IT appropriately for one's learning and employability. In 1993–94 when the list of skills was formulated and agreed, IT was in the penultimate list. We took it out of the final agreed list, as quite clearly some, perhaps many, courses did not then integrate it. Indeed, some would have questioned its relevance to a university education, particularly in their discipline, while many of us were concerned about the resource implications of such a commitment. By 1999 IT was widely seen as relevant both to employability and to how all or most courses were taught. We had moved on and skills had become further embedded.

COURSE-BASED AND PERSONAL PROFILING

Readers will recall that our institutional commitment (and our contract with the Department of Employment) was to ensure that 'all students graduate with a profile of their enterprise skills and qualities'. As we read the literature and considered the practice on profiling, we effectively took profiling in higher education to mean:

> the… processes of empowering students to be involved in the assessment, recording and reviewing of their own personal development and learning… The formative process, is then, at the heart of development but many would see the production of an end document… as equally important to students, employers and other end users… They provide a more rounded picture of an individual than a narrow list of examination results.
>
> (Assiter and Shaw, 1993: 20).

With declining resources we had (and have – for though the extra money has gone, the institution's stated commitment remains) to try to apply policies and practices that appeared, and still appear to many staff, to require more work. For profiling was clearly both a process and a product. In April 2000 we are still grappling with how – and perhaps whether – to do this.

By 1993–94 we had distinguished between two types of profiling, course-based and personal profiling, and defined a record of achievement. Course-based profiling is the process of reflection, recording and forward planning in relation to the learning that occurs in a particular course. Personal profiling is the process by which the individual student reflects on and records their learning while at university. This culminates in a record of achievement, prepared towards the end of a degree course, which records the achievements, knowledge and skills that a student has developed (Jenkins, Scurry and Turner, 1994).

Course-based profiling was initially a strange term to staff but could be delivered. All it required staff to do was to write a clear, brief statement on the principal knowledge and (discipline-based) skills developed on their course. This might then encourage them to review how the course was taught and assessed, and to consider how to bring out and perhaps further integrate opportunities for students to be aware of the knowledge and skills they were developing through the course. As to university policy, all that was and is required of course teams was producing a course profile and skills map. If, as we hoped, many would go beyond that to more systematically develop the process of course-based profiling, that was and remains their decision. No doubt tempted by money, some did, but the way they did so reflected the way the course was structured. Compulsory modules in the final graduating year enabled staff to ensure that all students reflected on and recorded their learning through the whole degree course in that subject, but whether they did so, and how, reflected disciplinary conventions and values. Thus those professional courses where profiling is built into professional requirements, such as some areas of health care, were and are more likely to develop these practices than the more 'academic' courses (Jenkins, 1996).

Some such 'academic' courses did develop their peculiar way of delivering reflective course-based profiling, but that was a product of local leadership, course structure and disciplinary practices. For example, English Studies requires all students in two compulsory modules, one at the end of year/stage one and one in a graduating synoptic module, to write an unassessed 500-word statement of what they have learnt through their English course. But this is a discipline with a strong emphasis on individual students writing and rewriting texts (Pope, 1994). Even in disciplines where such local practices have been embedded, this still fails to ensure that students get opportunities or are required to reflect on and record their learning across the whole of their formal course. (In the Oxford Brookes modular course many students are effectively studying two or more disciplines.)

Also, much learning occurs in what the US literature often calls the co-curriculum (Gaff, 1991), that informal environment of college and student life and paid employment in the university and the regional economy. During the Enterprise Programme we worked with and tried to respond to the capable student leadership in the Student Union and those students who were funded by our EHE contract to work in support of institutional policies. They played key roles in drawing up imaginative – and we thought deliverable – plans for recording and accrediting that formal and informal learning.

Two such proposals were: an optional module to enable students to bring together what they had learned in paid employment or as student representatives (Gaskell, Brookes and Brierley, 1994); and a 'long thin module' which effectively would have credited the personal tutor system (see below) and would have required students to bring together their learning, including of transferable or key skills, at various stages of their degree. We knew of other institutions that had developed or were developing or proposing similar schemes (eg Laycock 1994), but all our attempts at putting these into practice failed. Three central considerations shaped staff resistance to such proposals: resistance to the employability focus; suspicion and concerns about assessing the wider experience; and concern about further loads on an exhausted personal tutor system.

Personal profiling had come up against the harsh reality of a personal tutor system that was, as the inspectors observed in 1990, overstretched. For most staff, and for many of those of us developing the policies, it was an aspiration we could not deliver, or if we did, only in a very limited manner. Current university-wide policy is to stress that all courses should support students in being able to talk about and give evidence to employers of the skills they consider they possess. It is the student's responsibility (and that of the employer!) to demonstrate that any such statement has validity. The university does not validate or certify that students have developed these skills. Together with the, now usual, modular transcript that specifies the modules taken and grades obtained, all graduating students receive a statement from the Vice Chancellor which includes the claim:

> All our graduates will have developed a range of skills designed to be of practical value in the world of work... We have... put in place a university-wide system of 'profiling' that encourages students to reflect regularly on their progress and to explain their abilities. You should find that any student who has been through this process is able to discuss confidently his or her learning achievements.

But in no way does the institution guarantee to the employer, or more importantly to the student, that the student will be able discuss these issues confidently, and neither does it state the level of skill development.

A STEP BACKWARDS, A STEP SIDEWAYS OR JUST MOVING ON?

Certain developments during the period of the EHE contract and afterwards can be seen – well I sometimes see them that way – as steps backwards – 'towards' an institutional commitment to a skills-based curriculum. These include: changes in institutional leadership; the continuing impact of the Research Assessment Exercise; the growing importance of postgraduate courses; and perhaps the lack of a research base to the 'skills' movement and the overselling of skills-based curricula.

Over the past five years new leaders have been appointed in senior management, head of school and academic positions, for whom 'skills' are at best but one of many priorities. Like many other former polytechnics, Oxford Brookes sees itself as a university, and determines to increase its research base and performance in the national Research Assessment Exercise. A focus on skills can seem, indeed is, a distraction from the central agenda.

There is also a more subtle but perhaps a more deep-seated development that questions the list of skills we developed and the nature of the skills focus. Oxford Brookes, like many other higher education institutions worldwide, is developing an array of courses to meet the needs of a growing and diverse range of postgraduate courses. When we formulated the institutional policies on skills, and in particular the university list of skills and skills maps, we only made them a requirement at undergraduate level. Perhaps that was a sensible strategy at the time; for one thing, we were on surer ground on what were the key skills at that level. But as the institution becomes a more postgraduate institution, perhaps the skills focus has been bypassed or needs to be rethought.

What are the key skills at postgraduate level? (Cryer, 1998). Given what is a stronger research base to these courses, are the key skills at this level much more the skills associated with research training, which many would argue are the key employability skills for the 21st century? (Seltzer and Bentley, 1999). Similarly, while there may have been value at undergraduate level of agreeing on a university-wide list of skills, particularly since with a modular course students took courses from a wide range of disciplines, this common list may not be appropriate at postgraduate level. These courses are often much more targeted at particular areas of knowledge and geared to more specific labour markets or academic practices.

Perhaps also for some staff at Oxford Brookes – and certainly for myself – the limited research base on which these policies rested, and the overselling of the skills agenda, helped to draw a line beyond which these policies could not move. As an institution we discussed these issues; many staff, particularly from the social sciences (my territory) questioned from strong disciplinary research-based knowledge some of the intellectual and practical substance of the skills agenda. Some of their arguments parallel those in Chapter 18. Others argued that while something called 'skills' might exist, they were very context-based and calling them key skills had limited credibility. Calling them 'transferable' failed to recognize the research evidence as to whether and how 'skills' could 'transfer' (eg Norman, 1988). Also the dominant, or at least powerful, impact of class, gender and ethnicity shaping student employment after graduation further questioned a skills focus. In all intellectual honesty, those of us sympathetic to this agenda probably have to recognize that the institution's external reputation through research performance, etc may (also) be central to student employability.

So increasingly I – and I think many others at Oxford Brookes – look at this institutional skills focus as something that we have integrated into our institution, but it is now time to move on to more pressing concerns.

TWO STEPS FORWARD: RE-THINKING STUDENT SUPPORT AND THE POTENTIAL ROLE OF IT

Even in the context of moving onto a more research-based institution, an increased ability to effectively deliver skills and personal profiling may be deliverable, certainly at undergraduate level. If so, much of the credit for this will be due to the continued efforts of a number of staff in the Student Services Unit, which includes student employability in its remits. In two major ways they have long worked to help the institution find a way of giving effective support to individual students to get advice on, and reflect and record, their learning.

The increasing inability of the traditional personal tutor system to deliver this support has been a central theme running through this account. Student Services has run a rolling programme to help schools and departments to restructure student support. Their interventions parallel those of other institutions worldwide (Bochner, Gibbs and Wisker, 1995), including: rethinking the role of the personal tutor system; using school-based support staff as well as academic staff to advise students; setting up formal and informal systems to enable students to support each other; and integrating recording and reflecting on skills into the formal curriculum. The particular solutions sought reflect the local conditions in each department.

More speculatively, Oxford Brookes, like a number of other institutions, is proposing developing an IT-based electronic progress file to support individual students in reflecting on and recording their skills development. Again the modular system at Oxford Brookes offers support to this process, for we have long had a strong central IT-based student records system, which we hope to adapt using 'push' technology to encourage students to engage – with limited tutor support – in developing their own personal profile of skills. Whether this is effective is part of the future for skills at Oxford Brookes and elsewhere in the United Kingdom. One stimulus is the recommendation in April 2000 of the Quality Assurance Agency that all UK higher education institutions develop 'a Progress File (consisting... of two elements: a transcript recording student achievement... [and] a means by which students can monitor, build and reflect upon their personal development'. (QAA, 2000: 1)

LEARNING FROM OTHERS – IN PARTICULAR ALVERNO COLLEGE

As we developed these policies during the period of the Enterprise contract and after we benefited from working with other institutions that were themselves developing an ability-based curriculum. Three initiatives here were significant:

- At Brookes, we made strong contacts with Alverno College, for we quickly perceived they were the international leaders in this agenda (see Chapter 3).

- In 1994 we brought together for a closed three-day conference selected staff from Alverno and senior staff from five UK institutions that were developing institution-wide policies on skills: Brookes, De Montfort, North London, Northumbria and Wolverhampton. (Walker, 1995).

- With DfEE funding, we linked to Alverno and eight other UK institutions that were developing an 'ability-based curriculum' (Otter, 1997).

Much was learned from these contacts, but the main learning was informal support and awareness at an abstract level of the issues that such an institution-wide approach requires (Otter, 1997). While we might be interested in the peculiar practices of other institutions – eg Napier's work-based learning programme (see Chapter 4), seldom did we think of simply transferring structures and practices from one institution to another, and even when that occurred my impression is that what transferred was an abstract idea that was then reshaped to meet local conditions. Thus at Oxford Brookes we did learn from Alverno and have kept in close contact. But the central idea we took from Alverno was the research-based approach to analysing policy and practice. Perhaps paradoxically what most impressed many Oxford Brookes staff was the way that Alverno systematically researches student abilities (Mentkowski, 2000). This did help to buttress the intellectual arguments for a skill-based approach. But what mainly transferred from Alverno to Brookes was a strong institutional commitment to funding and supporting pedagogic research, eg on student perceptions of staff discipline-based research, the connection of which to the skills agenda is at most marginal. However, we also learnt from Alverno that such an institutional commitment to skills was and is a long hard road.

CONCLUSION: WHAT OF THIS IS TRANSFERABLE?

This chapter is clearly one interpretation of the development of policies and practices on skills in one UK institution. It does not pretend to be objective, and evidently others at Oxford Brookes would see these events and issues differently.

It does ask you to analyse and apply it to your own context, which clearly is shaped by your role and institutional and national context. In conclusion I want to assist that transference to your context and set out what I think of this is generalizable. In addition to my earlier observations of the period around 1978–1990, what is transferable to other institutions from this case study is:

- It is a long hard road. Any institution that commits itself to an institution-wide policy on key skills has to recognize that it will take much time and resources, and will involve many aspects of institutional policy and practice. Though one can accelerate institutional learning and practice by learning from others, it is still a long hard road, and should not be embarked on unless that is recognized. It is easy to state these policies in mission statements. Too often it is then others who have to deliver them.

- Leading and supporting staff along this road requires vision, and toughness, but most of all intellectual honesty, and one should only commit staff to policies for which there are effective resources and top-level commitment, and that top-level commitment has to be long term.

- How any institution develops effective policies will be highly context dependent, as is the list of what should be required or encouraged across all course teams or departments, and what should be locally determined.

- Disciplinary conventions and values will profoundly shape the locally specified material. Failure to value the disciplines will result in opposition and anger. In that context encouraging staff to work on national discipline-based projects on skills may be the best way to embed them inside an institution! Certainly at Oxford Brookes we had far more success at winning staff support when, a few years into our EHE contract, we arrived at the idea of a course-based profile that starts from disciplinary concerns.

- The focus on generic transferable skills can fail to recognize that the forms 'abilities' take on reflect the (disciplinary) context in which they are developed and practised. Here, as in many other areas, the experience of

Alverno is particularly relevant. For though at times outsiders describe the Alverno curriculum in terms of the abilities, the curriculum and the abilities are developed in the disciplines, and special attention is given to enabling their transfer (Schmitz, 1994).

- Whilst a discipline-based approach has great value, it needs to be complemented by strategies, policies and resources that enable students to pull together their learning across the whole formal and co-curriculum.

- National policies can support and can undermine an institutional commitment. That is certainly the case in the centralized political culture of the United Kingdom. For myself the EHE programme was a success in giving an infusion of money and support and in requiring institutions to deliver while giving them considerable control over what they delivered. However, it was then 'torpedoed' by the focus of the Research Assessment Exercise on research that did not necessarily connect to the curriculum.

- As throughout the whole of higher education, the need for effective resources to deliver these policies is ever more insistent. Thus I too am excited by the potential of information technology to support student profiling and recording of skills. In that sense Oxford Brookes is moving forward along the road. Indeed, I recently returned from a visit to Alverno where I saw a new IT-based system being piloted to support student learning and recording of skills. But that cost a great deal and in no way will replace the heavy staff and curriculum focuses on abilities. It adds value and resources to a strong tutor-based system.

- Finally we need – certainly in the United Kingdom – much greater awareness of the research evidence on the abilities, and the contexts that support their transference across the curriculum and into the world of employment. Relatedly, we need a far more sophisticated understanding of the appropriate abilities that should be developed at postgraduate level. In that context a focus on students' ability to do research may be a or the vital key skill. Perhaps – but we need more research-based evidence to guide practice and policy.

REFERENCES

Assiter, A and Shaw, E (1993) *Using Records of Achievement in Higher Education*, Kogan Page, London

Bochner D, Gibbs, G and Wisker, G (1995) *Supporting More Students*, Oxford Centre for Staff and Learning Development, Oxford

Cryer, P (1998) Transferable skills, marketability and lifelong learning: the particular case of postgraduate research students, *Studies in Higher Education*, **23** (2), pp 207–16

Department of Education and Science (DES) (1991) *The Modular Course at Oxford Polytechnic: A Report by HMI*, DES, Stanmore

Elton, L (1999) New ways of learning in higher education: managing the change, *Tertiary Education and Management*, **5**, pp 207–25

Gaff, J G (1991) *New Life for the College Curriculum: Assessing achievements and furthering progress in the reform of general education*, Jossey-Bass, San Francisco

Gaskell, G, Brookes, D and Brierley, S (1994) Accrediting students for extra-curricula learning, in *Developing Student Capability Through Modular Courses*, eds A Jenkins and L Walker, pp 101-07, Kogan Page, London

Gibbs, G, Rust, C, Jenkins, A and Jaques, D (1994) *Developing Students' Transferable Skills*, Oxford Centre for Staff and Learning Development, Oxford

Jenkins A (ed) (1996) *Course Based Profiling: Case studies from Oxford Brookes*, Oxford Centre for Staff and Learning Development, Oxford

Jenkins, A and Pepper, D M (1988) Enhancing students' employability and self-expression: how to teach oral and group work skills in geography, *Journal of Geography in Higher Education*, **12** (1), pp 67–84

Jenkins, A, Scurry, D and Turner, D (1994) Using profiling to integrate skill development in a large modular course, in *Developing Student Capability Through Modular Courses*, eds A Jenkins and L Walker, pp 132–42, Kogan Page, London

Laycock, M (1994) The use of learning contracts in undergraduate modular programmes, in *Developing Student Capability Through Modular Courses*, eds A Jenkins and L Walker, pp 125–33, Kogan Page, London

Mentkowski, M and Associates (2000) *Learning that Lasts*, Jossey Bass, San Francisco

Norman, G R (1988) Problem-solving skills, solving problems and problem-based learning, *Medical Education*, **22**, pp 279-286

Otter S (1997) The ability based curriculum – some snapshots of progress in key skills in higher education, www.brookes.ac.uk/services/ocsd/abchome.html

Pope, R (1994) A very 'English' profile, in *Developing Student Capability Through Modular Courses*, eds A Jenkins and L Walker, pp 70–76, Kogan Page, London

Quality Assurance Agency (2000) *Developing a Progress File for Higher Education: Summary report of the consultation exercise*, Quality Assurance Agency, Gloucester, www.qaa.ac.uk/HEprogressfile/contents.htm

Roper, B (1994) Capability and the future of modularity: an institutional perspective, in *Developing Student Capability Through Modular Courses*, eds A Jenkins and L Walker, pp 143–53, Kogan Page, London

Schmitz, J ed (1994) *Student Assessment as Learning*, Alverno Institute, Alverno College, Milwaukee, Wisconsin

Seltzer, T and Bentley, K S (1999) *The Creative Age: Knowledge and skills for the new economy*, Demos, London

Walker L ed (1995) *Institutional Change towards an Ability-based Curriculum in Higher Education*, Conference Report, Department of Employment and Oxford Brookes University

Watson D *et al* (1989) *Managing the Modular Course: Perspectives from Oxford Polytechnic*, Society for Research into Higher Education and Open University Press, Buckingham

18

Questioning the skills agenda

Len Holmes
University of North London
UK

SUMMARY

To question the idea of key skills may appear strange to many readers. It is now a commonplace notion (since the Dearing Report; NCIHE, 1997) that graduates should have what are called 'transferable', or 'key' skills, and that therefore universities should ensure that undergraduates are provided with opportunities to develop, and possibly be assessed in, such skills (Murphy and Otter, 1999). Yet this chapter *will* question this notion, or at least the currently orthodox way that the notion is presented. The aim in this chapter is to show why the orthodox view of key skills is problematic, and to present an alternative to that orthodox view.

INTRODUCTION

I emphasize at the outset that I am not arguing that higher education does not, or should not, have a role to play with regard to graduate employment. Far from it; in my view a university education *does* have a significant relationship to students' post-graduation lives, including their employment, and quite rightly so. My own personal career experience, my work with the students at the University of North London, and my research interests all lead me to have a deep concern about how higher education can and should relate to the lives of graduates. I believe that the issues concerned require the application of intellectual effort at least as much as that expended on other concerns within and about higher education. However, I fear that the arena of key skills has been somewhat poorly served on this score, and that the conventional approach suffers deeply as a consequence.

This is not to render all 'skills work' invalid. I believe that much of this work may be subsumable within the approach that will be elaborated below. Some skills work may have value *within* the educational setting, but have questionable utility in the setting in which new (and not so new) graduates seek entry to employment; in other words, it is what might be called 'ecologically invalid' (Usher and Bryant, 1989). However, the skills projects in some institutions may have deleterious effects, perhaps stigmatizing graduates of such institutions (Brown and Scase, 1994) or, at the very least, wasting the very limited time and efforts of staff and students. The aim of this chapter is therefore to present an approach for reframing the skills agenda, hopefully to help ensure that current approaches are reformed.

THE CONVENTIONAL MODEL OF SKILLS

To be clear what I am arguing against, I will briefly sketch what appears to be the underlying model of key skills that is conventionally adopted. Although there is much written *about* key skills, there is a notable lack of explanation of what the term 'skill' means; however, by attending to the language used *about* skills we can gain some understanding of the underlying assumptions. In the model's simplest form, the term 'skill' appears to be used to *refer to* (denote) some purported tool-like entity possessed by an individual, which is *used* in carrying out performances of particular kinds. Thus, someone *has* and *uses* the skill of problem solving to attempt to solve problems; one *uses* oral communication skill in conducting a business conversation, eg with clients, staff or peers; and so on. Of course, such entities are not immediately visible; they exist in some unobservable realm, eg 'the mind'. Their existence (*in* the individual) is *inferred* from what the individual *does*; skills are thus viewed as *instrumentally causative* of performance, the use of a skill *results in* some desired or required performance. The goal then becomes one of identifying what the main skills ('tools') are that are used in the work undertaken by graduates, then developing methods by which students can *acquire* or *develop* them (skills development) and demonstrate *possession* of them (assessment).

Protagonists of the key skills approach may balk at such a crude presentation, claiming that it is not what they are saying. But they would then have to explain what *they* mean by 'skills', and by 'acquiring', 'having' and 'using' skills. If they do not mean these terms literally, then it is probably better that they do not confuse people with such language but find ways of expressing what they mean more clearly. Some may claim to be using the term as a theoretical construct, part of a theoretical model that provides a mode of explanation of the phenomena under study. The usual suspect here is cognitive psychology, or at least rather simplified modes of theorizing based on the assumptions and methods of cognitive psychology. This tends to attempt to explain human action in terms of information processing 'modules', an approach that has been subject to considerable criticism (Harré, Clarke and de Carlo, 1985; Costall and Still, 1987). In any case, the actual implementation of key skills projects shows little indication of being based on a rigorous application of cognitive psychology principles.

THE LANGUAGE OF SKILLS

The term 'skill' is clearly used in a variety of types of contexts, and it is vital that no a priori assumption is made that the term is used with the same meaning in different contexts. We have to beware of the tendency to be confused by the different meanings that a term may have in different contexts in which it is used; there is the danger of our intelligence being 'bewitched by means of language', as Wittgenstein (1953) put it. Similarly, Andreski (1972: 61) reminds us that

> constant attention to the meaning of words is indispensable in the study
> of affairs, because in this field powerful social forces operate which con-
> tinuously create verbal confusion..

This observation is not new, as Aristotle drew attention to the 'systematic ambiguity' of some terms. Thus, he gives the example of 'healthy' as used about a person's body and when used about a city; there may be some relationship between the meanings of 'healthy' in these different cases, but whilst it would make sense to ask whether Edinburgh was a more healthy than London, it would be meaningless to ask whether either city was more healthy than my next door neighbour (see Flew, 1979). This should not be dismissed as mere hair-splitting, for as Hirsh and Bevan (1988) found in their empirical study of the way in which employers expressed their requirements of the skills and competencies of managers, although there was a high level of agreement over the terms used, there was not agreement at the level of meaning.

So what are the various kinds of ways in which the term 'skill' is used? For our purposes here we can distinguish:

- mundane, everyday, colloquial discourse;
- political-economic discourse, dealing with the requirements of and aspirations for the country's workforce in the emerging conditions of the coming decades;
- pedagogic discourse, concerning the form and processes of the undergraduate curriculum;
- the discourse of personnel or human resource management, particularly in the context of recruitment and selection;

- scientific psychology (as opposed to lay or 'folk' psychology), in which the concept of skill has meaning within particular frameworks of theory and research methodology.

There may be some similarity of meaning between one mode of discourse and another; however any such similarity should not be assumed to exist across all modes of use (Austin, 1961).

Space here does not allow for an extended analysis of the differences of meaning of the term 'skill' between these different language contexts. However, it may be noted that even a cursory examination of the use of the term 'skill' in political-economy discourse shows that it is very loose and general. As for employers, it is highly questionable whether they do, as is often claimed (NCIHE, 1997), express their requirements of graduates in terms of explicitly identified skills. Prior to the NAB/UGC joint statement in 1984 (NAB/UGC, 1984), there is little evidence that employers did in fact express their requirements in terms of skills. Certainly such terminology is absent from the study by Roizen and Jepson (1985), particularly in their chapter 3, which is titled 'A degree and what else?' – precisely where we might expect to find employers using skills terms. Even in the more recent study by Harvey *et al* (1997), close examination of the material presented shows that employers by and large do *not* express their requirements either in terms of 'skills' or even of 'attributes'. For example, in the discussion of what Harvey *et al* refer to as 'self-skills' (cf Association of Graduate Recruiters (AGR), 1995, on 'self-reliance skills') five extracts from interviews are presented, *none of which* includes the word 'skills'. The language of skills, it may be argued, is not the way that graduate employers normally articulate what they require in prospective recruits and actual employees, but is more an artificial vocabulary of analysis, superimposed on discussions about the education–employment relationship.

PROBLEMS WITH THE SKILLS AGENDA

The skills agenda, as conventionally conceived, has been shown to be fraught with many difficulties and problems (Wolf, 1991; Bridges, 1992; Barnett, 1994; Holmes, 1995, 1999). From a practical standpoint, there is the problem of the multitude of models, the plethora of lists. A large number of institutions have devised their own lists or frameworks, often on the basis of what appears to be little more than brainstorming exercises by small teams of staff. Some have adopted the limited list of four key skills emphasized by Dearing (NCIHE, 1997), or the QCA framework of key skills, or some variation of these (see the Key Skills Dissemination project Web site: www.keyskillsnet.org.uk). More ambitiously, Allen (1993) posited 104 skills in eight categories across four zones. Overall, there is no *rational, technical* basis for selecting from this multitude of approaches any single one that may be deemed to be valid.

Protagonists for the skills agenda might argue, as do consultants PriceWaterhouseCoopers (Committee of Vice Chancellors and Principals (CVCP), 1998), that 'there are many lists of skills being produced but considerable similarity between them'. Even one of the key protagonists for key skills, Otter (1997), warns 'the use of the same ability in different universities does not mean that they necessarily share common understanding, and it often obscures fundamental differences of principle'. Such a view is consonant with the conclusions reached by Hirsh and Bevan in their study of 'managerial skills language':

> ... if we ask the question 'is there a shared language for management skills?', the answer seems to be 'yes' at the level of expression but 'no' at the level of meaning.
>
> (Hirsh and Bevan, 1988: 45)

The fact that there is such variety of skills terms, and a plethora of lists of purported skills, is understandable when we look at the methods of enquiry which their protagonists adopt. In many cases, it seems that lists have been drawn up by select groups of staff engaging in nothing more rigorous than a form of brainstorming. Whilst such groups may gain a sense of achievement, the conceptual validity of their products must surely be rated as low. Where it is claimed that 'research' has been undertaken, this usually involves nothing more systematic than surveying a sample of employers (or students, or staff, or some combination of these) with a predetermined list of purported skills. No details are provided about how the lists were devised. Again, such efforts should be treated with care, as there is little evidence that the respondents to such surveys share the same meaning for the skills terms used. Moreover, such research might be accused of putting words into the mouths of the respondents. Thus, from their empirical research, Mangham and Silver (1986) report that:

> Many of the individual replies were only secured *after* considerable prompting; the qualities, attributes and skills of effective performers *do not* appear to be common currency.
>
> (Mangham and Silver, 1986: 32; emphasis in original)

Overall, the methodology typically adopted for identification of skills does not provide a sound basis for relying on the purported empirical findings.

Key skills are presumed to be transferable, capable of being carried from the educational setting to the various employment contexts into which students go after graduation. Yet it is clear that the concept of transferability is rarely subject to critical scrutiny by protagonists for the skills agenda. Indeed, Griffin refers to the 'aura of untouchability' of the concept of transferability:

> That transfer takes place was and is so powerful an assumption as to be deemed beyond discussion: what we think or can do just *does* transfer from one situation to another.
>
> (Griffin, 1994: 134)

There are many published critical analyses of the concept (Wolf, 1991; Bridges, 1992; Barnett, 1994; Griffin, 1994; Gubbay, 1994; Holmes, 1995; 1999; Hyland, 1997). Bridges (1992) challenges that the notion of transferability of skills is neither intelligible nor applicable *without a theory of social domain*. Similarly, Wolf argues for 'the primacy of context' in our understanding of skills.

> ... these skills are by definition inseparable from the contexts in which they are developed and displayed, and... they only make sense (or, rather, the same sense) to those who have the same recognition and understanding of those contexts.
>
> (Wolf, 1991: 194)

The concept of transferability of key skills thus appears to be highly questionable.

PERFORMANCE

The methodological and conceptual difficulties with the skills agenda suggest that we need to reconsider the matters in question. The main concern is that of preparation for graduate employment; we might therefore start by considering the nature of performance in such employment. The skills agenda assumes that what a person does, their *performance*, is objectively observable, so that descriptions of desired performance may be articulated and used to assess actual performance. However, this assumption is flawed, as it fails to distinguish between behaviour, actions and acts (Harré, Clarke and de Carlo, 1985). Once this flaw is remedied by recognizing the distinction, an alternative approach is suggested to address the issues that the skills agenda seeks but fails to address.

If we distinguish between *activity*, as bodily movement and utterance of sounds, and *performance*, as socially meaningful action within particular situations, then the question arises as to how what is perceived as activity is transformed through its interpretation into performance. This is clearly not a matter that is solely under the control of the individual who engages in the activity; it also involves processes of interpretation by those who are party to the situation. This is not a new insight, but is central to the interpretive traditions within sociology, particularly symbolic interactionism (Rose, 1962; Blumer, 1969) and social constructionism (Berger and Luckmann, 1966). It is also a key element within linguistic philosophy, particularly in the work of Wittgenstein (1953) and Austin (1962).

Performance, then, is an interpretative construction and not in itself objectively observable. For any particular situated activity to be construed as performance-of-a-kind, it appears that there are two key criteria:

1. There must be some set of social practices, appropriate to a social arena, such that the current situation is located within that arena by the actors involved and the activity is taken to be an instantiation of one of such practices;
2. There must be a set of identities or positions (Harré and van Langenhove,1999) appropriate to that social arena, such that the individual whose activity is under interpretation in the current situation is deemed to occupy one such identity.

This is represented pictorially in Figure 18.1, showing the elements within this process of the interpretive construction of performance, which we might therefore refer to as the 'practice–identity model of performance'.

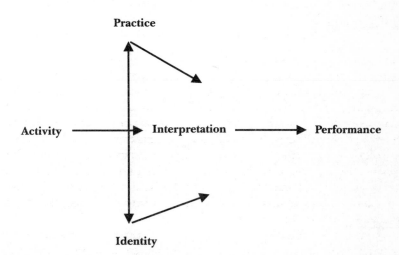

Figure 18.1 Practice–identity model of the interpretation of performance

Applying this to the issues of concern here, we may say that we are dealing with some form of understanding of what constitutes the practices of the social arenas into which graduates typically enter, and the nature of what may be called the 'graduate identity'. So, if we are attempting to analyse the work of graduates in employment, and what counts as capable or competent performance or the expression of skills in such work performance, then it is necessary to establish the answer to two questions. First, how is that performance construed as the instantiation of the practices within that occupational arena? Second, how are the persons undertaking the work accepted as having a distinctive identity *as graduates* relevant to such work performance?

PRACTICES AND PERFORMANCE

The interpretative traditions within social science emphasize that social life is produced collectively by conscious human beings. We do not merely and non-consciously react to events, but initiate action and respond to events according to an understanding of the meaning others attribute to events and in anticipation of the effects of our actions and responses (Blumer, 1969). In interaction, humans thereby reproduce certain patterns of meaning and construct a degree of familiarity, and so predictability, about social life. Thus, we *typically act* on the basis of a 'stock of knowledge' (Schutz, 1967), or ready-made classificatory schema by which social meaning is attributed to particular features of what would otherwise be merely indeterminate happenings. The term 'social practice' is used to address this feature of the conditions of social life, engaging both the patterning of meaning and the typicality of action.

If we consider a graduate in employment, in order to understand how their activity is interpreted as performance of some kind, it would be necessary to have some framework of practices relevant to the context. It is important to recognize that differences in social practice arise within different contexts, because differences in memberships within varying contexts of action will give rise to *divergence* in practices. Part of the process of joining and becoming a 'competent' member of an employing organization involves familiarization and engagement in the local practices. However, we should also note that arenas of social practice are characterized by tendency towards *convergence*. So, whilst in principle every organization, and every department within an organization, may be taken as a unique arena of social practice, we routinely act on the basis of similarity between departments and organizations.

The language of skills may be seen as a set of generalized terms for the practices typically undertaken within the occupations for which graduates are deemed to be suited, broadly professional–managerial occupations

(Holmes, 1995, 1999). That is, the vocabulary of skills provides a way of talking (and writing) about the activities undertaken in such occupations, such that they are seen as having significant similarities. This enables the parties to these arenas to share understanding of what is required, at a level of generality that enables the social setting to maintain continuity. As the ethnomethodologists have shown, meaning is constructed in on-going social life, and is not prerequisite (Garfinkel, 1967). Graduates need to develop their understanding of what is required of them *within* their employing organization; this cannot be done beforehand, although there may be ways of them preparing for it.

GRADUATE IDENTITY

Identity is a concept that has come to take a major part in recent social science theorizing. This is particularly so in recent social psychology seeking to address the nature of the *social*, and in sociological analysis concerned with understanding the *individual* actor within the structured social world (see Jenkins, 1996). Thus, the concept of the person as a monadic entity, a sovereign self acting freely and totally rationally, is replaced by that of a 'social self' (Burkett, 1991). This social self is situated within social relations and a moral order, whose actions are based in explicit or implicit understandings of what *should be done* (morally and/or pragmatically) given their social positioning.

This concept of identity thus provides an analytical link between the social and the personal, and between structure and action. The processes of social life have their structural form only in so far as there is patterning of the actions of members of the social world. Such patterned action is *'as it should be'*, that is, taken for granted, expected and predictable, because of *who* those members are *in relation to each other*. This involves a continuing process whereby the individual person engages in self-identification, and significant others ascribe attributes and characteristics to the individual (social ascription).

This suggests that it is appropriate to adopt the term *emergent identity* to distinguish this analysis from one based either on identity as social ascription (social identity) or on identity as self-concept (personal identity). What is socially salient is neither the one nor the other, but the situated outcome of the interaction between both. Another way of considering this is that of claim (by the individual) and affirmation (by significant others), or their contraries, disclaim and disaffirmation. The relation between these may be shown by the model in Figure 18.2, whereby different *modalities of emergent identity* arise from the interaction between claim/disclaim by the individual, and affirmation/disaffirmation by significant others (Holmes, 2000).

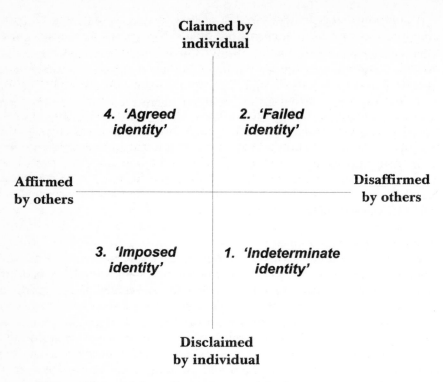

Figure 18.2 Claim–affirmation model of emergent identity

The concept of *graduate identity* should be understood in this interactionist sense; what is *socially salient* is not so much the formal award of a degree, but the extent to which an individual who has graduated is successful in gaining affirmation of their identity as a graduate in relation to the social settings for which this is deemed relevant. From the model, we might take cell 1, 'indeterminate identity', as the student's starting point. Their aspiration would be to make a transition to the position of cell 4, ie they 'really are' a graduate. Gaining a post that is explicitly regarded as a 'graduate job' would be the obvious case, whereby others (the recruiters) are in effect expressing the view that the individual is indeed a graduate worthy of being employed by the organization. However, for some this may not be a smooth transition, such that their position becomes that of cell 2, 'failed identity', ie significant others (such as graduate recruiters) are not prepared to accept them as worthy of employment *as a graduate*. Of course, all emergent identities are fragile, subject to potential challenge; so the graduate positioned in cell 3 may yet gain a 'graduate job', or may seek affirmation of their claim on the identity by re-entering higher education at postgraduate level.

A question that now arises is that of how identity claims, and affirmation/disaffirmation of such claims, are made. To understand this, we may draw upon the notion of 'warranting', the process whereby, of all the possible ways of construing a certain situation, one particular way is presented as correct. Gergen (1989) argues that this is accomplished by the parties to interaction drawing upon certain 'conventions of warrant'. This notion may be applied to identity claims and affirmations/disaffirmations. So, the individual will attempt to present him- or herself as someone worthy of entering the type of occupation for which being a graduate is normally deemed necessary, making such presentation on the basis of what they anticipate will be seen as legitimate grounds. Similarly, those who are 'gatekeepers' to such occupations will seek to justify their decisions to allow or disallow entry by making reference to certain legitimated grounds for such decisions. The language of skills may be seen as constituting such a 'convention of warrant' in respect of 'graduate identity' (Holmes, 1995, 1999).

It is vital here to distinguish between the approach adopted by the conventional skills agenda, and this graduate identity approach, in respect of their different implications for the language of skills. The skills agenda seeks to engage in definition, in precise usage of language; a skills term, a word or phrase, will be taken to denote some particular skill. In contrast, the graduate identity approach recognizes the rich diversity in the language of skills, and seeks to understand how it enables the interaction between the parties engaged in the processes (of claim and ascription) by and through which emergent identity arises. It is the extent to which an individual is able to express their claim on the graduate identity through the use of skills language that is likely to improve their prospects of being selected, rather than some bogus 'proof' that they possess certain entities called 'skills'.

APPLYING THE MODEL

The practice–identity model provides the conceptual and theoretical basis for understanding how the activities of a graduate may be interpreted as performances of particular kinds, in their specific contexts. We might say that it enables us 'to get behind the meaning of' skills (Harvey *et al*, 1997). Whilst skills terminology may be seen as providing a generalized vocabulary, related to the practices typical of the arenas into which graduates enter, this is insufficient without reference to issues of identity formation. Taking both practice and emergent identity as the key issues, the model may be used in research on graduate employment and the trajectories taken by students into their post-graduation lives. It may also be used to reframe existing 'skills development' work, and to suggest new ways of helping students to make successful transitions into the occupational and other arenas to which they aspire.

The model has already been applied in published research on graduates in smaller business (Holmes, Green and Egan, 1998). A major research project on employability amongst graduates from under-represented groups (in terms of ethnicity, age and socio-economic class background), currently underway at the University of North London, is informed by the model. In terms of fecundity, the fruitfulness of the model in generating research issues and projects, it scores highly. The different trajectories and experiences of graduates, from different courses, institutions, backgrounds, and so on would be the focus of identity-oriented research. By contrast, the conventional skills model is *reductionist*, focusing on students or graduates as sets of supposed skills.

In educational terms, the model also has significant benefits. Much existing material may be reframed within the terms of the model, so long as the terminology of skills is seen as practice-vocabulary and provided that identity issues are also addressed. So, for example, rather than presenting students with activities that are predetermined as involving particular, named skills, students may be helped to articulate what they are doing in skills language, ensuring that the full richness and diversity of such language is allowed and encouraged. In a word, students must become fluent in skills-talk. There are many opportunities for this, and for reflecting in students' assessed work the types of practices they may encounter as graduates (Holmes, 1999).

CONCLUSION

This exposition of the graduate identity approach, as an alternative to the skills agenda, has been necessarily brief. Compared to the Goliath of the conventional skills approach, what has been presented might be regarded as a puny David. Hundreds of millions of pounds have been spent on initiatives and projects premised on the conventional notion of skills; the resulting product is very meagre, with little sound evidence that it does achieve what is claimed. Very little funding has been provided for the development of coherent alternatives. Perhaps we may yet see this situation change, and the graduate identity approach begin to be taken as a serious contribution to debate.

REFERENCES

Allen, M (1993) *A Conceptual Model of Transferable Personal Skills*, Employment Department, Sheffield
Andreski, S (1972) *Social Sciences as Sorcery*, André Deutsch, London

Association of Graduate Recruiters (AGR) (1995) *Skills for Graduates in the 21st Century*, AGR, Cambridge

Austin, J L (1961) *Philosophical Papers*, Oxford University Press

Austin, J L (1962) *How to do things with words*, Oxford University Press

Barnett, R (1994) *The Limits of Competence*, Open University Press, Buckingham

Berger, P and Luckmann, T (1966) *The Social Construction of Reality: A treatise in the sociology of knowledge*, Doubleday, New York

Blumer, H (1969) *Symbolic Interactionism: Perspective and method*, Prentice-Hall, Englewood Cliffs, New Jersey

Bridges, D (1992) Transferable skills: a philosophical perspective, *Studies in Higher Education*, Summer, **18** (1), pp 43–51

Brown, P and Scase, R (1994) *Higher Education and Corporate Realities*, UCL Press, London

Burkett, I (1991) *Social Selves*, Sage, London

Committee of Vice Chancellors and Principals (CVCP) (1998) *Skills Development in Higher Education*, CVCP, London

Costall, A and Still, A eds (1987) *Cognitive Psychology in Question*, Harvester Press, Brighton

Flew, A ed (1979) *A Dictionary of Philosophy*, Macmillan, London

Garfinkel, H (1967) *Studies in Ethnomethodology*, Prentice-Hall, Englewood Cliffs, New Jersey

Gergen, K (1989) Warranting voice and the elaboration of the self, in *Texts of Identity*, eds J Shotter and K Gergen, Sage, London

Griffin, A (1994) Transferring learning in higher education: problems and possibilities, in *Academic Community: Discourse or Disorder?* ed R Barnett, Jessica Kingsley, London

Gubbay, J (1994) A critique of conventional justifications for transferable skills, in *Transferable Skills in Higher Education*, ed D Bridges, University of East Anglia, Norwich

Harré, R, Clarke, D and de Carlo, N (1985) *Motives and Mechanisms: An introduction to the psychology of action*, Methuen, London

Harré, R, and van Langenhove, L (1999) *Positioning Theory*, Sage, London

Harvey, L *et al* (1997) *Graduates' Work: Organisational change and students' attributes*, Centre for Research into Quality, University of Central England, Birmingham

Hirsh, W and Bevan, S (1988) *What Makes a Manager? In search of a language for management skills*, Institute of Manpower Studies Report no. 144, Institute of Manpower Studies, Brighton

Holmes, L (1995) 'Skills – a social perspective', in *Transferable Skills in Higher Education*, ed A Assiter, Kogan Page, London

Holmes, L (1999) Competence and capability: from 'confidence trick' to the construction of the graduate identity, in *Developing the Capable Practitioner: Professional capability through higher education*, eds D O'Reilly, L Cunningham, and S Lester, Kogan Page, London

Holmes, L (2000) What can performance tell us about learning? Explicating a troubled concept, *European Journal of Work and Organizational Psychology*, **9** (2), (in press)

Holmes, L, Green, M and Egan, S (1998) *Graduates in Smaller Businesses: A pilot study*, Management Research Centre, University of North London (also available at www.legacy.unl.ac.uk/relational/gisme/gismesum.htm)

Hyland, T (1997) The skills that fail to travel, *The Times Higher Education Supplement*, 2 May, p 12

Jenkins, R (1996) *Social Identity*, Routledge, London

Key skills in higher education dissemination project (2000) www.keyskillsnet.org.uk

Mangham, I and Silver, M (1986) *Management Training: Context and practice*, ESRC, Bath

Murphy, B and Otter, S (1999) A common sense issue, *The Times Higher Education Supplement*, 6 August

NAB/UGC (National Advisory Board for Public Sector Education/University Grants Committee) (1984) *Higher Education and the Needs of Society*, National Advisory Board for Public Sector Education, London

NCIHE (National Committee of Inquiry into Higher Education) (1997) *Higher Education in the Learning Society*, The Stationery Office, London

Otter, S (1997) *The Ability-Based Curriculum, or Key Skills in Higher Education: some snapshots of progress*, report to Ability-Based Curriculum network (available through www.keyskillsnet.org.uk/supportpack/reports/welcome.html)

Rose, A ed (1962) *Human Behaviour and Social Process: An interactionist approach*, Routledge and Kegan Paul, London

Roizen, J and Jepson, M (1985) *Degrees for Jobs*, SRHE and NFER-Nelson, London

Schutz, A (1967) (original German Edition, 1932) *The Phenomenology of the Social World*, Heinemann, London

Usher, R and Bryant, I (1989) *Adult Education as Theory, Practice and Research*, Routledge, London

Wittgenstein, L (1953) *Philosophical Investigations*, Basil Blackwell, Oxford

Wolf, A (1991) Assessing core skills: wisdom or wild goose chase?, *Cambridge Journal of Education*, **21** (2), p 194

Part 3

Conclusions

19

Concluding observations and plans for institutional implementation

Stephen Fallows and Christine Steven
University of Luton
UK

INTRODUCTION

The first part of this book provided an introduction to the justifications for the adoption of a skills-recognizing curriculum. The second group of chapters provided illustration of (mostly) institutional initiatives undertaken at a wide range of higher education institutions in the United Kingdom, United States and Australia with respect to skills. This chapter moves the discussion on to provide a number of observations based on these earlier chapters and includes a concluding commentary which focuses on the process of skills policy implementation at the broad institution or departmental level. The final chapter which follows takes implementation a stage further by considering actions that might be taken by individual teachers within the modules and courses for which they are responsible.

KEY OBSERVATIONS

From the preceding chapters and knowledge of other skills programmes not described here it is possible to make a number of observations that provide the basis for subsequent discussion.

- There is widespread acknowledgement of the benefits that accrue to students from participation in a skills development programme. Employers particularly welcome as new employees those graduates who are able to demonstrate skills-related attributes in addition to having the relevant subject knowledge.

- Skills development programmes around the world are all designed to facilitate the students' progression on graduation into employment and into the wider community. Programmes also aim to provide the life skills necessary for future personal development through lifelong learning.

- Although there is a fair level of agreement about the general nature of skills deemed desirable for students to develop, there is no single, universal, model. Institutions place different degrees of emphasis on the particular skills attributes: this will reflect institutional philosophies, histories and organizational structures.

- There is substantial variation in the implementation strategies adopted by different institutions. Some embed skills across the entire curriculum for everyone. Others offer specialized skills modules or courses as part of every student's degree. Finally, there are instances in which skills programmes are provided as an additional element of the student experience.

- Similarly, there is variation in the manner and in the extent to which seemingly universal skills schemes are applied as different disciplines adapt the essentially generic models for the perceived needs of their students. In some instances, if not carefully applied, this can perpetuate prejudices and stereotypes if (for example) the numerate disciplines avoid oral and written skills whilst the arts eschew numerical analysis.

- There is no consensus view on terminology. There is variation at programme level with a variety of terms in use: transferable skills, key skills, core skills, graduate attributes, tertiary literacies. Variation also applies when describing the skills expectations. The manner and extent to which expectations are detailed is also subject to significant variation.

  Table 19.1 summarizes the skills descriptors used at some of the institutions whose staff have contributed to this volume. There is interesting variation in the relative specificity used by institutions. This indicates a desire for tight central managerial control in those with detailed specifications and greater institutional devolution of responsibility to departmental capabilities in those institutions that are operated on a more collegiate basis.

- Assessment of skills remains problematic and the most favoured approach is to record that the student has engaged with the skills programme but not to specifically assess in a formal manner the student's performance in the individual skill areas. However, it is broadly recognized that the presentation of conventional academic works requires the utilization of a range of skills and also the achievement of a high grade will require full engagement with these skills. Students may be given clear feedback on skills as a part of the general feedback on assessed work.

- Whilst skills may not be assessed in an individual formal manner, a number of institutions provide students on graduation with a skills transcript that details the manner in which skills development has been addressed.

- It must be remembered that skills are being developed throughout each and every student's education, at whatever phase or level, whether these are formally recognized or otherwise. In some instances it is the recognition of these 'naturally occurring' skills that forms the foundations of an institutional skills programme.

- Perhaps the greatest benefit of many skills programmes is that the students recognize that they are developing these skills and gain full confidence in their utilization.

The above observations make it very clear that any expectation of a single implementation model is unrealistic. Each institution has its own historical baggage of traditions and its own perspective on the future. Similarly, we live in a competitive age and it has to be recognized that skills have become a selling point when the institution is recruiting students. If every institution used the same terminology and descriptors (see Table 19.1), there might be the possibility of an 'ill-informed outsider' making an over-simplistic comparison between them: each is unique in its approach and this diversity should be applauded.

Table 19.1 Examples of terminology and skills descriptors used in selected institutions

Institution	Principal terminology	Descriptors[1]
University of Luton UK	Core skills	• Information retrieval and handling • Communication and presentation • Planning and problem solving • Social development and interaction (Each of the above is further subdivided — this yields a total of 13 skills expectations at Levels 2 and 3)
Alverno College USA	Abilities	• Communication • Analysis • Problem solving • Valuing in a decision-making context • Social interaction • Global perspectives • Effective citizenship • Aesthetic responsibility
Napier University UK	'Toolkit skills'	• Study skills • Communication skills • IT skills • Library/information skills • Quantitative skills (Each of the above is further subdivided — this yields a total of 20 skills expectations)

Table 19.1 (continued)

Institution	Principal terminology	Descriptors[1]
University of South Australia Australia	Graduate qualities	• Ability to operate effectively upon a body of knowledge • Preparation for lifelong learning • Effective problem solving • Working autonomously and collaboratively • Commitment to ethical action and social responsibility • Communicating effectively • Demonstration of international perspectives
University of Nottingham UK	Key skills	• Builds upon the students' 'naturally occurring' key skills in accordance with departmental expectations and practice. No institution-wide list of required skills.
Middlesex University UK	Key skills	• Personal and career development • Effective learning • Communication • Teamwork • Numeracy • Information technology
University of Wollongong Australia	Tertiary literacies	• Commitment to continued and independent learning, intellectual development, critical analysis and creativity • Coherent knowledge of subject, appropriate ethical standards and professional skills • Self-confidence plus communication skills • Teamworking skills • Ability to analyse issues logically and implement decisions

Table 19.1 *(continued)*

Institution	Principal terminology	Descriptors[1]
University of Wollongong Australia *(continued)*	Tertiary literacies *(continued)*	• Valuing of diversity – ability to function in a multicultural or global environment • Information literacy and specific skills in computer-based activities • Acknowledgement of individual responsibilities and obligations
Bowling Green State University USA	'Springboard' competencies	• Communication • Analysis • Problem solving • Judgement • Leadership • Self-assurance
De Montfort University UK	Key skills	• Application of number • Communication • Improving own learning and performance • Information technology • Problem solving • Working with others (This list is derived from the national key skills framework as defined by the Qualifications and Curriculum Authority[2])

Notes

1. This table has been extracted from material presented earlier in this volume. In some cases it has been necessary to abbreviate descriptors.
2. The Graduate Apprentice Scheme at the University of Luton also utilizes the QCA skills descriptors.

INSTITUTIONAL IMPLEMENTATION

As stated previously, many of the contributions to this book have addressed the matter of what may broadly be termed 'institutional implementation'. The next section of this chapter seeks to consider the various steps that need to be taken and the questions that must be addressed when considering the implementation of a strategy to implement a skills-recognizing curriculum.

The progression to the recognition that the skills agenda must be addressed has tended to rest on the two main parameters of national initiatives and the local institutional agenda. These parameters are not mutually exclusive and often they have operated together to provide the impetus for the initiation of skills development.

In the United Kingdom, perhaps the most significant stimulant for skills development programmes was the Enterprise in Higher Education Initiative (EHE) (see Chapter 17). It was involvement with EHE that initiated the activities that subsequently led to the development of the formal skills development activities in the authors' home institution from 1992 onwards.

More recently in the United Kingdom, the report of the National Committee of Inquiry into Higher Education (the Dearing Committee) (1997) suggested that recognition of key skills should be a part of the experience of every student in higher education. The political influence of this has been sufficient to encourage further activity.

Finally, in the United Kingdom – partially as a response to the Dearing Report – the Department for Education and Employment has funded a number of experimental skills initiatives (see for instance Chapters 6, 9 and 10).

The institutional agenda is less easily defined. However, in recent years many educational institutions have developed a close relationship to (particularly the larger) business interests in their locality. This relationship is not merely with respect to the possible placement of students in employment with these organizations (though in certain instances this could be important). Rather it is through these links that higher education institutions have been made fully aware of the current needs of employers when selecting new graduate employees. For a minority of posts, a particular subject specialism continues to be relevant, but for the majority of new graduates, employment will be gained on the basis of the non-specific skills that exist in addition to the subject-specific knowledge. The skills development initiatives in many institutions are intended to provide the graduating students with a comparative advantage in an increasingly competitive external environment.

Following initiation, the key point to note is that the first step has been taken. The exact steps that follow will depend on the nature of the institution. The consideration presented below is a mix of the hypothetical and the practical. In reality, no institution would ever follow rigorously the processes outlined here: hence it is hypothetical. However, an attempt has been made to address the key issues in a logical manner that will be useful to readers: hence it is practical.

In order to make progress from conception to implementation of a skills programme institutions will need to address a number of key issues or questions. As stated previously, there is often no one correct answer to each question; rather the answers will reflect the nature of the institution and its established culture and organization. Actions and decisions will include:

Establishing a committee

It is common practice for a committee or working party to be established to act as either the decision-making group or a body charged with providing advice to senior decision makers. As with all committees, careful consideration needs to be given to the make-up of this body. The group will need to be chaired by someone with recognized enthusiasm for skills development; this could be a member of the institution's management team (if the group is to be decision-making) or a senior teacher (if it is to be advisory). Appointment to the chair of someone with doubts would undoubtedly impede progress. Membership should include a mix of individuals; those in managerial positions (budget holders able to comment on any cost implications), front-line teachers (able to comment on the day-to-day pedagogical implications), quality assurance/academic standards (to ensure that the scheme has a positive effect on the institution's academic standing) and last but not least representatives of the student body.

When establishing the group consideration should be given to the inclusion of one or more employer representatives. Such individuals are able to stand back from the institution's internal agenda and give independent advice from their professional perspective. As outsiders they are also better placed to comment on the external public relations aspects of the introduction of the skills development programme.

It will be the task of this group to provide locally appropriate answers to the issues and questions that are outlined below.

Nominate a champion

A champion may arise from the committee or working party or from the institution at large. There are essentially two types of champion in this setting. The first is a member of the institution's senior management team (perhaps a pro-vice-chancellor – in the authors' home institution the skills agenda was championed by the then deputy vice-chancellor). The second type of champion is the person appointed or seconded to steer the scheme on a day-to-day basis as a project manager. Each successful skills programme will have at least one visible champion.

Timescales

A key decision will have to be taken concerning the speed of implementation. Clearly, once the decision to go ahead has been taken people will wish to get on with the task. Institutions may like to consider a phased implementation over a number of years.

The authors' home institution phased in the introduction of its skills programme over a period of three years: in year 1 it was applied to Level 1 programmes, in year 2 to Levels 1 and 2, and in the year 3 to all three undergraduate levels). This phasing meant that there could be a clear distinction of students who had experienced the programme (necessary for production of skills transcripts at graduation). It also meant a phasing in of the workload for staff.

Other institutions may favour a 'big bang' once-and-for-all implementation but may phase in other ways.

Universal implementation or department by department?

This issue is one that tends to reflect the institutional culture. Some institutions operate in a manner in which a strong central managerial steer is the norm, with departments falling into line as a matter of course. In others academic departments may operate as autonomous units within a collegiate setting. The universal approach (everyone will do... by...) fits the first model but would not find favour in the second.

The Nottingham model presented in Chapter 6 has focused on phasing the initiative in to a small number of departments in the first instance.

Single model or multiple?

In many ways this question follows on from the previous one. Is it preferable to implement a single skills development programme across the institution? Or is there merit in different programmes for different disciplines? There is, of course, no correct answer. For institutions that operate a major modular credit scheme that encourages students to consider a diverse range of joint honours or major/minor combinations a single universal scheme is the simplest means of ensuring the desired level of engagement with the skills programme. But for institutions in which departments and the degrees they offer are largely self-contained there can be merit in developing targeted skills development programmes.

Different levels or single expectation?

There remain differences of opinion over whether it is best to set out a single set of skills expectations that can be achieved by the completion of a student's time with the institution or alternatively to set out progressively more onerous expectations for each level of study.

Focused skills module or embedded into general curriculum?

This too is a fundamental question. A one-off module that deals specifically with skills has its attractions and can be modified if necessary to suit the particular balance desired by specific disciplines. However, the alternative approach of embedding skills work within the general curriculum highlights the fact for everyone, staff and students alike, that skills can be developed in a wide range of academic situations.

The two models can have quite different staffing implications. With the embedded approach, skills development becomes a universal responsibility with the expectation that each and every lecturer recognizes the skills content of all modules taught. With the one-off model, it is necessary to ensure that a person or team is employed specifically to deliver the programme.

Which skills?

This book has indicated how a number of higher-education institutions have defined skills expectations in different ways (see Table 19.1). There is a common need to recast the generic descriptors to yield a local understanding of skills. The development of a new, in-house, set of descriptors leads to local ownership since it allows for the skills programme to take account of local circumstances, mission and aspirations.

It is interesting to note that none of the skills initiatives detailed in this book has suggested competence in a second language as a desirable skill. But with increased globalization, in both business and government, there is a growing demand for multilingual employees. This apparent omission is likely to reflect the fact that all contributors are based in English-speaking countries. Academic competence and ability to operate professionally and socially in a second or third language is an accepted norm for students in most countries; this usually means competence in English. The institutions featured in this book all offer language tuition for their students but this is under quite separate arrangements.

Assessment and recording?

Recording of students' achievements with respect to skills remains an issue for many institutions. A mere 'tick the box' approach seems inadequate for the amount of effort expended in setting up these skills programmes. Formal summative assessment requires formal and specific criteria against which staff may make consistent judgements. It can be argued that skills assessment is unavoidably a feature of all assessment within education since the students must use some or all of their skills to produce the work that is assessed.

Some institutions provide a separate assessment (and certificate) for certain of the skills, particularly in the use of communications and information technology. This is feasible for a restricted range of skills for which objective criteria can be established but not so simple for the wider range of expectations set out by many institutions. Furthermore, there are a number of skills that are deemed to be desirable but which it is difficult, if not impossible, to define in clear objective terms.

To be meaningful any skills assessment must have wide recognition and consistency – at present there is no universal system able to provide this.

A number of institutions have taken the position that it is most appropriate to provide students, at graduation, with a transcript statement that records the students' engagement with skills as a part of their university experience.

Communication with teaching staff

Whilst it is appropriate for the development work to be undertaken by a small group, it is essential that the full corpus of teaching staff is kept informed about the initiative. This is particularly true if the embedded model is to be utilized, since this could be considered to be placing an additional workload on the teaching staff. Communication may take place through a variety of mechanisms but should definitely include the use of appropriate open meetings at which teaching staff may ask questions of those responsible for development of the skills programme.

In certain circumstances, it may be necessary for the management to discuss implementation with the relevant teachers' unions.

Communication to students

Consideration should also be given to how the skills programme is to be communicated to the student body. Inclusion of a student representative on the development group provides one channel for communication. Once the skills strategy has been finalized, and later whilst it is being implemented, there is a need to inform students; this should include provision of information to prospective students, since a well-thought-out skills programme could feature in choice of study institution.

It is likely that many institutions will wish to include information on the skills programme on a Web site. The nature of the information presented will depend to a significant extent on whether it is to be for local consumption only or if it is to be presented more widely.

Resourcing

The cost of operating the skills programme will inevitably have to be considered. If carefully managed, a good deal of the resource costs can be met through pre-existing commitments.

For instance, if the embedded model is used, there may be no additional staff costs and communication of skills expectations can be within course/module handbooks, which are generally revised and updated on a year-by-year basis, as are prospectuses which provide the chief route for communication with prospective students.

In all institutions of higher education, as with many other organizations, the principal cost will be people. If it is decided to employ a specific person as 'skills coordinator' or to establish a skills team, then there are clear cost implications.

Staff development

Undoubtedly, if a skills programme is to be implemented there will be a need to address the personal and professional development of those who are expected to deliver the programme. Such development will be needed for both new appointees to the institution and those who are established members of the teaching staff.

An initiative such as this can be utilized as a lever to engage all teaching staff in discussions with respect to the development of learning and teaching for the 21st century.

FINAL COMMENT

The list of issues and questions introduced briefly above is not exhaustive: each of those responsible for the skills programmes discussed in this book will undoubtedly have other issues to add. It does, however, provide the reader with an indication that this is not a simple and straightforward matter. Rather the adoption of a skills programme requires careful consideration and skilled management.

Part 4

Guidance on 'How to...'

20

'How to' at the module level: a selection of practical skills implementation tips

Christine Steven and Stephen Fallows
University of Luton
UK

INTRODUCTION

The previous chapter, along with many of the case examples, has considered the adoption of a skills-recognizing curriculum from the strategic viewpoint – that is, from an institutional or departmental perspective. No matter how the individual institution operates, from the perspective of the front-line teacher, this level of approach tends to have a managerial or enthusiast (rather than collegiate) feel about it.

Announcements such as the totally hypothetical one (invented for this chapter) that follows have been circulated in universities around the world:

> ... It is recognized that in the context of changing circumstances in the world of work, it is essential that all students with the University of... develop a range of transferable skills during their time with the University.
>
> Following a period of local consultation, it has been decided that the University is to adopt a transferable skills programme. This skills programme will ensure that students will experience and demonstrate competence in the following skill areas [local list then follows]. The transferable skills initiative will apply across the entire University [or Department] and will be implemented from the start of academic year [generally the next].
>
> A summary of the skills programme is given in Figure...

In order to maintain the University's academic standards, the development of these skills will be in addition to the students gaining the recognized level of expertise for their chosen discipline.

In order to ensure that the transferable skills programme progresses successfully, all teaching staff will need to identify how each of their courses develops students' transferable skills. This exercise will be completed by [date]. In support of this programme all lecturers should submit a skills development plan for each of their courses by [date].

As indicated, the above announcement is hypothetical and deliberately more heavy-handed than would be the case in most higher-education institutions. However, it does indicate a commonly held view that skills programmes can be imposed from the top or by a small group of enthusiasts who are particularly vociferous and influential. The majority of teaching staff may feel that they have little influence on the situation, and this view is likely to prevail even with the most extensive consultation. Many academic teaching staff may believe that they are too busy doing their 'day job' to focus much on consultation papers. Similarly, the membership of advisory groups, working parties, committees, etc tends to reflect status – with the majority of more junior teachers being (thankful that, for the present, they are) excluded – and more senior staff wishing that they could be.

The announcement appears to impose an additional workload upon the teacher – the skills programme will be implemented on top of the maintenance of academic competence within the students' chosen discipline. It will be achieved by a named deadline (which usually appears to be not too distant).

So the front-line teacher may often appreciate the skills initiative as a 'good thing' that brings benefits for the students and will support the concept, but may be less certain of the new personal role and responsibility that the institution's initiative is to place upon them.

One point of view that is heard commonly is:

> We accept that this skills business is good for the students and is something we have got to do, but how do we do it? How do I build skills into my teaching without disrupting years of course development and long-term planning? Won't the skills take away from the already limited curriculum time?

As before, this is an invented statement, but it is one that brings together a number of front-line concerns about skills initiatives that we are sure will be familiar to many.

The viewpoint is not negative to the skills concept – rather it indicates doubt faced by the individual lecturer at a time of change: doubt that is couched in terms that indicate an unwillingness to compromise the existing academic standards despite a perception of additional workload.

The statement above is indicative that university teachers as facilitators of students' learning may often be taking a less than positive look at the prospect of having to teach skills. However, we believe that a focus on skills can be used positively; it can be something used to enhance our time with the students, be it in lectures, tutorials, and practical sessions or even when assessing their progress. If used positively, then a skills-recognizing course can be particularly stimulating and can make the experience more enjoyable for teachers as well as for students.

Practicalities do of course come into the equation. It is rare for establishments to provide large amounts of money for additional resources to facilitate this venture. In some instances project funding may be made available from either national initiatives or local resources. But in most instances, teachers must be innovative and find ways of using and enhancing what is already available.

IMPLEMENTATION

In the following section, the core descriptors adopted by the University of Luton (as discussed in Chapter 2) will be utilized as a convenient base on which a discussion of practical skills implementation can be introduced. The Luton model is obviously the one with which the authors are most familiar; it is also one in which the skills expectations have been divided into manageable elements rather than remaining as broad headings. As stated earlier, the Luton model reflects different outcomes and expectations at each of the undergraduate levels. Other institutions adopt an alternative approach and do not make this distinction.

For this discussion, only those skills descriptors pertaining to Level 3, the final year, of an undergraduate programme will be considered. This level represents the culmination of both the academic and skills aspects of the undergraduates' work. It must be remembered that the skills content of the students' work must be seen in the context of their academic development and it is anticipated that at this level in their studies they will be able to demonstrate a high level of confidence in the core knowledge base of their chosen discipline area. They will also be able to critically evaluate new and abstract data presented to them using a variety of techniques appropriate to that discipline.

The Luton model divides the core skills descriptors into four main areas and at Level 3 these have been subdivided into more detailed descriptors, totalling 13 in all. It is recognized that in practice it is extremely difficult to isolate each skill area and that almost every task undertaken will impinge on at least three of the skills areas, namely those of planning and problem solving, information retrieval and handling, and communication and presentation.

The challenge is to incorporate skills development in a meaningful way even when the skills are not seen as obvious or of immediate use to that discipline. Many mathematics and science graduates, and indeed their tutors, find it difficult to see the relevance of being able to assess the quality of their own oral communication skills or to produce a complex piece of written work. Similarly, English and other arts graduates often fail to recognize the importance of handling and analysing numerical data and using IT. Clearly, the depths of usage and understanding of many of the techniques can be varied, but a basic awareness is vital to the survival of all new graduates in the world of work. Real-world examples tend to inspire students (Fallows and Ahmet, 1999) as do practical exercises (Steven and Fallows, 1999). It must be remembered that for the majority of students their education is not simply an abstract activity but one that is related to long-term requirements.

With the above provisos in mind it must be said that it is easier to isolate the skills areas for the purposes of highlighting some examples of the practical techniques that have been utilized successfully in the past. The examples given are intended to be generic and are provided as an introductory guide to help teachers through the process of incorporating skills into the curriculum. Clearly, in a few pages, it is not feasible to discuss each and every possible technique; however, we hope that the points suggested below will give readers a few ideas that can be built into their teaching.

Planning and problem solving

Within the Luton model, the university sets out the following expectation:

> It is anticipated that by the end of Level three the learner will be able to take a well-defined problem, apply given tools and methods both accurately and creatively to a set of abstract data or concepts and produce conclusions appropriate to those data.

Bullet points below follow on from the above – the text that follows each bullet point gives a short discussion of how the university's expectations might be achieved. As indicated previously, it is likely that almost every task presented to students will involve the use and development of more than one skill).

In particular, the student will be able to:

● Decide on action plans and implement them effectively.
  This skill area is concerned with encouraging the students to become better organized in the way that they manage their work. It is vital to encourage the students to stage their work, to break it down into manageable portions and to organize their materials in accordance with a logical plan of action.

The final year research project provides the highest test of whether students have acquired this skill. The student will have to set out a logical programme of work, negotiate access to the necessary resources (particularly true for laboratory-based disciplines), conduct the work effectively and in time present the necessary report or dissertation.

However, students need to build their capabilities whilst with the university. Initially the tasks set will be relatively small, but even here the students should be encouraged to think through what needs to be done ahead of diving in. Group activities can be used to illustrate how a task may be addressed, since the action plans will not only break down the task but will allocate it between group members; successful completion requires that the various elements are coordinated effectively.

Remember there is major benefit in relating tasks to meaningful examples from the 'real world' wherever this is possible. What needs to be done in a public inquiry –what evidence/information will be required? How are large-scale computer software products produced – what are the key steps? The specific tasks will also need to be tailored to the individual disciplines.

● Manage time effectively in order to achieve intended goals.

This takes the efforts of the previous action plan a step further. Now the student needs to recognize the need not only for planning but also for timing.

Time management is a major skill demanded by all employers. But it is also one that students can struggle with, with assessed assignments completed at the last minute and often submitted late. The strict application of deadlines may be deemed to be harsh, but it does impose criteria that equate to those found in the 'real world', where missed deadlines can mean lost orders.

In lecture or tutorial situations the facilitator can set tasks under tight time constraints. A set of gapped handouts summarizing the previous session's work that requires completion in five minutes at the beginning of a lecture usually works well. In tutorial sessions a paper related to the lecture that requires summarizing and delivering to the rest of the group on one overhead slide often produces some interesting results. If the students become accustomed to completing tasks in a set time they will begin to respond by setting their own targets.

As above, the production of the final-year dissertation or major project report requires professional-level time and project management skills, as this work is generally implemented over an extended period of as much as a year. Similarly, for students undertaking research degrees such as the PhD, time and project management are crucial and yet evidence suggests that there is a significant need for these students to work on their skills in this area in order to ensure that the thesis is submitted on time.

- Clearly identify criteria for success and evaluate their own performance against those criteria.

  If students are to achieve the above expectation, they must be made fully aware of the criteria for success. This puts the onus on the lecturer to give clear guidelines as to what is required of the student. This guidance should, wherever possible, give an indication of what is needed in order to achieve excellence as well as describing criteria for lesser grades.

  When this has been provided the task is then to show, first by example, why the student has achieved the grade they have. This may involve provision of feedback against specific criteria. The next step is to let the students themselves give a grade, with justification for a piece of work; there can be clear benefit in negotiation of grading criteria for the work of themselves and their peers (Fallows and Chandramohan, in press).

  Another very successful approach is to use anonymous work from previous years that has already been graded by at least two people. The students also learn more about the topic being accessed.

  For more senior students it can be a useful test to ask them to referee a piece of academic writing against the criteria set out by the editors of a journal in their discipline. Use of appropriate refereeing criteria in this manner helps to prepare these students for the possible publication of their work whilst clarifying the nature of refereed journal articles.

  It is also a useful exercise to get students to consider technical papers against their set criteria for what is acceptable and what is not. In this context technical papers could include for example instructions for the use of equipment or software.

- Produce creative and realistic solutions to complex problems.

  Some courses have a requirement that students study problem solving as a theoretical exercise. Traditionally this has been achieved by using a standard lecture to deliver the theory and then following this with tutorial exercises. A more successful approach has been shown to be that of using experiential exercises, deriving the results and then progressing to the theoretical aspects. This method can be used for many 'dry' theoretical subjects. The students become involved and at times excited by the subject.

  As with all skill areas, it is often useful to build up to the complex problem through phased use of minor and even trivial problems. Understanding of how problems may be addressed can be initiated through use of simple puzzles followed by discussion – teachers should not be afraid to utilize quite simple exercises since it is the analysis of how the solution was achieved that is important rather than the solution per se.

Again it is very useful to utilize authentic 'real world' examples, the nature of which will vary with the discipline. Students appreciate and enjoy having to tackle apparently bizarre scenarios. Ommundsen, (1999) suggests the use of the acronym 'DENT' – students should Define the problem, Explore the solutions, Narrow the choices and Test their ideas.

Information retrieval and handling

Again, the Luton model will be used to give structure to the discussion. The university expects that:

> By the end of Level 3 the learner should be able to find, describe and interpret data and interpret information within the context of the discipline(s).

In detail this will mean that the learners will be able to:

- Identify their own information needs in order to support complex problem requirements.

  Whatever problem is being solved there is information to be obtained. When the student has decided what is to be done he or she then needs to establish what information is required in order to complete the task successfully. The task set may vary from a relatively straightforward one being set within the lecture or tutorial situation to a more complex piece of assignment work.

  A now more popular assessment that requires the student to think of more novel information needs is that of producing a poster. The student needs to establish what the poster is being used for: is it a substitute for an abstract or is it to interest and stimulate discussion? These two different uses will require the collection of different types of information.

- Complete an information search using a wide range of appropriate primary and secondary sources.

  In this area the students should be encouraged to look in a variety of places for information. The resource centres of most universities now cover books, journals, microfiche, CD ROMs and the Internet. There are also inter-library loans between universities and national resources (such as, in the United Kingdom, the British Library).

  The use of this nice diversity of information sources can be encouraged by setting appropriate tasks: perhaps begin by using marking criteria that clearly state that the students must be able to show they have used at least three different types of source. This will encourage them to draw upon a range of sources for future pieces of work.

An interesting activity for both student and lecturer is trying to find out how many references can be found to the lecturer's work on the Internet or in a particular journal (this is of course more interesting the more prolific the lecturer).

But it is not simply the matter of finding information that is important. The students need to be able to evaluate the quality of sources: the Internet in particular offers access to the full range of quality.

- Analyse data using appropriate techniques.

'Data' in this context can have a variety of meanings, depending on the discipline, and can be interpreted to include more qualitative and quantitative sources.

It is not enough for the student to complete a course in, say, statistics. It is also necessary that this be applied into other items of work and most particularly into the final year research project and dissertation.

When setting data-analysis tasks there is very considerable merit in utilizing authentic data that have relevance to the students' specific personal and professional background. (See Fallows and Ahmet, 1999 for several case studies that focus on this issue.)

It is very useful if the data have currency: one colleague, who teaches epidemiology, was utilizing data from the case of the serial murderer Harold Shipman within days of the completion of the trial. The gruesome nature of the data also caught the attention of his students.

Where possible students should analyse data that they have collected themselves. This gives 'ownership'. It is also a useful exercise that helps students to realize that often in research there is no absolute correct answer to many real world circumstances.

The use of computer-based analysis packages should be encouraged where this is appropriate, but a key issue is the need to ensure that the student is able to select the most appropriate test and can interpret the outcomes.

- Support previously identified areas by using appropriate IT resources.

As an absolute minimum this area can be interpreted as referring only to the standard software suites that include packages such as word processors, spreadsheets, databases and presentational software.

It can also refer to computer-aided learning (CAL) or computer-based assessments (CBA). Many students do not know when it is appropriate for them to utilize these resources. They can be encouraged throughout their time at the university to use CAL and CBA to help them to learn.

It should also include an opportunity to utilize specialist software that is available for use in specific disciplines; for instance, someone studying nutrition and dietetics would use one or more of the dietary analysis packages.

The use of IT resources needs to be introduced as an extension of other resources; how much more effective a table is than lots of writing, using a spreadsheet instead of a calculator (it is so much easier and there is no erasing!). Where better to store the data you have spent so long collecting than in a database and of course it is so much easier to read a word-processed essay than a handwritten one (it spell checks for you too).

Communication and presentation

The University of Luton expectations are:

The learners... should be able to communicate effectively in context, both orally and on paper.

('In context' means at the correct level for the defined audience and using the correct medium.)

The learners should be able to:

- Produce a piece of work that demonstrates that they have a grasp of the vocabulary of the subject and deploys a range of skills of written expression appropriate to the subject.

    This aspect should be demonstrated throughout students' time at university. They are continually (or so it seems) being given assignments where they are required to write a paper or an essay.

    Maybe a more effective way would be to ask for an executive summary of some aspect being studied. For example, students could be asked to prepare a range of documents on a current topic. The documents could include briefing notes for the board of directors of a company on a recent scientific development, or the draft of a minister's answer to a parliamentary question on a current issue.

    Students could be given a recent paper from a scientific journal and asked to prepare a (say) 500-word article on the issue in the style of a (named) national newspaper or popular science magazine.

    The production of slides to accompany an oral presentation again requires a different range of skills. Students need to be taught (or shown) what constitutes good handouts and slides (bullet points, uncluttered overheads).
- Assess the quality of his or her own oral communication and identify areas for improvement.

It always seems to be difficult for students to assess how effective they have been at delivering presentations. One method that can demonstrate this to them is first to make them give a brief presentation (10 minutes maximum) to their peers, then get the student and the rest of the group to award marks for various aspects of the presentation. See how these agree with each other and the lecturer's perception. It is even more effective if the group themselves have devised the criteria.

Don't be afraid to lead by example, for instance, by giving a short but deliberately bad presentation and getting the students to criticize constructively. Students remember these performances and are more likely to avoid the flaws when putting together their own presentations than if all they ever experience is the perfect lecture.

- Deliver a paper or presentation that succeeds in communicating a series of points effectively.

This area is probably one of the most difficult to succeed at. Many experienced lecturers display problems when delivering a conference paper to a group of people who are not familiar with their work. This can be a difficult skill to acquire and there are many so-called professional lecturers who never achieve it.

One technique that can be adopted is to get the students to analyse a technical paper and make them write down what they think the important points are. The next step is for them to consider how they would present these same facts to different audiences, their peers, their tutors, an open meeting, a group of sixth-form pupils who want to study this subject when they leave school.

Presentation skills, the ability to write good, clear overheads and the ability to speak clearly and concisely all play a part here.

Don't just limit the students to live presentations. It is very useful to get them to produce a video of their presentation (in a group is very effective). It also means that you can mark the work at leisure rather than attend all the presentations, and it is available for next year's students to watch. This could be how to or how not to do presentations!

Social development and interaction

At Level 3 the University of Luton expects that learners 'should be able to work with and meet obligations to others (tutors and/or other students)'

In particular this means that the learners are expected to be able to:

- Formulate effective strategies for achieving goals when working with others.

It has become increasingly popular for students to be given group work activities. The student often begins by thinking this will be good fun and ends up by hating the mere mention of group work. Often this is because the students are not given any help or advice about how to set up or work within groups.

Initially the lecturer is likely to form the teams (almost arbitrarily) and to designate role-playing activities. Ultimately it could become the group's responsibility to divide up the tasks.

'Working with others' can be interpreted into a range of situations. The 'others' could be colleagues within the university (other students, teaching staff, technical staff, librarians, etc), participant subjects in research studies, or clients in a professional setting.

- Participate effectively in the operation of a team and collaborate with members of the team.

Within this skill area, the students have to learn how to work within groups and recognize the strengths and weaknesses of all those in the group, including themselves. They will need to be able to give and accept criticism in a constructive manner and to distinguish between personal views and corporate policy, resolving any conflict they may have.

Many group activities can be constructed in a manner that requires each group member to take on a specific role. In such exercises, it can be useful to provide each role with an incomplete set of background information, as often happens in practice. In order to complete the assigned task it is essential that all roles participate and make their contribution. If circumstances permit it can be a useful tactic to set a problem that cannot be completed using the information provided initially and then to provide additional information to specific roles only.

An exercise that can be useful is to make each group put forward two policies having totally conflicting interpretations of an issue. This works well for debates. The tutor may wish to provide a deliberately provocative stance.

The interaction may, of course, be with teams from the outside world in the form of work placements, external research projects, work-based learning activities and ultimately at job interviews. The same rules apply in that the students must learn to recognize strengths and weaknesses and must whilst building on their strengths learn to minimize their personal weaknesses.

The formation of groups to perform tasks does itself create potential problems for the facilitator. How do we assess these group tasks? How do we ensure fairness in the allocation of grades?

It should be noted that it is this skill that is most often cited in the case against the formal assessment of skills per se, since aspects such as 'collaboration' are very difficult to score in a meaningful manner.

CONCLUDING COMMENTS

We begin with a reminder: the University of Luton model for skills development has been used here to provide structure to the discussion; our choice of this structure reflects local experience. The university's breakdown of skills expectations into 13 items at Levels 2 and 3 allows Luton staff to examine each and every module taught with a view to identification of the skills opportunities.

The Luton system permits the construction of a matrix for each degree programme. The x axis is the list of skills whilst the y axis is the list of modules. Using this matrix it is possible to identify where each skill is being addressed and developed. From the staff perspective, the early editions of the matrix identify any gaps in skills provision and also any instances where a skill seems likely to be developed on (say) just a single occasion. Each of these problems can easily be rectified to ensure that skills development is well-rounded and takes place (for each skill) on a number of occasions. The system ensures that the development of each skill is embedded into several modules, each of which may utilize a quite different approach to achievement of the skills expectation.

We have utilized the Luton model as the basis for our discussion and think it would be useful for readers in other institutions. However, we believe that readers from other institutions that have a less specifically defined model than that operated at Luton will find a similar mapping exercise to be of benefit.

A general observation that can be made from the preceding paragraphs is that success in skills work follows a couple of basic general principles that can be employed throughout education.

If students are enjoying their learning activities, and especially if they find them to be fun, they learn more than if the approach does not stimulate (bores). As always, key elements for learning success include use of:

- Active sessions that use rather than merely talk about the skill area.
- A variety of approaches for each skill. Repeated use reinforces learning.
- Authentic and credible material that provides genuine 'real world' learning experiences rather than abstract and less believable examples.

Our final comment is that skills can be developed in every learning activity and if the reader is working within an institution that prescribes a specific skills module this should be considered as the mere foundation and not the end of the skills experience. We all owe this to our students.

REFERENCES

Fallows, S and Ahmet, K (1999) *Inspiring Students: Case Studies in Motivating the Learner*, Kogan Page, London

Fallows, S and Chandramohan, B (in press) Multiple approaches to assessment: reflections on use of tutor, peer and self assessment in *Teaching in Higher Education*

Ommundsen, P (1999) Problem based learning, in *Inspiring Students: Case Studies in Motivating the Learner* eds S Fallows and K Ahmet (1999) pp 25–32, Kogan Page, London

Steven, C and Fallows, S J (1999) Skills in the curriculum: implementing a university-wide initiative, in *Managing Learning Innovation: The challenges of the changing curriculum*, ed G Windle, Proceedings of a Society for Research in Higher Education conference (pp 93–99), University of Lincolnshire and Humberside, Lincoln

Appendix 1: Contributors' contact details

The contributions included in this book have all been created by practitioners in higher education for the benefit of colleagues throughout the worldwide community of higher education.

It is increasingly the case that the primary mode of communication within the international higher education community is by means of e-mail. This mode has been utilized extensively throughout the development of this book. For many authors, the sole mode of communication with the editors has been via e-mail. Since is e-mail is a preferred and rapid mode of communication for our contributing authors we list the e-mail addresses of all contributors.

For readers who prefer to use more traditional communications route, postal addresses are also given.

Chapter	Contributing author	Academic institution	E-mail addresses	Postal address
Chapters 1, 2, 19 and 20	Stephen Fallows Christine Steven	University of Luton	stephen.fallows@luton.ac.uk sjfallows@aol.com christine.steven@tesco.net	Centre for Quality Assurance University of Luton Luton Bedfordshire LU1 3JU England
Chapter 3	Kathleen O'Brien	Alverno College	kathleen.obrien@alverno.edu	Alverno College 3400 S 43rd St PO Box 343922 Milwaukee, WI 53234 USA
Chapter 4	Phyllis Laybourn Nancy Falchikov Judy Goldfinch Jenny Westwood	Napier University	p.laybourn@napier.ac.uk n.falchikov@napier.ac.uk j.goldfinch@napier.ac.uk j.westwood@napier.ac.uk	Napier University 219 Colinton Road Edinburgh EH14 1DJ Scotland
Chapter 5	Ted Nunan Rigmor George Holly McCausland	University of South Australia	ted.nunan@unisa.edu.au rigmor.george@unisa.edu.au holly.mccausland@unisa.edu.au	Learning Connection University of South Australia Magill Campus St Bernard's Rd Magill South Australia 5072
Chapter 6	Mary Chapple Harry Tolley	University of Nottingham	mary.chapple@nottingham.ac.uk harry.tolley@nottingham.ac.uk	University of Nottingham School of Nursing Faculty of Medicine and Health Sciences Queen's Medical Centre Nottingham NG7 2UH England

Chapter	Author	Institution	Email	Address
Chapter 7	Judith Harding	Middlesex University	j.harding@mdx.ac.uk	Centre for Learning Development Middlesex University Bounds Green Road London N11 2NQ England
Chapter 8	Catherine Milne	Previously University of Wollongong, now University of Pennsylvania	cemilne@gse.upenn.edu	Department of Chemistry University of Pennsylvania 231 S 34th street Philadelphia, PA 19104–6323 USA
Chapter 9	Becka Currant Pete Mitton	University of Bradford	r.currant@bradford.ac.uk p.r.mitton@bradford.ac.uk prmitton@btinternet.com	University of Bradford Great Horton Road Bradford BD7 1BP England
Chapter 10	Sue Drew	Sheffield Hallam University	s.k.drew@shu.ac.uk	Learning and Teaching Institute Sheffield Hallam University Adsetts Centre City Campus Sheffield S1 1WB England
Chapter 11	Stephen Fallows Gordon Weller	University of Luton	stephen.fallows@luton.ac.uk sjfallows@aol.com gordon.weller@luton.ac.uk	Centre for Quality Assurance University of Luton Luton Bedfordshire LU1 3JU England
Chapter 12	Milton D Hakel Eleanor A W McCreery	Bowling Green State University	mhakel@bgnet.bgsu.edu emccree@bgnet.bgsu.edu	Bowling Green State University Bowling Green Ohio 43403 USA

Chapter 13	Dick Glover Maggie Boyle	University of Leeds	dick.glover@ukonline.co.uk m.m.boyle@leeds.ac.uk	Learner Support Office University of Leeds Leeds LS2 9JT England
Chapter 14	Sue Bloy Jean Williams	De Montfort University	sbloy@dmu.ac.uk jwilliam@dmu.ac.uk	De Montfort University The Gateway Leicester LE1 9BH England
Chapter 15	Barbara de la Harpe Alex Radloff	Curtin University of Technology	b.delaharpe@curtin.edu.au a.radloff@curtin.edu.au	Centre for Educational Advancement Office of Teaching and Learning Curtin University of Technology GPO Box U 1987 Perth Western Australia 6845
Chapter 16	Donna Wood McCarty	Clayton College & State University	donna.mccarty@mail.clayton.edu	School of Arts and Sciences Clayton College and State University 5900 N Lee Street Morrow Georgia 30260 USA
Chapter 17	Alan Jenkins	Oxford Brookes University	alanjenkins@brookes.ac.uk	Oxford Centre for Staff and Learning Development Oxford Brookes University Oxford OX3 0BP England
Chapter 18	Len Holmes	University of North London	l.holmes@unl.ac.uk	The Business School University of North London Stapleton House 277–281 Holloway Road London N7 8HN England

INDEX